Managing Performance through Training & Development

Monica Belcourt
Associate Professor
Atkinson College
York University

———

Phillip C. Wright
Associate Professor
Faculty of Administration
University of New Brunswick

Nelson Canada

I(T)P An International Thomson Publishing Company

Toronto • Albany • Bonn • Boston • Cincinnati • Detroit • London • Madrid • Melbourne
Mexico City • New York • Pacific Grove • Paris • San Francisco • Singapore • Tokyo • Washington

I(T)P"
International Thomson Publishing
The ITP logo is a trademark under licence

© Nelson Canada
A division of Thomson Canada Limited, 1996

Published in 1996 by
Nelson Canada
A division of Thomson Canada Limited
1120 Birchmount Road
Scarborough, Ontario M1K 5G4

Canadian Cataloguing in Publication Data
Belcourt, Monica Laura, date
  Managing performance through training and
development

(Nelson Canada series in human resources management)
Includes bibliographical references and index.
ISBN 0-17-604258-X

1. Employees – Training of. 2. Performance.
I. Wright, Phillip Charles. II. Title.
III. Series.

HF5549.5.T7B45 1995   658.3'124   C95-931265-X

Acquisitions Editor	John Horne	Interior Design	Holly Fisher
Managing Editor	Margot Hanis	Cover Design	Liz Harasymczuk
Developmental Editor	Edward Ikeda	Composition Supervisor	Zenaida Diores
Senior Production Editor	Tracy Bordian	Input Operator	Elaine Andrews
Art Director	Liz Harasymczuk	Senior Production Coordinator	Sheryl Emery

Printed and bound in Canada

1 2 3 4 (BBM) 99 98 97 96

To my mother, Mary Harrison,
who taught me to value education
and training.
— M.B.

◆

To my wife, Barbara,
and to Sara and Kenneth,
who make my life interesting,
stimulating, challenging,
and worth living.
— P.W.

Contents

◆

About the Series

There is one resource in organizations that competitors can't easily imitate or duplicate: human resources. The management of this resource makes the difference between a mediocre organization meeting some goals and a superior organization surpassing its objectives. We see and feel the result of the management of this asset in our daily lives. At fast food outlets, we are interacting with a workforce that has been selected, trained, and compensated in a way to minimize cost and maximize output. In newspapers across Canada, we read about the results of poor human resources planning leading to layoffs of thousands of competant employees. As students entering professions, we need to know about career development strategies and company recruitment practices. Thus, the effective management of human resources touches not only the employees and managers of the organizations, but all those with whom they interact. Knowledge of this field is critical, and so Nelson is publishing a series of texts dedicated to those managers and human resource professionals who are responsible for people.

The texts in the *Nelson Canada Series in Human Resources Management* include: *Managing Performance Through Training & Development, Health & Safety, Human Resources Management Systems, Human Resources Planning, Staffing,* and *Compensation.*

The *Nelson Canada Series in Human Resources Management* is important for many reasons. Each book in the series (except for *Compensation*) is the first Canadian text in the area. Human resource practitioners in Canada must work with Canadian laws, Canadian statistics, Canadian policies, and Canadian values. This series serves these needs. The series also represents the first time that practitioners have access to a standardized guide to the management of the various HR functional areas. This one-stop resource will prove useful to anyone involved in the management of people.

The publication of this series signals that the HR field has advanced to the stage where theory and applied research guide practice. Because the HR field is still emerging and new tools and methods are being invented, the theory and research is being supplemented with common methods shared among Canadian HR professionals. The books in this series cover the dominant HR functional areas and are based on applied HR research. This research is supplemented with examples of best practices used by Canadian companies who are leaders in the HR area. Each text identifies the process of managing and implementing HR strategies, thus serving as an introduction to the functional area for the new student of HR and as a validation manual for the more experienced HR practitioner. Cases, exercises, discussion questions, and supporting references contained at the end of each chapter provide opportunities for further discussion and analyses.

As you read the texts, I hope you share the excitement of being involved in the development of an extremely important profession.

Monica Belcourt
SERIES EDITOR
MAY 1995

About the Authors

MONICA BELCOURT

Professor Belcourt is currently an Associate Professor and Coordinator of Human Resources Management in the Department of Administrative Studies, Atkinson College, York University. She holds a B.A. in psychology from the University of Manitoba, an M.A. in organizational psychology from York University, an M.Ed. in adult education from the University of Ottawa, and a Ph.D. in administration from York University. She is a certified human resources professional.

Dr. Belcourt has extensive experience in human resources management as Director of Personnel for CP Rail, Manager of Employee Development for the National Film Board, Manager of Consumer Services for the Quebec Region of Consumer and Corporate Affairs, Personnel Administrator for the Federal Government, and as a consultant. Serving as Director on boards such as CIBC Insurance and the Human Resources Professionals Association of Ontario has given her a strategic perspective on the HR function. In addition, she has received over $200,000 in research grants and published over 30 articles on human resources and entrepreneurship. She is founding Chair of the Human Resources Research Institute of the Human Resources Professionals Association of Ontario. Dr. Belcourt is Series Editor of the *Nelson Canada Series in Human Resources Management*.

PHILLIP C. WRIGHT

Professor Wright is Associate Professor of Human Resources Management in the Faculty of Administration at the University of New Brunswick in Fredericton. During an academic career spanning 20 years, he has taught part-time at Conestosa College, York University, and the University of Guelph, while holding full-time positions at the Humber College School of Business and most recently at the University of New Brunswick, Fredericton, where he is a recipient of UNB's Excellence in Teaching Award.

An active management consultant, Dr. Wright has helped a variety of clients, both private sector and not-for-profit, in Canada, the United States, Hong Kong, and China. His current interests focus strongly on the Far East, where he is involved in a number of projects involving the export of vocational education.

His volunteer activities include more than 12 years as Academic Dean of the Canadian Institute of Management. As well, he has served as Chairman of the Board of The New Brunswick Youth Orchestra.

Dr. Wright received a B.A. (Hons.) from Bishop's University, a M.Ed. from the University of Toronto, an M.A. from Wilfrid Laurier University, a M.Sc. from the University of Guelph, and a Ph.D. from Penn State University. Other qualifications include a diploma in general business from Seneca College and a fellowship (FIPD) in the British Institute of Personnel and Development.

Dr. Wright has published more than 80 refereed and professional papers, four books, and a number of monographs. He has been Associate Editor of the *Journal of European Industrial Training* for almost 10 years.

Preface

The Western world is going through a period of adjustment as profound and as far-reaching as the Industrial Revolution that ended almost a century ago. Where the last great spirit of industrialization lasted almost 300 years, the present revolution (couched in terms like "globalization") is proceeding at a pace that astonishes even those who spend their professional lives predicting change and developing change management programs. It is against this background of chaos and rapid industrial and human displacement that this text is written.

This is a book about Canada. Like anything else in our workworld, training and development will undergo a fundamental restructuring within the next few years. Trainees and the managers who employ them will need to rethink the philosophies, missions, and roles surrounding all human development activities, otherwise their organizations will cease to be functional in an increasingly effectiveness-conscious world. For the first time, a distinctly Canadian text is being created to guide them.

This book is part of the *Nelson Canada Series in Human Resources Management*, which examines the functional areas of human resources management. The purpose of the series is to profile the best thinking and research in the human resources (HR) field, while demonstrating how each functional area is related to overall HR strategy. Training and development is one such area, a subsystem within the human resources management function. For example, information from human resources planning, job analysis, and performance appraisals drives the type of training to be developed. Legislation and programs in employment equity and safety determine new types of training. In these ways, training and development can be seen to be tightly integrated with other HR areas.

We begin this book with chapters that develop the theme that training is an investment, and that this investment in human capital must be managed. Chapter 1 introduces the importance, history, and role of training and development. This chapter introduces the first of many Canadian facts, practices, and stories in the text. Chapter 2 outlines the roles and responsibilities of those in human resources development (HRD). Although this text is concerned primarily with HRD within organizations, the training of the workforce is of great interest to a larger constituency. These stakeholders have a vested interest in the performance and continued employment of workers, and in the performance of companies and their continued viability. Their roles and resources are identified and described in Chapter 3. The next nine chapters identify the key steps in the process of training, that is, the steps most likely to result in an effectively trained workforce.

The process starts with the delineation of the need for training, accomplished through needs analysis at three levels (Chapter 4). Once these needs have been established, the next step is the setting of measurable goals (Chapter 5). These quantifiable goals allow trainers to determine if training is the best solution. Throughout the text, the emphasis is that training is an expensive solution and not always the most effective option for improving performance. These ideas about investment, positioning, and analysis serve as a springboard for one of the primary intellectual threads woven throughout the text: it is not training activity that is important, but employee effectiveness. Hence the title of this book focuses on managing *performance*, not *performers*.

Methods for increasing employee effectiveness are explored (Chapter 6). Program design (Chapter 8) must take into account knowledge of adult learning principles (Chapter 7) and equitable training practices (Chapter 10). Obviously, the ultimate goal of all training and development is the transfer of the new skills or knowledge to the job (also Chapter 7). Certain methods are more effective for adults and for ensuring transfer (Chapter 9). The loop is closed by costing the training intervention (Chapter 11) and establishing if the investment achieved a return (Chapter 12).

The development of managers is of principal concern to organizations. Because management development differs in time and focus from other training efforts, it is the focus of a separate chapter (Chapter 13). The final chapter (Chapter 14) describes trends in HRD and looks into the future of the field.

Each chapter begins with a description of the key learning within the chapter to orient the reader. A summary of these key points is provided at the end of the chapter. Mini-cases, discussion questions, and/or exercises, with supporting references, are included to allow students the opportunity to analyze and to apply the theory.

Acknowledgments

As with most authors, we have used not only our own thoughts and experiences, but we have also drawn on the experiences and published work of a large number of practitioners and academicians throughout North America and Europe. Of major benefit to our research was the several computerized databases that allowed us to access a large number of sources quickly and easily. Reference citations from this and many other sources are consolidated at the end of each chapter.

We wish to thank our reviewers: Hermann Schwind, Saint Mary's University, and Bill Hooper, Sir Sandford Fleming College and York University. Each one contributed to this text by lending us their expertise and by taking the time to share experiences and to make insightful comments.

As well, we have been helped immensely by our students, our former students, and by the participants in the many management development programs with which we have been associated.

Similarly, we would like to express our appreciation to our many colleagues who have given freely of their expertise; in particular: Francisco Arcelus, Dan Coleman, Jim Tolliver, Gary Geroy, Nancy Myers, and Francis Randle.

We are grateful to the team that helped to develop and produce this text. The authors wish to acknowledge the entrepreneurial spirit of Peter Jackson, the Acquisitions Editor at Nelson Canada who first recognized the need for a Canadian series in human resources management. Peter moved on, passing the torch to John Horne, who while nurturing the project through its many frustrating phases, never failed to be encouraging and optimistic. Edward Ikeda and Tracy Bordian moved the text through its final stages efficiently and effectively.

Our greatest indebtedness, however, is to our families. The craft of authorship takes time, energy, and emotion, often at the expense of those whose lives we share. To them: Michael, Marc, and Brooker Belcourt, and Barb, Sara, and Kenneth Wright, a sincere thank you for the tolerance you have shown.

Monica Belcourt
YORK UNIVERSITY

Phillip C. Wright
UNIVERSITY OF NEW BRUNSWICK

Managing Performance Through Training and Development

◆ ◆ ◆

INTRODUCTION

ntelligence—the ability to acquire and apply knowledge—is the new source of wealth. Singapore, an island very poor in material resources, is one of the strongest economies in the world. Singapore, which calls itself "The Intelligent Island," is wealthy because of its educated, multilingual workforce (Handy, 1994). Organizations can benefit by increasing the value of their human capital, as Singapore has done. Other sources of capital such as raw material and patents become depleted, obsolete, or worn out. Human capital is the one asset that grows more valuable as it is used. Some of the most successful organizations are buying into the concept that human capital—or an intelligent and effective workforce—can be a firm's principal competitive advantage.

Examples from two organizations (one small and one large) in North America illustrate this new reality.

> *"We want to be the best resort in Canada at exceeding customer expectations," said Gordon Canning of Blue Mountain Resorts in Collingwood, Ontario. Working on the knowledge that it costs five times more to get new customers than to keep existing ones, the employees at Blue Mountain ski, golf, tennis, and waterslide operations set out to provide superior service. Each employee was given about nine hours of training designed to enable them to provide superior service to customers. The result was that 50 percent of customers said that Blue Mountain was better than other resorts in Canada, and employees each received a 2 percent bonus. In 1994, they shared a 4 percent bonus when customer satisfaction reached the same level.*

In 1991, Saturn sold more cars than any other manufacturer. These results were achieved by a substantial investment in training. At Saturn, each new employee goes through a week of orientation training before the job is started. Production workers spend only half their time on the factory floor in the first three months; the rest is spent in a classroom or on-the-job training. Besides technical training, the employees learn "soft" skills such as conflict resolution, problem-solving, and communication. Employees spend at least 5 percent of their time in training—92 hours a year. Saturn takes this goal seriously— unless an employee meets this target, he or she receives only 95 percent of his or her wages.

The executives of these organizations have learned that human capital investments pay off in higher wages and job growth. For a long time, executives have been mouthing the cliché that "people are our greatest asset." Indeed, Dofasco's company slogan is "Our product is steel; our strength is people."

However, most organizations do not measure their human assets, or even begin to estimate the costs associated with a poorly trained workforce. Manufacturing companies, for example, have good cost accounting systems for measuring scrap material and work that must be redone, but do not assess in quantifiable terms the cost of incompetent employees who necessitate this work.

There is a calculable benefit in training employees. Trained employees can do more work, make fewer errors, require less supervision, have higher morale, and have lower rates of attrition (Bowsher, 1990). Half a dozen studies done in the late 1980s concluded that company-sponsored training programs boost workers' wages by 4 to 11 percent over the long run (Mandel, 1993). Other studies found that a 10 percent increase in training produced a 3 percent increase in productivity over two years (Mandel, 1993). Training does result in performance improvement.

The purpose of this text is to identify the key processes involved in achieving these returns on investment through the development of people. This chapter provides a brief history of training, a definition of key terms, an examination of the state of training in Canada today, and a model of human resources development (this model serves as the framework for the text). Let us begin what we hope will be a lifelong journey of learning about human resources development.

◆ ◆ ◆

THE HISTORY OF TRAINING

STAGE ONE: CRAFTS

Before the year 1400, most training was done on the job. Ninety-five percent of workers were employed in agriculture; the rest were craftsmen working at or near their homes. Training, except for the military, was informal and consisted of imitation or oral direction, because most people could not read. The trainee was expected to observe and imitate what he had seen.

Systematic training began with the introduction of apprenticeship training in 1459 in England. (Apprenticeship systems, which were not encoded in law, had been practised in earlier times in other countries.) The earliest programs consisted of a father teaching his son his trade, or locating a master craftsman to train him. The training period was seven years, formalized by a written contract with rules and regulations (Dunlop, 1912). The apprenticeship program was not only a technical training one, but often the only means to an education. Nor was it limited to the trades. Lawyers, doctors, and teachers were trained in this manner—it was vocational education. Girls in the home were also trained through this system, learning trades and crafts such as weaving. These "cottage industries" were the beginning of the seeds of mass production.

STAGE TWO: MASS PRODUCTION

The Industrial Revolution shifted the production of goods from homes to factories, from rural areas to urban areas, from small-scale craft production to mass production. The need for mass training of workers followed. When factory owners were unable to find skilled workers, they opened factory schools that provided technical training. The trainers were skilled workers with experience. The training was of shorter duration than an apprenticeship program and focused on a small set of job skills. The concept of "the one best way to do a job" (resulting from time and motion studies) diffused into training, allowing a set of simple skills to be acquired efficiently. Cooperative education was introduced during this time, in which students would attend school and work at a factory for equivalent amounts of time.

During this period, the government became involved in training, first through agricultural colleges, then through schools for general education. Vocational training in teaching, home economics, and industrial skills followed. Correspondence schools opened in the 1920s, which allowed workers to complete their basic education while working (Watkins and Wright, 1991). The Industrial Revolution also influenced the way training was conducted. From the see-and-do methods, trainers moved to principles of efficiency. Training content, like jobs, was broken down into steps, and evaluation of learning first introduced. For the first time, workers tried to control the content of training by setting up training programs run by unions.

STAGE THREE: EMPLOYEE-CENTRED TRAINING

After the end of World War II, a shift from employer efficiency to employee satisfaction occurred. It was widely believed that a satisfied employee was a more productive employee. To create satisfied employees, supervisors were trained to manage the satisfaction as well as the productivity of employees. Managers attended interpersonal-skills classes and sensitivity training. This period was important because it introduced the concept that the needs and desires of workers were important variables in productivity.

STAGE FOUR: SATURATION TRAINING

Currently, there is a movement to relate training content more closely to job requirements, and to move training from a distant classroom to instruction on the job (using technology, not human coaches). Competency-based training reflects the concept behind this strategy. Jobs are analyzed for the core abilities or competencies needed to do the job, and workers are trained specifically to attain these competencies. As much as possible, training is located at the work station, using technology. Some observers estimate that by the year 2010, only 5 percent of all training will be conducted in the classroom.

Coupled with the "here and now" focus on training is the "everywhere and forever" perspective on the development of employees. There seems to be an emerging requirement to train employees in all areas from basic literacy to personality attributes, and in all places from the work station to the corporate "university" (an off-site location where all training takes place). Learning organizations continually expand their ability to shape the future of the work environment. They encourage employees to identify and solve problems by giving them training and experience in problem-solving, quantitative analysis, and other process skills. The goal is to make everyone smarter at their jobs.

The words "training" and "development" will be scattered extensively throughout this text. An understanding of their meanings will assist the reader in the learning process.

◆ ◆ ◆
DEFINITIONS

Learning within organizations occurs at three levels: training, development, and organizational development. *Training* refers to the acquisition of knowledge, skills, and attitudes that result in improved performance in the current job. *Development* focuses on the acquisition of knowledge and attitudes that may be required in the long-term achievement of individual career goals and corporate objectives. *Organizational development* (OD) is the process of making the organization work better, and a better place to work.

From an organizational perspective, *the development of human resources refers to the process of assessing the abilities of employees, and the formation of programs to enable employees to achieve their full potential to meet organizational objectives.* It also refers to the creation of an organizational environment that is conducive to optimum performance. OD enhances the effectiveness of an organization and the well-being of its members through planned interventions that apply behavioural science concepts (Harris and DeSimone, 1994).

Obviously, training, development, and OD are intertwined. All are concerned with the goal of improving organizational effectiveness through the improvement of human resources. The development of human resources begins the moment an employee is hired. A fully trained and developed employee might experience a scenario like the following:

> *Imagine that you are a newly hired customer-service representative for a major Canadian consumer products company. You have been carefully hired for your ability to learn and adapt,*

not just for your skills and experience. Before you even start the job, you receive reading material from the company about its history, mission, products, and services. Orientation takes three days, including the normal benefits information session. However, most of the time is spent training you in company processes and your job responsibilities. Your supervisor then spends one prearranged hour every day listening to you and coaching you.

Because you are working as part of a team responsible for a territory, you receive off-the-job training in team building, problem identification, and conflict resolution. In addition, your team spends several hours per week in quality improvement sessions. Every member of the team is trained in meeting management. As a group you identify a need for better ways to handle complaints. The training facilitator suggests a multi-media program, which you can use at your work station and learn during scheduled training breaks. The company also encourages you to attend university in the evening to complete your degree and reimburses your tuition.

You are selected by your team to be its representative in the company's organization development effort to improve service quality. All representatives are sent to Germany to analyze competition and identify innovative practices. This trip is preceded by training in development of service performance standards. The trip is beneficial to you because your career goal is to become VP of Marketing, and international experience is a job requirement (along with the degree).

These learning experiences are fairly typical of an organization committed to investing in human resources. This is what is known as *saturation training* in a learning organization. The majority of Canadian organizations have a long way to go to replicate this experience, as shown by the statistics on training presented in the next section.

◆ ◆ ◆
TRAINING AND DEVELOPMENT TODAY

A recent $1-million study of the Canadian economy by Michael Porter of Harvard University warned that unless Canada invests in training and education in the workplace, Canadians will face a declining standard of living in the future (Toulin, 1991). As a direct response to this challenge, Ontario and the federal government announced an 83 percent increase in spending on training programs for an estimated 500 000 Ontarians. The expenditure of $1.6 billion on training is an attempt to make the skills of the workforce meet the needs of the economy (Maychak, 1991). Americans have underlined their commitment to training, as evidenced by a job program that requires employers to spend 1.5 percent of their payrolls on training (Mandel, 1993).

Aware of this emerging emphasis on the profit-generating potential of a trained workforce, Canadian human resources directors view employees as important assets, as the root of competitive advantage, and are very supportive of spending for training (McIntyre, 1994).

◆ ◆ ◆
TRAINING FACTS IN CANADA

Canadian companies spend $4 billion annually on training and development. On average, Canadian companies spend only one-half of what is spent by American firms (Larson and Blue, 1991). This gap may now be narrowing because training budgets in Canadian companies are increasing at a higher rate than inflation (McIntyre, 1994). Significantly, most companies surveyed have maintained or increased their training staff and are planning to increase the number of consultants, contract staff, or outside organizations for training activities (Mandel, 1993).

The amount of training provided varies by company size and industry sector. Most American surveys show that training expenditures increase in proportion to organization size. However, on a per-capita basis in Canada, smaller companies (less than 1000 employees) spent more than larger companies. The transportation, communications, and utilities sectors provide more training than the manufacturing sector.

Canadian companies spend about half of their training budget on courses from external suppliers, hiring consultants, and attending conferences. By

FIGURE 1.1 Training and Development as a Subsystem

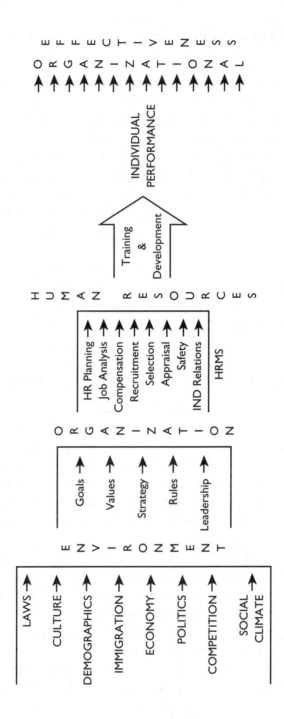

contrast, American organizations spend only 20 percent on external resources (Larson and Blue, 1990).

The average training-and-development expenditure per employee is $849 in Canada. Profitable companies spend the most on training. Those rated as one of the 100 best companies to work for in Canada spend the most per employee.

The average Canadian worker receives 7 hours of training annually compared with 200 hours in Japan and 170 hours in Sweden (*Globe and Mail*, 1992). According to a 1991 survey by the Canadian Labour Market and Productivity Centre, which covered 9.3 million employees, Canadian employees are more likely to receive health-and-safety training than any other kind of training. Orientation was the next most common type of training. Surprisingly, only 11 percent of employees received computer training, although one-quarter of the companies surveyed said they would like to provide it but did not have the funds (*Globe and Mail*, 1992). Professional and technical workers receive the most training days per year; clerical workers received the least (McIntyre, 1994).

Another indication of the growing importance of training is the push to certify trainers, thus ensuring the professionalization of the industry and the ethical conduct of its practitioners. Those responsible for the development of human potential in the firm have been transformed from seminar leaders to organizational development experts, human-performance technologists, behaviourial engineers, instructional technologists, and facilitators.

The next section outlines the systems relationship of training and development within the larger environment.

◆ ◆ ◆
THE TRAINING AND DEVELOPMENT MODEL

Unfortunately, many training departments operate much like the continuing education department of the local university: attempting to attract "customers" by mailing glossy catalogues of the newest and latest programs (Noel and Dennehy, 1991). Instead, initiatives within human resources development should be aligned with key organizational objectives and visions. Training initiatives should result from strategic planning and environmental analysis, as portrayed in Figure 1.1.

It will be argued throughout the text that training and development are not isolated activities, independent of the surrounding organization and its processes, values, etc. Training and development should be tightly integrated within an organizational context dedicated to improving performance. The standards of effective performance are in turn influenced by factors in the environment, such as competitors. Figure 1.1 makes these relationships clearer.

ENVIRONMENT

The first box in Figure 1.1 suggests that *environmental* variables such as legislation, the economic climate, demographics, and social values will impact the organization. For example, if a competitor introduces a lower-priced product, the organization will have to decide to match the competitor's actions or compete in other ways, such as providing superior service. This strategic decision will in turn affect costs, the ability to pay employees, or the necessity to train and reward employees for effective performance.

ORGANIZATION

The next box in Figure 1.1 suggests that the goals, values, rules, and managerial processes of the *organization* determine human resources management practices. For example, if the goal is to provide inexpensive fast food (a McDonald's strategy), then costs of employees must be kept to a minimum. Thus the human resources (HR) strategy is to compensate at minimum wage and have short, low-cost training programs to deal with rapid turnover. Obviously, some of the factors on this list, which is not exhaustive, have more impact at certain times and for certain types of organizations.

HUMAN RESOURCES

Training and development programs should be integrated not only within the larger organizational context but within the HR web of activities. The objective of the human resources management (HRM) function is to attract, motivate, develop, and retain employees in a safe, equitable environment. HRM accomplishes these objectives through the provision of counsel and services in HR planning, organization design and job analysis, compensation and benefits, recruitment and selection, orientation, training and development, performance appraisal, industrial relations, health and safety, employment equity, and HRM information systems. Each function should feed information into a related subsystem, such as training or recruitment.

The training and development model presented in Figure 1.1 provides a clear illustration of the links between the organizational goals and the impact that human resources development (HRD) activities should have on the achievement of these goals. This is a traditional perspective; i.e., the needs of the organization, which are influenced by the environment, determine the nature of all HRM activities, including training and development activities.

An emerging viewpoint flips this model: the knowledge and influence of a firm's human resources influence the nature of the business. We would argue that the intellectual capital of employees is the most important resource in an organization. The intelligence, abilities, and skills of employees determine which markets an organization should enter. Employees are the organization's competitive advantage.

◆ ◆ ◆
LOCATING THE FUNCTION

The development of HR is traditionally the responsibility of the training section located within an organization's HRM department. However, titles and locations are changing. The traditional training unit might now be called the department of organizational effectiveness, organization development, human resources development, performance support, etc. These new titles reflect the expanding role of HRM.

The newly titled department might report directly to the president of a company, rather than through a vice-president of HR. In some organizations, the head of development reports directly to a line manager, such as the VP of the plant. A recent Conference Board of Canada survey reports that 45 percent of all training staff operate out of line divisions (McIntyre, 1994). This placement underlines the importance of the training function to the operations and profitability of the company.

◆◆◆
THE TRAINING AND DEVELOPMENT PROCESS

Training and development are imbedded within environmental and organizational contexts. They flow from these contexts, impacted by other HR processes such as safety and performance appraisal. But training is itself a process—a series of steps designed to improve performance. The cycle starts with current performance and ends with improved performance. Various stakeholders (employers, unions, governments) have a vested interest in the development and continued employment of workers. Stakeholders influence the training process as part of the environmental input.

Step one in the training process is similar to an itch—something in the organization is not quite right, is of concern to someone, is an "itch." Perhaps customer complaints are too high, quality is low, market share is being lost, or employees are frustrated by management or technology. If some part of the organization "itches," then a needs analysis is performed to determine the difference or gap between the way things are and the way things should be. The needs analysis results in the setting of objectives—or measurable goals—to improve the situation and reduce the gap. Before training is determined to be the best solution to the problem, alternatives to this very expensive option must be assessed. The needs analysis, the setting of objectives, and the consideration of alternatives force the trainers to focus on performance improvement, not the delivery of a training program. Training is only one solution—and not necessarily the best one—to performance problems.

If training is the solution, a number of factors must be considered in the development of the course or program. Using the objectives as guidelines, the course designer determines the best training methods for achieving these objectives. Principles of equity must be incorporated into the design to ensure fair access and treatment of employees. Fundamental learning theories and practices must be built into the process before, during, and after the course to optimize the transfer of learning to the job.

After the program has been implemented, the key questions become: Did the program accomplish its objectives? Was the gap reduced? Was it worth it? The sections on costing (Chapter 11) and evaluation (Chapter 12) discuss methods for answering these questions.

TABLE 1.1 THE PERFORMANCE IMPROVEMENT/TRAINING MODEL		
Step 1	Survey stakeholders	Chapter 3
Step 2	Conduct a needs analysis	Chapter 4
Step 3	Set objectives	Chapter 5
Step 4	Explore alternatives	Chapter 6
Step 5	Design program:	Chapter 9
	• maximize transfer	Chapter 7
	• choose methods	Chapter 8
	• incorporate equity	Chapter 10
	• cost the program	Chapter 11
Step 6	Evaluate the program	Chapter 12

An understanding of this model, presented in Table 1.1, will facilitate the reading of the text. The purpose of all training and development efforts is ultimately to improve organization performance.

◆ ◆ ◆
SUMMARY

This introductory chapter stressed the importance of viewing training as an investment in human capital. The history of training was reviewed, ending with a picture of training in Canada today. Training is part of a larger HR strategy, which in turn is dependent on the strategy of the organization, and the influence of the environment. Model-development interventions start with the identification of needs, the development of objectives, the planning of the intervention, and the evaluation of the effectiveness of the intervention.

E X E R C I S E S

1. Phone the 10 largest employers in your area. Determine the term or label for the department responsible for the development of human resources. Identify the reporting relationship. Arrange to interview a trainer to determine where the requests for training originate, and the types of training required. See if you can determine a pattern. For example, if the training department reports to a plant manager, then the training might be very technical and initiated in response to department problems of inefficiencies.

2. Make a list of all the training and development activities that you have undergone since high school. Include everything from highly structured education (such as a degree program) and training (a course in computers or driving) to informal development, such as your efforts to become better in a certain sport or to write better essays. Compare your list to those of others in your group. Divide the activities into organizationally sponsored or initiated, and those undertaken because you wanted to learn something. Prepare a separate list of other development activities you wish to do in the near future. This is lifelong learning.

References

Bowsher, J., 1990. "Making the Call on the CEO." *Training and Development Journal* (May): 65–66.

Dunlop, O.J. 1912. *English Apprenticeship & Child Labour: A History.* New York: The MacMillan Company.

The Globe and Mail. 1992. (15 September): B26.

Handy, C. 1994. *The Age of Paradox.* Boston, Mass.: Harvard Business School Press.

Harris, D.M., and R.L. DeSimone. 1994. *Human Resource Development.* Toronto: The Dryden Press, Harcourt Brace College Publishers.

Larson, P.E., and M.W. Blue. 1991.*Training and Development 1990: Expenditures and Policies.* Conference Board of Canada, Report 67–91.

McIntyre, D. 1994. *Training and Development, 1993: Policies, Practices, & Expenditures.* Toronto: Conference Board of Canada, Report, 128–94.

Mandel, M. 1993. "Jobs, Jobs, Jobs." *Business Week* (22 February): 76.

Maychak, M. 1991. "1.6 Billion Allotted to Train Ontarians." *The Toronto Star* (25 October), p. 4.

Noel, J.L., and R.F. Dennehy. 1991. "Making HRD a Force in Strategic Organizational Change." *Industrial and Commercial Training* 23, no. 2, 67–70.

Toulin, A. "Economy Crumbling: Report." 1991. *The Financial Post* (25 October), p. 6.

Watkins, B.L., and S.J. Wright. 1991. *The Foundations of American Distance Education.* Dubuque, Iowa: Kendall/Hunt Publishing Co.

2

The Training Function

◆ ◆ ◆

INTRODUCTION

Training, the diffusion or spreading of work-related knowledge, skills, and attitudes from person to person, from person to group, or even from generation to generation, has been part of both organizations and societies for more than 1000 years. Only recently, however, have we progressed beyond learning by watching others, or learning through trial and error. Despite the existence of apprenticeships and other vocational learning opportunities, it was not until World War II that formal industrial-training activities became widespread throughout Western societies. During the last five decades, expenditure on training throughout North America has grown steadily, so that by 1994, more than $100 billion will be spent on formal and on-the-job training (Carnevale et al., 1990; Lombardo, 1989). Although separate data for Canada are not available, one study found that average per-employee expenditure in North America was $849 in 1993, up considerably from the $659 per capita in 1992 (McIntyre, 1994).

Justification for this massive spending has required a fundamental change in management thinking. In the past, training was often seen as an unnecessary expense. The myth of training suggested that trainers were always the last hired and the first fired. Although, obviously, one can still find organizations in which this tradition is followed—allowing for training budgets to fluctuate with profit levels—there is now an unmistakable trend toward viewing human resource development (HRD) as an investment. Where this change in attitude has occurred, trainers can play a more proactive role in managing the organization (Sinclair and Collins, 1992).

◆ ◆ ◆

POSITIONING THE TRAINING FUNCTION

Based on the assumption that people are a valued and an appreciating (versus a depreciating) asset, human resource (HR) considerations should be incorporated into strategic decision-making. Sweet's (1981) model is still one of the best illustrations of this process (see Figure 2.1). Here, Sweet (1981),

Wright (1983), and Wright and Geroy (1991) have illustrated that strategic planning has at least two streams: a technical planning component and a human resources management and development component. Without adequate attention to human resource management (HRM) functions (including training), long-term organizational goals can be placed in jeopardy. At the Travelers Corporation, for example, "top management committed extensive ... [funding toward training] after corporate training officials demonstrated that the company's strategic goals would be unattainable without timely, cost-effective training" (Casner-Lotto, 1989, 5).

Further, companies such as NCR are anchoring their HR strategies in their mission statements, allowing the HRD function to depart from the traditional passive role and enter the mainstream of corporate planning and decision-making. Thus, management support for HRD is slowly increasing, as training in many large companies is positioned at, or near, the vice-presidential level (Garavan, 1991; Gunnigle, 1991).

FIGURE 2.1   Integrating Human Resources Development and Tactical Activity Functions

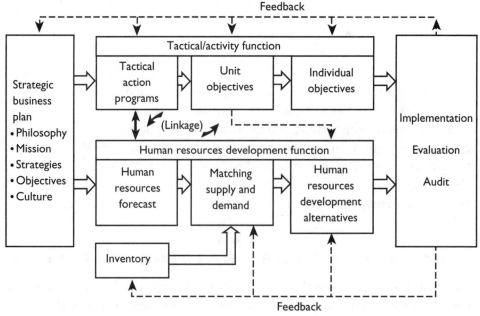

Source: Adapted from J. Sweet, "How Manpower Development Can Support Your Strategic Plan," *Journal of Business Strategy*, no. 2 (1981). Reprinted by permission.

A "full-service" training organization in a large company, therefore, might be centralized and organized into a series of divisions (London, 1989). By separating the HRD function from the personnel management unit or department, access to the highest levels of decision-making is made easier (see Figure 2.2).

Of course, smaller firms would have a much less elaborate structure, especially as the amount of training done outside the firm appears to increase with decreasing company size (Bishop, 1982). As well, it appears that government-supported vocational education is the most significant system of formal training for most small employers. The small business community will

FIGURE 2.2 The Structure of a Full-Service Training Organization

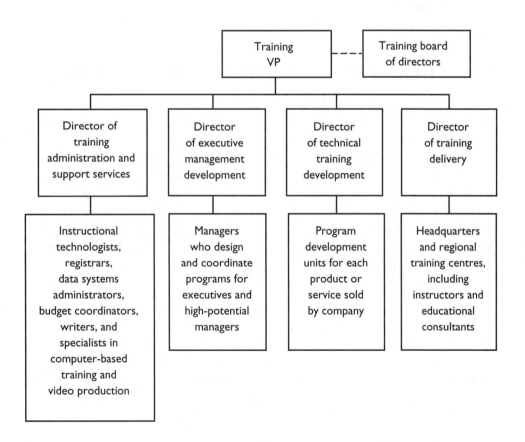

Source: M. London, *Managing the Training Enterprise*. San Francisco: Jossey-Bass, p. 65. Reprinted by permission.

have to overcome its reluctance to pay the often higher training costs associated with improved technology, given the need to upgrade basic workplace skills (Lichenstein, 1992). Even in the smallest organizations, therefore, training should either be positioned near the top and/or, if there is no formal training function, HRD considerations must be made part of the strategic planning process.

It is impossible to develop this strategic emphasis without the increased involvement of line personnel in the training function. Traditionally a weak subunit within a weak personnel organization, HRD now commands the attention of managers at all levels. Indeed, a recent United Kingdom Industrial Society Training Survey confirmed that this trend is gathering pace. In 71 percent of companies surveyed, training departments were no longer the prime initiators of training. Instead, the role was shared with line management (McKibben, 1991).

◆ ◆ ◆
ORGANIZING THE TRAINING FUNCTION

Given the increased importance of developing human assets and the relatively recent line involvement in training, how the HRD function should be organized has generated considerable debate. Of primary importance is the centralization/decentralization controversy. While management in some organizations have found it more efficient to centralize training efforts, others have tried a decentralized approach. British Columbia Telephone (BC Tel), for example, created a model city to train employees, while Control Data Corp. has a somewhat decentralized training program aimed at keeping decision-making close to the customer (Gerber, 1987; Lee, 1988). As there are advantages and disadvantages to both systems, in some cases training policy is set centrally, but delivery is controlled regionally. The best approach depends on an individual organization's need and on the type of training being delivered. Hence, Johnson Controls and BCTel may use learning centres, while San Diego County in California, with 13 000 employees, operates a decentralized training function. In this instance, the potential advantages of centralization (control, economy of scale, consistency of content, commonality of values, superiority of design and presentation) are sacrificed for customization, ownership, and local budget control (Tovar et al., 1989; Carnevale et al., 1990).

Another important trend concerns the trainer's traditional status as staff, rather than as a line professional. It has been suggested that trainers relinquish their staff status by accepting assignments in specific departments, working directly with line personnel as part of a managing team, so that training better reflects company needs (Piskurich, 1991; Pace et al., 1991). Indeed, Zemke (1987) went one step further in reporting on a successful training approach in which at least half the staff were not professional trainers but line managers "cycling" through the training department as part of their career development plan.

This approach could lead to a more knowledgeable and supportive attitude toward HRD. As Yeomans (1989) has suggested, one of the HRD professional's most important functions in the 1990s will be to train managers to become trainers and developers. Thus, the training process should be organized so that managers at all levels learn to understand that every action they take either produces healthy growth or inhibits it (Webster, 1990; Markowich, 1989).

Involvement with line managers can become so intense that the training department may become obsolete as training returns to a master/apprentice approach (Tritsch, 1987). While this concept represents a minority view, there are those who would replace the training function with a vastly broader mandate based upon human resources performance rather than human resources development (Fierstein, 1988; Arcelus and Wright, 1993).

This scenario is based on Gilbert's (1978) early work in human competence engineering. Here, training is but one activity that focuses on what employees do to further organizational goals. The training department becomes the performance management department, where approximately 80 percent of the effort is spent fixing the environment and 20 percent training the employee, with a focus on creating world-class performance, no matter what has to be done to get there (Arcelus and Wright, 1993).

Thus far, we have not drawn an organization chart to show the "correct" structure of a training department, since every organization is different and this variety should be reflected in training organization design. Whatever formal structure prevails, however, it should revolve around some key concepts. The overriding centralization/decentralization issue has been discussed. To this background, we have added the concept that line managers can and should be included in every step of training design, delivery, marketing, analysis, and evaluation (Grace and Straub, 1991). As well, the training function should report to a position close to the centre of power, so that input into the strategic planning process is assured. Finally, it has been suggested that HRD might be organized around a much broader role that focuses on HR results rather than competence (McLagan, 1989).

Whatever the final configuration, the organization chart must indicate how training interacts with the other HRM functions. The idea is to create a corporate entity whose members, at all levels, spontaneously learn and innovate in ways that promote the well-being and mission of the organization (Kramlinger, 1992). As organizations are changing rapidly, it is difficult to suggest appropriate structures. HRD, however, has been described as an "organizational fishbowl" that must focus on the organization's most pressing business needs in a manner that leads the way in terms of management style and employee empowerment (Kahnweiler, 1991; Stuelpnagel, 1989).

Where training fits within the organizational matrix, then, is not important, as long as the function can influence organizational direction in both a strategic and a day-to-day sense. Every organization is unique; what works in one may fail completely in another. The task is to design structures that either allow trainers to participate directly in achieving corporate goals, or (if there is no formal training function, as in smaller organizations) to use training as a tool that accomplishes the same ends.

◆ ◆ ◆
MANAGING THE TRAINING FUNCTION

Based on the complexity of HRD and the necessity to integrate this function into the broad range of HRM activities, managing training requires skills far beyond technical knowledge as well as the ability to present learning sessions. The training manager must:

◆ learn training (as a discipline) well and keep up with trends in both the discipline and the manager's industry;

◆ learn about the informal power structure by astutely observing human behaviour;

◆ understand and concentrate on the organization's mission, culture, and core competencies;

◆ cultivate widespread management support for training activities;

◆ handle resistance creatively;

- carefully build up a power base;

- develop credibility by modelling effective behaviours;

- learn to work within the cultural and the political limitations imposed by the organization (Petrini, 1989; Kirby and Ginzel, 1989; Burack, 1991).

As Warshauer (1990) indicates, the ability to play organizational politics is often just as important as technical expertise. With these skills, the training manager must do two things: plan and integrate training (or performance improvement) into the very fibre of the firm, and create a training team capable of meeting the organization's HRD needs. This process is complicated further by the trend to involve line personnel in training and by the rate of change in most corporate environments (Wellins and George, 1991).

As organizations must plan strategically, so too must the training manager or individual responsible for HRD. The key concept is to operate as if internal contracts (e.g., internal departments) are paying customers (which they may be) by developing a strategy-to-practice model that meets their real (as opposed to perceived) needs (McDermott, 1989). This approach will avoid the problem described by the following conversation:

> **Line Supervisor:** *"Did you see the personnel department's new training catalogue? I can't believe the number of programs offered. You'd never know we're supposed to be cutting budgets!"*

> **Manager:** *"Yeah, not only are there a lot of programs, but I'd like to know what "Advanced Oral Presentations" and "Managing Your Boss" have to do with getting the job done. They never asked me what skills my people really need. It makes me wonder if we could get better services from people outside the organization. And who knows, it might cost less!" (McDermott and Emerson, 1991, G1).*

When conversations like this one occur—Sebrell (1990) calls this the "student's return quotient"—it is almost certain that the person responsible for training has failed to develop an appropriate strategy that links training to business needs (Robinson and Robinson, 1989).

Credible plans are difficult to develop, however, if a training management system is not in place. The training manager needs access to information. Cohen (1989a; 1989b; 1989c) has written a series of papers that outline both data-base construction techniques and the type of information that should be collated. These methods will not be expanded upon here, as they will be detailed in Chapter 4. In brief, however, Cohen suggests that data be collected from several areas:

1. organizational—relating to the strategic plan

2. position—an analysis of actual tasks or duties required for world-class performance

3. performance—involving the line manager and the employee in training design and implementation

4. employee—individual values, desires, and personalities.

These data, then, are applied in the learning process, as training becomes the result of employee/manager analysis that has helped identify precise needs. The better the data base, the more likely it is that appropriate management decisions will be made. Cohen (1989a) even suggests that it is the responsibility of HRD managers (or those responsible for training) to show line managers how to "facilitate quality people decisions."

Aside from decision-making data, training managers require a system for analyzing and reporting activities. The maintenance of trainee records, training histories, customized learning opportunities, schedules, and course and material inventories is a routine but necessary activity. As well, the system should be able to handle registrations for in-house courses, public seminars or classes, and self-study (Sebrell, 1989). To this inventory might be added the capacity to track individual career development and learning plans.

An important dimension, too, is the training manager's ability to manage the in-house, external training balance. Kaeter (1990) has produced a detailed analysis of this subject. In some instances, off-site training is beneficial; but in other cases, especially where sensitive material is involved or the skills needed are very organization-specific, in-house training is preferable. Cost is also a consideration, and the ability of trainees to apply their training to the job must always be considered.

Finally, any training management system must have auditing capacity. There are two major facets to auditing training: auditing the training system and auditing each training program or learning event. Auditing a training system requires an analysis of the quantity, quality, and breadth or variety of learning activity. Special emphasis should be placed on the analysis of the interaction between training and the meeting of both strategic and short-term goals, especially from the line manager's perspective (Anif, 1989; Bramley and Hellah, 1987).

These data analysis and auditing functions do not occur by themselves. They must be performed by people who are properly selected, trained, and then motivated to do the job. In smaller organizations, one person may be responsible for the entire HRD process, but the activities and system characteristics remain the same as in larger organizations, even if they are not sophisticated or are informal extensions of someone's main duties.

Again, bearing in mind that every organization is different, individuals who are skilled (or can become skilled) problem-solvers and change agents will become the most successful HRD practitioners. Conflict resolution and meeting management also are prime prerequisites. The training team, then, needs to be moulded into an effective unit like any other subgroup (Wellins and George, 1991; Kirkpatrick and Smith, 1991).

A reward structure that is both valued by trainers and recognized by line personnel should be developed. Few organizations offer tangible rewards to their HRD staff. Even the best paid training professionals and managers appear to want more recognition and respect from line managers; as a result, many competent training directors and trainers have left HRD positions in corporations to become consultants (Gerber, 1988).

More thought could be put to the use of nontraditional reward systems like profit sharing, lump-sum bonuses, pay-for-knowledge, earned time off, and two-tier salary systems. Some research suggests that while recognition is appreciated by employees, more tangible rewards are better received. Managers responsible for HRD should avoid overdependence on the most favoured method of recognition/reward: sending trainers to professional-development conferences (Gerber, 1989).

◆ ◆ ◆
THE TRAINING BUDGET

The myth that training budgets are always the first to be cut in recessionary times does not appear to apply to the last decade (Gerber, 1987a). In a study on the state of training in mid-sized Canadian companies, more than 60 percent indicated that growth rates in training budgets had exceeded inflation, and 75 percent expected either stable funding or increases in the future (McIntyre, 1992).

It is still wise, however, to expect close scrutiny of the training budget and to be prepared to defend it. The importance of HRD expenditures should be explained long before the formal budgeting process begins. Aid can be solicited from allies outside the HRD function. Another method is to find less-expensive methods of training and to link these savings to cost reduction of goods and services. Of course, a sophisticated, believable cost/benefit analysis system, combined with an effective reporting structure, is the best defence against budget cuts (Lloyd, 1989; Phillips, 1991).

From a budget-management viewpoint, one must not ignore those who suggest that training should be (or should attempt to be) self-financing. There are two main avenues of revenue enhancement. The HRD function can work on a "chargeback" basis, whereby internal budget transfers are made when other units send their people for training, or outside clientele can be actively solicited. This latter activity turns the HRD department into a possible profit centre (Long, 1990; Fazio, 1988).

The advantages of these cost-recovery or "chargeback" systems are that, in general, they are viewed favourably by upper management, and the learning programs offered to internal clients, of necessity, must be relevant (Hequet, 1991). As well, the extra income—if not matched with comparable budget cuts—can be used to improve the training environment.

Conversely, what the clients think they need may not be compatible with corporate strategy and shorter-term plans. As well, the search for profitability may syphon energy and talent away from HRD's main role, that of orchestrating strategic culture change (Burack, 1991; Hequet, 1991).

◆ ◆ ◆
MARKETING THE TRAINING FUNCTION

HRD professionals frequently fail to demonstrate the value of what they do. As a result, many trainers labour in obscurity. The failure of HRD to sell itself is well known (Lookatch, 1991).

Credibility, then, has to become the operational objective for all training professionals. Part of this process involves traditional marketing activities performed internally, e.g., selecting a target market, analyzing market needs, and developing the capability to address these needs (McDermott, 1989;

Nathan and Stanleigh, 1991). Another part concerns developing measurement techniques so that trainers can speak the quantitative (profit/loss) language of senior managers (Lookatch, 1991; Nachshen, 1987). A third part is the formation of strategic alliances, beginning with the president or CEO. In fact, one of the most important tasks for a newly appointed training manager may be to bring senior managers (and other individuals with influence) "on side" (Gerber, 1988). While "most" HRD directors complain that their CEO is not interested in employee education programs, most CEOs indicate that they do not "hear" from their training directors (Bowsher, 1990). This internal selling process, then, must be planned as carefully as any other facet of departmental management.

Companies have found that training is less expensive than ignorance (Tritsch, 1987). But the training profession, or the training craft, is still coping with the radical changes in corporate needs and expectations caused by global restructuring and the increased need to be competitive. This chapter has suggested how the training function should be positioned and managed in order to cope with rapid change and the intense need to transform corporate cultures into true learning organizations. Because the field is changing so rapidly, we have avoided "how to" prescriptions. Rather, we have presented concepts and, where possible, alternative views. This approach should provide the student or the practitioner with sufficient background to analyze individual, unique work environments and to develop appropriate HRD structures that can cope with constant change.

◆ ◆ ◆
SUMMARY

Modern training, as we know it today, became widespread during World War II. Because expenditures have risen sharply since then, there is an unmistakable trend toward the view that training is an investment that must compete with other activities for funding.

In sophisticated organizations, however, training is part of the strategic plan, and trainers are now behaving more proactively. Whether centralized or decentralized, training is no longer a weak subunit but now commands the attention of all levels of management, so much so that line managers are becoming more and more involved.

There is no "correct" HRD structure, then, as long as the training function can influence where the organization is heading. This responsibility probably requires that training be positioned near the top of the organization.

Managing the training function will also require new skills. Not only must the training manager of the future have excellent presentation skills, but high-level expertise in conflict resolution and networking will be a must. Similarly, the ability to speak the language of top management must be combined with the abilities to manage staff, develop budgets, and market the training function both internally and externally.

EXERCISE

The Day They Hired Jenny

"Great course, Sam!" they chorused as they trooped out the door and headed for the parking lot.

Sam Harris, a veteran trainer with Flotation Ltd., a manufacturer of life jackets and other flotation devices, smiled as he gathered his notes together. He had just finished two hours of wisecracking and slightly off-colour storytelling as he worked his way through the third session of a Human Relations course for supervisors. "Keep 'em happy" was Sam's motto. Give the troops what they want, keep your enrolments up, and no one will complain.

Sam was good at it, too! For 20 years, he had earned an easy living, working the politics, producing good numbers (of trainees) for the top brass to brag about ("we give each employee up to 26 hours of training every year!"), and generally promoting his small training group as a beehive of activity.

Everybody knew Sam; everybody loved Sam! His courses were such fun. He had no trouble convincing managers to send their people. He put out a little catalogue with his course list every year in January. He hadn't had a cancellation in more than 10 years. Some managers said that training was the best reward they had! Now only three years from retirement, Sam intended to coast comfortably into pension land. All his favourite courses had long been prepared; all he had to do was to make adjustments here and there and figure out some new jazzy titles.

But times were changing. Elsewhere, someone was thinking differently.

" ... and I need somebody to take a close look at our training function." Sitting in the presidents' office, Jenny Stoppard, the newly hired VP of Human Resources, wondered what he meant. Flotation Ltd. had a reputation as a company with a well-trained workforce.

"We need to increase our productivity per person by 50 percent over the next three years," he continued "... and you are going to spearhead that effort ... yes, we spend a lot on training ... yes, we cycle people through a lot of courses ... but I'm not satisfied with the bottom line. I know that while Dad was president he swore by old Sam ... said he was the greatest ... I don't know anymore ... maybe a whole new approach is needed ... anyway, I want you to take a close look at Sam's operation."

Later in the day, the president called Sam into his office.

"Sam, I want you to meet Jenny Stoppard. I've just hired her as VP of Human Resources. She's your new boss, Sam. I think the next three years are going to be very exciting around here, and Ms. Stoppard is going to be a key player in the drive to increase our competitiveness. I want you to do everything in your power to cooperate with her."

Questions

1. Comment on Sam's approach to training, e.g., would you want him working for your company? Why, or why not?

2. What skills of a trainer has Sam not developed?

3. Compare Sam's traditional measures of training with the president's ideas.

References

Arcelus, F.J., and P.C. Wright. 1993. "On the Implementation of CIM in Small Manufacturing Firms." *Technology Analysis and Strategic Management* 6, no. 4, 403–413.

Anif, A.R. 1989. "Performance Audit of Human Resource Management." *International Journal of Government Auditing* 16, no. 2, 9–11.

Bishop, J. 1982. *On the Job Training in Small Business.* Washington: US Small Business Administration.

Bowsher, Jack. 1990. "Making the Call on the CEO." *Training and Development Journal* 44, no. 5, 64–66.

Bramley, P., and H. Hellah. 1987. "Auditing Training." *Journal of European Industrial Training* 11, no. 6, 5–10.

Burack, Elmer H. 1991. "Changing the Company Culture—The Role of Human Resource Development." *Long Range Plan* 24, no. 1, 88–95.

Carnevale, A.P., L.J. Gainer, and J. Villet. 1990. *Training in America.* San Francisco: Jossey-Bass.

Casner-Lotto, J. & Associates. 1989. *Successful Training Strategies.* San Francisco: Jossey-Bass.

Cohen, Stephen L. 1989a. "Managing Human-Resource Data: Information, Please." *Training and Development Journal* 43 no. 7, 28–35.

_____. 1989b. "Managing Human-Resource Data: Keeping Your Data Clean (part 2)." *Training and Development Journal* 43, no. 8, 50–54.

_____. 1989c. "Managing Human-Resource Data: Applying the Data Base." *Training and Development Journal* 43, no. 9, 65–69.

Fazio, Robert A.1988. "Beyond Bureaucracy: Riding the New Wave in HR." *Personnel* 65, no. 2, 28–35.

Fierstein, Jeff. 1988. "Let's Get Rid of the Training Department." *Training* 25, no. 6, 63–66.

Garavan, Thomas N. 1991. "Strategic Human Resource Development." *Journal of European Industrial Training* 15, no. 1, 17–30.

Gerber, Beverly. 1987. "It's a Whole New Ball Game at B.C. Tel." *Training* 24, no. 1, 75–81.

_____.1987a. "Training Budgets Still Healthy." *Training* 24, no. 10, 39–45.

_____. 1988. "The Care and Feeding of Trainers." *Training* 25, no. 8, 41–46.

_____. 1989. "Rewarding and Recognizing Trainers." *Training* 26, no. 11, 35–41.

Gilbert, T.F. 1978. *Human Competence: Engineering Worthy Performance.* New York: McGraw-Hill.

Grace, Paul, and Carrie Straub. 1991. "Managers as Training Assets." *Training and Development* 45, no. 6, 49–54.

Gunnigle, Patrick. 1991. "Personal Policy Choice: the Context for Human Resource Development." *Journal of European Industrial Training* 15, no. 3, 22–31.

Hequet, Marc. 1991. Selling In-house Training Outside." *Training* 28, no. 9, 51–56.

Kaeter, Margaret. 1990. "Off-site vs. In-house." *Training* (supplement): 5–7.

Kahnweiler, William M. 1991. "HRD and Empowerment." *Training and Development* 45, no. 11, 73–76.

Kirby, Paula, and Linda Ginzel. 1989. "Look Smarter in Your First Training Job." *Training and Development Journal* 43, no. 8, 69–72.

Kirkpatrick, Tom, and Bryan Smith. 1991. "Team Development for Real." *Industrial and Commercial Training* 23, no. 4, 3–8.

Kramlinger, Tom. 1992. "Training's Role in a Learning Organization." *Training* 29, no. 7, 46–51.

Lee, Chris. 1988. "Where Does Training Belong?" *Training* 25, no. 2, 53–60.

Lichenstein, J. 1992. "Training Small Business Employees: Matching Needs and Public Training Policy." *Journal of Labor Research* 13, no. 1, 23–40.

Lloyd, Terry. 1989. "Winning the Budget Battle." *Training* 26, no. 5, 56–62.

Lombardo, Cynthia A. 1989. "Do the Benefits of Training Justify the Costs?" *Training and Development Journal* 43, no. 12, 60–64.

London, M. 1989. *Managing the Training Enterprise.* San Francisco: Jossey-Bass.

Long, Ralph F. 1990. "Protecting the Investment in People—Making Training Pay." *Journal of European Industrial Training* 14, no. 7, 21–27.

Lookatch, Richard P. 1991. "HRD's Failure to Sell Itself." *Training and Development* 45, no. 7, 47–50.

McDermott, Lynda C. 1989. "Strategic Marketing for HRD." *Training and Development Journal* 43, no. 6, 64–67.

McDermott, L.C., and M. Emerson. 1991. "Quality and Service for Internal Customers." *Training and Development Journal* 45, no. 1, 61–64.

McIntyre, David. 1992. "Training Budgets Weather the Recession."

Canadian Business Review 19, no. 2, 33–34, 37.

_____. 1994. *Training and Development 1993*. Report 125–94. Ottawa: Conference Board of Canada.

McKibben, Jenny. 1991. "When Training Becomes Part of the Job." *Industrial Society* (March): 16–17.

McLagan, Patricia S. 1989. "Models for HRD Practice." *Training and Development Journal* 43, no. 9, 49–59.

Markowich, M. Michael. 1989. "Every Manager a Trainer." *Supervision* 50, no. 4, 3–5.

Nachshen, Bernie. 1987. "The Value of Training in Dollars and Cents." *Computerworld* 21, no. 14, 69–76.

Nathan, Anthony, and Michael Stanleigh. 1991. "Is Your Department Credible?" *Training and Development Journal* 45, no. 1, 41–45.

Pace, R.W., P.C. Smith, and G. E. Mills. 1991. *Human Resource Development: The Field*. Englewood Cliffs: Prentice Hall.

Petrini, Cathy. 1989. "Getting a Foot in the Door." *Training and Development Journal* 43, no. 4, 13–18.

Phillips, Jack J. 1991. "Measuring the Return on HRD." *Employment Relations Today* 18, no. 3, 329–42.

Piskurich, George. 1991. "Training: The Line Starts Here." *Training and Development* 45, no. 12, 35–37.

Robinson, Dana G., and Jim Robinson. 1989. "Training for Impact." *Training and Development Journal* 43, no. 8, 34–42.

Sebrell, Bill. 1989. "A Training Management System." *Computerworld* 23, no. 15, 134.

_____. 1990. "Calculating Training Quality." *Computerworld* 24, no. 24, 120.

Sinclair, John, and David Collins. 1992. "Viewpoint: Training and Development's Worst Enemies—You and Management." *Journal of European Industrial Training* 16, no. 5, 21–25.

Stuelpnagel, Thomas R. 1989. "Total Quality Management in Business and Academia." *Business Forum* 14, no. 1, 4–9.

Sweet, J. 1981. "How Manpower Development Can Support Your Strategic Plan." *The Journal of Business Strategy* no. 2, 79–84.

Tovar, Roberta T., Allison Rossett, and Nancy Carter. 1989. "Centralized Training in a Decentralized Organization." *Training and Development Journal* 43, no. 2, 62–65.

Tritsch, Catherine. 1987. "Training in the 1990s: Boom or Bust." *Successful Meetings* 36, no. 11, 29–35.

Warshauer, Susan. 1990. "Setting the Stakes for Success." *Training and Development Journal* 45, no. 4, 26–31.

Webster, Bryan. 1990. "Beyond the Mechanics of HRD." *Personnel Management* 22, no. 3, 44–47.

Wellins, Richard, and Jill George. 1991. "The Key to Self-Directed Teams." *Training and Development Journal* 45, no. 4, 26–31.

Wright, P.C. 1983. "Strategic Planning and Human Resource Development: The Vital Link." *Training and Development* 1, no. 9 (January): 16–18.

Wright, P.C., and G.D. Geroy. 1991. *Experience Judgement and Intuition: Qualitative Data-Gathering Methods and Aids to Strategic Planning.* Bradford: MCB University Press.

Yeomans, William N. 1989. "Building Competitiveness Through HRD Renewal." *Training and Development Journal* 43, no. 10, 77–82.

Zemke, Ron. 1987. "Bill Yeomans: Making Training Pay at J.C. Penney." *Training* 24, no. 8, 63–64.

3

Stakeholders
in Training
and
Development

◆ ◆ ◆

INTRODUCTION

A large manufacturer of soap products is automating its production line. Robots and other types of technologically advanced production equipment will replace the manual operation. The manual operation has been staffed by a largely immigrant population with an average education level of Grade 9. The new operation needs workers who can read and work in English, understand basic arithmetic, electronics, and some computer-software programs. In addition, they will have fewer levels of supervision and will work mainly in teams.

Who can help the manufacturer retrain and identify skilled and literate employees? The task of converting unskilled employees into literate and skilled workers, and identifying Canadians with advanced skills, does not have to be done in isolation, without assistance, by the manufacturer. An understanding of the programs of governments, unions, and other stakeholders will save the manufacturer time and money. These stakeholders can offer literacy, software, and soft-skills training; identify qualified workers and offer relocation assistance; develop apprenticeship programs; offer outplacement services for those unable or unwilling to train; offer adaptive services for those with special needs, etc.

It pays to know the stakeholders.

The term *stakeholder* refers to those institutions or associations that have an established interest in training and development. These stakeholders include governments at all levels, unions, associations, employers, and educational institutions. Their interests lead these parties to research the employment market in order to determine the need for training. They then develop programs for funding and supplying training. The goals of these programs are to ensure that the right number of trained workers is ready for available jobs.

Stakeholders play two important roles in training and development: *supply-side training* and *labour market* adjustment services.

◆ ◆ ◆
SUPPLY-SIDE TRAINING

The supply of trained workers rests on the assumptions that there are labour market imbalances and that these change slowly enough that over time, individuals can be trained in response to shortages in the labour market. Anyone reading the classified advertisements of a local newspaper will notice that there are many vacancies in one skill area (engineering technologists, for example) and none in another (advertising managers).

> *A $10-million precision-tool manager at Northwestern Tool and Die recently tried to fill two openings: one for a toolmaker and another for an accountant. For the toolmaker's position, he placed 10 ads. Response: zero. For the accounting job, he took out one ad. Response: 167* (Inc. Magazine, *1992).*

One solution to this labour market imbalance is to provide training to prepare individuals for anticipated shortages. Training for anticipated shortages is done by many types of organizations including community colleges and private schools. For example, Humber College in Toronto sells about $30 million a year worth of education to the private sector. Privately owned career colleges (1100 of them in Canada) teach vocational skills such as typing, accounting, and electronics.

The link between the skills taught and the job obtained is often left to the individual. The plight of Peggy Lohse highlights the difficulty of establishing the link between the right training and obtaining a job. Ms. Lohse did all the right things: a university science degree and a diploma in the environmental effects of toxic agents. Yet she was unable to find a job, and went back to school (Little, 1993).

One researcher estimates that 22 percent of the unemployed are jobless because their skills don't match employer needs (Little, 1993). Researchers at the University of Alberta have found that high-school and university graduates take two to four years to settle into careers, and this period is marked by frequent job changes (Little, 1993).

Despite the uncertain link between training and entry-level jobs, the belief persists that training will, ipso facto, result in a job. The economic strategy of the province of New Brunswick embodies this belief (Freeman, 1993).

The provincial government has tied New Brunswick's economic future to the development of human resources. The increased value of the human capital is perceived to be the province's competitive edge.

Besides ensuring the supply of trained workers, stakeholders try to help those unable to get into the workforce, or those who have lost their jobs.

◆ ◆ ◆

LABOUR-MARKET ADJUSTMENT SERVICES

Stakeholders try to provide assistance to those who cannot get a foothold in the labour market, or those who have suffered job loss.

ENTRY/RE-ENTRY TRAINING

Stakeholders assist those individuals who have difficulty entering or re-entering the labour market. Programs in this category include assisting young people who may never have had a job, women who wish to re-enter the labour force after a period of family time, and immigrants who have never had a job in Canada. For example, Manitoba spends over $1 million assisting individuals to identify realistic vocational goals, and provides counselling and job placement to those who have occupational handicaps. Another Manitoba program places volunteers in government jobs that are related to their career aspirations.

JOB-LOSS SUPPORT

Not only do stakeholders supply training for individuals entering the job market, they also attempt to mitigate the effects of job dissolution. The effects of job dissolution are wrenching, affecting the lives of former workers in profound ways. The social and human costs are higher than the annual $12 billion spent on Unemployment Insurance. Studies of people who experience sudden, involuntary unemployment show that plant closures change the lives of workers entirely through higher rates of physical and mental illness, marital discord, alcoholism, suicide, and crime (Premiers Council, 1989).

Stakeholder policies and programs can ease the impact of job loss by providing training, counselling, information, and financial support. Unions, businesses, and even the community can play roles in the adjustment infrastructure by sharing the costs and by providing programs to speed re-employment. However, programs of the past may not serve the next generation as well if the fundamental nature of the economy continues to change.

The next sections describe the policies and programs of the major stakeholders: governments at the federal, provincial, and municipal level; unions; private organizations; associations; and educational institutions.

◆ ◆ ◆
GOVERNMENT ROLES

Government-sponsored training programs are delivered by community colleges, employers, private agencies, schools, community-based organizations, and government departments. Funded clients include immigrants, people with physical and mental challenges, towns seeking assistance for former employees of a closed factory, young dropouts in need of job-search skills, or employers seeking to upgrade staff.

The money is spent not only on training and development programs but also on income support, child care, transportation, and other subsidies. The Ontario Ministry of Education and Training estimates that for every $100 spent on actual training costs, the province spends another $120 in income support, and $30 in additional subsidies (Gibb-Clark, 1993).

All levels of government play three generic roles in training: funding, labour-market research, and leadership.

FUNDING

According to a study conducted by The Canadian Labour Market and Productivity Centre, Canadian governments spend about $50 billion a year on education and training, which makes Canada one of the biggest such spenders in the world. Besides financing the education of children, this money is spent on training support for adults and school-to-work transitional arrangements. Monies spent by all levels of government directly on training are estimated to be $4 billion annually (Gibb-Clark, 1993).

Governments, however, do not want to be the sole source of training funds. Through tax incentives and policy directives, they attempt to induce organizations to fund most of their own training. Other countries also do this. Britain levies a tax on all firms; this fund is then redistributed to companies that do conduct training.

Although governments in Canada spend more money than others on education and training, Canadian companies spend less than other industrialized companies on training (one-half as much as American companies; one-quarter as much as German companies) (Premiers Council, 1989). Governments are now developing policies to increase the contributions of employers. For example, Québec uses a refundable tax credit that is to be used by companies primarily for increasing access to training, upgrading, and retraining (Government of Québec, 1991).

LABOUR-MARKET RESEARCH

Governments provide information on labour market and employment opportunities. The nature of this information includes the prediction of job vacancies, the estimation of the quantity of workers, and the documentation of available training courses. Human resource (HR) planning initiatives occur at the national (pan-Canadian) level and can be conducted by region, industry, occupation, etc.

LEADERSHIP

Governments attempt to envision the future and prepare the players in the development process to be ready for it. They do this by preparing policy papers that generate discussion, and, it is hoped, action plans and programs. For example, the Ontario government published a document suggesting that the results of education and training must be measurable, that graduates of science and technology programs must be doubled, and that 90 percent of all Canadians should earn a high-school diploma, etc. (Geis, 1991). This paper, particularly its stance on the measurement of education, generated much public debate and has resulted in province-wide exams for high-school students.

Governments also play an advocacy role. Through money designated to assist occupationally disadvantaged groups, the government can ensure that people within these groups receive training, counselling, or work experience. The money allocated to apprenticeship programs, for example, is tied partially to the number of registered apprentices who are women, aboriginal, physically challenged, or part of a visible minority.

Although all levels of government incorporate these three roles into their training initiatives, each level has staked out different sectors for which it assumes primary responsibility.

◆ ◆ ◆
FEDERAL GOVERNMENT
RESPONSIBILITIES

The federal government focuses on initiatives in labour-market adjustment and funding, including income support. The target groups are the unemployed, the disadvantaged, and immigrants. Through information and counselling, and the funding of specific programs by a number of departments, the government hopes to achieve a skilled, employed workforce. Some examples of programs targeted at these groups follow.

THE UNEMPLOYED

Employment and Immigration Canada has a program entitled "Canadian Jobs Strategy" that focuses on individual training and development. The goal is to integrate selected individuals into the workforce by providing counselling, training, work experience, mobility assistance, and income support.

THE DISADVANTAGED

Women, aboriginals, visible minorities, and the physically and mentally challenged are of particular concern to the federal government as part of its equity programs. The federal initiatives have rewards and punishments built in to achieve equity programs. An example is the federal government contract program to help the physically and mentally challenged.

The physically and mentally challenged made up 5.4 percent of the general workforce in the 1985 census (*Globe and Mail*, 1993). Their unemployment rate is about 50 percent (compare this to around 11 percent overall for Canada). Discriminating against those with physical or mental challenges is illegal in Canada, and the federal government requires all major contractors, such as Canadair, to file employment-equity plans as a condition for landing government contracts.

IMMIGRANTS

The focus of federal programs for immigrants is on language training to overcome barriers to integration.

Besides the initiatives targeted at these three groups, the federal government offers significant support programs in the areas of information and research, skills improvement, labour-market adjustment, and community development. (Readers requiring more specific information about federal programs may either consult the blue pages of the telephone book, which lists government programs, or phone Employment and Immigration Canada.)

◆ ◆ ◆
PROVINCIAL GOVERNMENT RESPONSIBILITIES

Jurisdiction over job training is a contentious issue in federal–provincial relations. The provinces want more control. Indeed, Québec wants exclusive control over job training in its jurisdiction. Within provincial jurisdiction, training tends to be as fragmented (among many departments) as it is federally. At the provincial level, the target groups tend to be the employed or the recently displaced. Provincial governments also provide labour-market information and act as consultants and advocates to employers, unions, and community groups. The provincial governments provide no income support. Their objective is to ensure the continuing employability of workers, and the survival of employers through the advantage of a trained workforce.

This section describes some of the key responsibilities and programs of provincial governments.

BASIC EDUCATION

The provinces have constitutional responsibility for training and to provide the bulk of financial support for it. (The federal government, however, supports higher education through transfer payments and research grants.) Employers have a vital interest in an educated workforce; i.e., a literate and numerate workforce. Surveys have shown that about 30 to 40 percent of the workforce in Canada cannot read simple directions or do the basic arithmetic required to add up a restaurant bill or complete a mail-order invoice (Geis, 1991).

New Brunswick is the only province that integrates education and labour-market strategies within one department, in the belief that growth industries, such as those in the high-tech sector, will locate where they can find the best workers (Freeman, 1993). Even programs that create jobs in highway construction are perceived as building the infrastructure necessary to attract global corporations. New Brunswick is following the philosophy of

Robert Reich of Harvard University, who believes that the way to attract these corporations is by investing in human capital.

REGULATORS OF PRIVATE TRAINERS

Provinces, which have the primary responsibility for education, also regulate the provision of education by private organizations. Anyone who wishes to train people to become certified barbers or chefs, for example, must be approved by officials in provincial departments of education.

APPRENTICESHIP PROGRAMS

Apprenticeship training is long-term training that combines classroom and on-the-job training. As registered apprentices, students can train to become carpenters, mechanics, electricians, etc. Although the provincial governments control this type of training and certification, the federal government pays the bulk of the institutional portion of apprenticeship training, as well as income support to apprentices while they are in school. Canada plans to spend over $300 million in 1997–98 to create 60 000 apprenticeship positions (Menyasz, 1993).

EDUCATION AND TRAINING INFRASTRUCTURE AND STANDARDS

The certification of workers such as carpenters and barbers is a provincial responsibility. Barriers between provinces are being reduced so that, in time, skilled workers will write a single examination and be certified across provinces. This program recognizes about 40 skilled trades. Interprovincial barriers to mobility for professionals, such as accountants, are also being removed.

STIMULATION OF WORKPLACE TRAINING

Through policies of tax incentives, grants, consulting, and funds designated to offset the cost of training, governments try to stimulate and increase the amount of training conducted by companies. For example, the Ontario Skills Development office used to spend $18 million per year to help clients identify training needs, to develop plans to address those needs, and to evaluate the success of these programs. Assisting in this process were 188 consultants. In addition, in 1990 an incentive fund of $35 million existed to provide partial support for the direct costs of training. The purpose of these programs was to encourage clients to offer more flexible, relevant, and high-quality training.

◆ ◆ ◆
MUNICIPAL GOVERNMENTS

Municipal governments are very active in joint programs of community development with both the federal and provincial governments. Community-development programs refer to those activities designed to increase local employment opportunities and manage disruptions in the labour market. Examples of programs include on-the-job training in community-improvement projects (parking surveys, downtown marketing studies, etc.) and support for those interested in careers in municipal management.

◆ ◆ ◆
PROBLEMS WITH MACROTRAINING SERVICES

The end of the 19th century was known as the "gay nineties." This century will end with a different term "the nervous nineties." As a direct result of an economic recovery in which, contrary to predictions, no surge in jobs occurred the recession has challenged many firmly held economic assumptions, including: full employment should be a goal; successful companies hire more people; and governments should create jobs when the private sector cannot.

Existing training and education programs are clearly inadequate when growth in output is not accompanied by growth in employment, when industries that traditionally hire low- and semi-skilled workers are disappearing, and when few employment opportunities exist in successful high-tech firms. Combine these factors with general attitudes of downsizing, doing more with less, and outsourcing (hiring contractors to do organizational work, such as running the cafeteria and cleaning), and machine-intensive production techniques: the result is a skew in traditional rehiring and training practices.

Production workers are not the only ones affected. The process of work itself is altered when organizational hierarchies are flattened by networking, teamwork, and elimination of middle-management levels. Dofasco, IBM, and the Canadian banks are shedding up to 20 percent of their workforces. The revenues of a highly successful Canadian software-development company, Corel Systems Corp., grew 80 percent in one year, but it only hired 20 percent more employees.

The impact on training policy is to shift resources from short-term job training and job creation, to working with individuals and employers, to providing portable and basic skills. The goal is employability. An example of this shift occurred in the Brockville plant of Shell Canada. After laying off 165 people with little education, Shell hired 40 who were screened for their technical skills, ability to learn, and aptitude for teamwork (Little, 1993). The hiring emphasis was on those who were ready to "learn a living, not just earn a living."

Skills for learning, such as English as a second language, mathematics, computer awareness, and communication skills, provide the groundwork for more trade-specific training programs. The Toronto plant of Honeywell Ltd. used both the local school board and the Metro Toronto Labour Council to instruct its employees in these types of programs and achieved a 40 percent increase in productivity. These generic skills may become the focus of future labour-market adjustment programs.

◆ ◆ ◆
REACTION TO GOVERNMENT PROGRAMS

There is widespread dissatisfaction with the role of governments in training. More than half the firms surveyed in a report on people and skills in the global economy reported that government-sponsored training programs were not particularly useful (Premiers Council, 1989). The emphasis has been placed on short-term training for entry-level jobs that tends to be nontransferable. Of those surveyed, 10 percent felt that government programs discouraged training. Many of the complaints by both companies and individuals using the program concerned excessive paperwork, cumbersome bureaucracies, and the running of the maze required to identify the right programs (Premiers Council, 1989).

The multitude of programs is due to the reactive nature of training policies in general. The public experiences a crisis (factory closure) or perceives a need (disadvantaged youth) and demands that the government do something. Often, several levels of government jump on the same bandwagon, resulting in overlapping programs.

Most parties to the process are demanding an end to this reactive style. Some provinces (Québec, Ontario, New Brunswick) have prepared papers outlining the need for better analyses of the labour market (shortages, surpluses), long-term training and development strategies, investment in vocational training, and more effective alliances among all the partners.

An example of this type of strategy and cooperation occurred in 1987 at the Firestone plant in Hamilton. Nearly 1300 people received notice of the plant closure 18 months in advance. The union, the company, and the community worked together creatively. A highly motivated adjustment committee was able to accommodate 95 percent of the laid-off workers through training programs, new jobs, and retirement programs.

Critics contend that in order to implement timely programs, an information system that speeds up the labour-market adjustment processes and alleviates skill bottlenecks is needed. Such a system is in the works. The Canadian Occupational Projection System (COPS) uses top-down, input-output information to forecast occupational demand combined with the bottom-up approach, using the judgments of the private sector and public agencies. The system is not ideal, as forecasting is limited by interoccupational mobility, changing participation and retirement patterns, and shifting macroeconomic conditions (Simpson, 1988). These limitations suggest that in a global environment with constantly shifting demands, short-term technical training should be replaced by flexible and transferable generic skills.

◆ ◆ ◆
UNIONS

Unions combine forces with other stakeholders to provide training in order to decrease the effects of drastic restructuring within their trades. A typical program uses funds generated by employee deductions to set up training funds. Federal and provincial governments often contribute. Two examples illustrate the use of these funds to assist laid-off workers and to provide training to upgrade skills. The 1980–81 recession eliminated about 40 percent of steel-making jobs in Ontario. Through the formation of the Canadian Steel Trade and Employment Congress, programs to assist laid-off workers were developed. Since 1988, about 70 percent of laid-off steelworkers were trained for new livelihoods (Southerst, 1993). Likewise, various unions in the construction industry created Training Trust Funds to provide training in current skills and new skills because most construction firms were too small to provide the training needed. By 1989, there were 37 Training Trust Funds with almost $5.5 million in contributions.

Besides the roles of HR planning and funding, unions also advocate for changes in the training process. The Auto Parts Sectoral Training Council wants to establish the right for workers to learn on paid company time, the right to technical awareness and training, and the right to negotiate the definition of required workplace skills (Hynes, 1993).

◆ ◆ ◆

EMPLOYERS

Organizations train their own employees because they cannot locate or afford highly skilled employees, and because they wish to maintain or improve the skills of current employees.

Businesses sometimes avoid training employees because they fear that trained workers will be more marketable and will quit to work for the competition. Others view labour as they do machinery: when the part wears out, replace it with a new one. Still others worry that workers will lack the aptitudes or motivation to learn new skills (Overman, 1992).

However, most firms that provide formal training view it as a necessary part of doing business. Their primary objective is to obtain a competitive edge through a well-trained and skilled workforce. A Statistics Canada 1991 survey on adult education and job training reported that 30 percent of Canadian employees participated in employer-sponsored programs and courses (Statistics Canada, 1991). The average employee receives two days of training per year (Canadian Labour Market Productivity Centre, 1991). These numbers may change significantly over the next few years as organizations seek to gain a competitive edge through the knowledge and skill bases of their employees. One organization, Circo Craft of Montreal, has a goal of 100 training hours per employee per year, to teach its workers to work in teams, to gather data to document sources of problems, and to resolve these problems (Gibbon, 1993).

◆ ◆ ◆

PROFESSIONAL ASSOCIATIONS

Associations, like the Human Resources Professionals Association of Ontario, provide training for their members. This training includes courses that lead to formal certification and informal courses on topics of interest to its members. Their program is typical of most trade and professional associations. In addition, most associations educate their members through newsletters and annual conferences.

Not all associations that deliver programs for their members are professional associations. For example, organizations such as The Native Women's Association and the YWCA deliver training in life skills, job upgrading, and job readiness on a contract basis for the government of the Northwest Territories (Fogwill, 1989).

♦ ♦ ♦
EDUCATIONAL INSTITUTIONS

Educational institutions offer training and development programs beyond their basic mandates of primary, secondary, and post-secondary schooling. Most universities have a noncredit continuing education department. Some school boards play an active role in community development by assisting employers, unions, and communities with labour-market adjustments. For example, the Peel Board of Education in Ontario works directly with employers who are downsizing by providing vocational counselling and generic-skills training for displaced workers. This board also assists the employed to do their jobs better by promoting a multimedia software program that teaches both safety and reading skills.

The leadership role is an important one for some educational institutions. Cambrian College is a leader in providing students with technology that allows them to focus on abilities, not disabilities. A student with a severe learning disability can use a Personal Reader that scans typewritten material and turns it into synthetic speech, a tape recorder to tape lectures, and word processors with spell-check and grammar-check functions (*Globe and Mail*, 1993).

♦ ♦ ♦
PARTNERSHIPS

All stakeholders in the business of training realize that working in isolation is not the best method to improve skills. Partnerships among employers, unions, governments, and educational institutions may prove to be the best method for ensuring the employability of workers. One example of this type of partnership occurred in Ontario. Zehr's (located in Cambridge) and the

United Food and Commercial Workers train workers for different jobs and careers. Dissatisfied with 18-month community college programs, union and management agreed in a contract proposal to do their own training. Now, a butcher can be trained in 16 weeks. Workers can apply to be retrained for many positions, and one impact has been the placement of women and night-shift workers in nontraditional jobs with more opportunity for advancement. Funding for the program comes from payroll deductions (Galt, 1991).

Another form of partnership is the community-based, volunteer-driven organization. Working with local employers, unions, educators, and community groups, these Community Industrial Training Committees identify needs, arrange training programs using government funds, and advocate for training and jobs in their communities. The most comprehensive effort to form these partnerships has been the creation of the Ontario Training and Adjustment Board (OTAB). This organization does not deliver programs, but will make broad design and funding decisions over direct suppliers of programs. There are about 20 local boards across the province. The boards are composed of eight business representatives, eight labour representatives, four social-action groups, two educators/trainers, and are co-chaired by both business and labour representatives.

Sometimes, a group of local businesses will become partners in training, sharing the costs of establishing courses. This occurs where no employer has enough employees needing training to justify the costs of development or to realize economies of scale in purchasing training. For example, The British Columbia Training Consortium, which has 11 participating organizations, uses its collective purchasing power in the marketplace (McIntyre, 1994). Partnerships serve two needs: cost effectiveness and the development of programs designed to satisfy real, not perceived, needs.

All stakeholders recognize that lifelong training is part of the workforce culture. Industry representatives estimate that, in the past, one set of skills would guarantee a person a job for 10 or 20 years (Overman, 1992). Now the assumption is that workers will train and retrain for the rest of their lives.

◆ ◆ ◆
SUMMARY

This chapter has outlined the roles of the various players in the training and development field. In addition, problems in managing macro-issues in training have been identified. To ensure the effectiveness of this ongoing learning, all stakeholders must themselves learn to manage the HR planning function. With an effective forecasting system, stakeholders can plan the funding and provision of training programs to meet the goals of full and equitable employment. Cooperation among the stakeholders will facilitate this process.

E X E R C I S E S

Stakeholder Analysis

1. Read again the opening paragraph of this chapter. Identify the stakeholders that the soap manufacturer should contact. After you have identified the stakeholders who could assist the manufacturer, consult the list below to see if you were correct.

Literacy training → educational institutions (local school board)

English as a second language → local school board or federal government

Software training → private company or community college with funds from provincial government

Certification of workers → provincial government

Identification of qualified workers → federal government

Apprenticeship programs → provincial government

If a federal contractor using designated workers → federal government

Assistance accommodating the physically challenged → educational institutions, with funds from federal government

Assistance with outplacement → municipal and federal governments, some unions

Assistance with unemployment → federal government

Assistance with re-employment → some unions, municipal governments, and federal government

2. Imagine that you are the general manager of a large manufacturing organization that has just been awarded a substantial contract. This contract will result in the tripling of production. Dozens of skilled workers will have to be found. You know from past experience that the workers are not available from the local labour pool. You wish to identify skilled tradespeople within Canada to fill these vacancies. If there are none, your organization is willing to train them, but with government assistance.

Using the blue pages of the telephone book, identify the specific federal, provincial, and municipal programs that will help you fill these vacancies. Describe which stakeholders might be potential partners in training.

References

Canadian Labour Market Productivity Centre. 1991. *National Training Survey, 1991*. Ottawa.

Fogwill, L. 1989. "Adult Training in the Northwest Territories: A Review and Assessment." Prepared for the Legislative Assembly's Special Committee on the Northern Economy. Government of the Northwest Territories.

Freeman, A. 1993. "New Brunswick Hits Books After Years of Hard Knocks." *Report on Business Magazine* (16 January): 16.

Galt, V. 1991. "Skills Made to Order." *Report on Business Magazine* (15 October): 19.

Geis, G. 1991. "As Training Moves Toward the Next Decade." Toronto: Ontario Training Corporation.

Gibb-Clark, M. 1993. "Job Training Trail a Maze-ing Venture." *The Globe and Mail* (7 August): B15.

Gibbon, A. 1993. "How Training Primed the Pump." The Change Page, *The Globe and Mail* (16 November): B22.

The Globe and Mail. 1993. (5 February): C9.

Government of Québec. 1991. *Policy Statement of Labour Force Development*. Ministere de la Main-d'oeuvre, de la Sécurité du revenu et de la Formation professionnelle. Bibliothèque nationale du Québec.

Hynes, M. 1993. "Report on the 'What's Training Got to do with It' Workshop." *Newsletter of the Centre for Research on Work and Society at York University. North York, Ont.*

Inc. Magazine. 1992. (15 October): 67–69.

Little, B. 1993. "Workers in 1990's Must 'Learn a Living.'" *Report on Business, York University Magazine* (12 January): 34.

McIntyre, D. 1994. *Training and Development: Policies, Practices & Expenditures 1993*. Toronto: Conference Board of Canada.

McPherson, DoLo., V.V. Murray, D.M. Robertson, G.S. Saunders, J.T. Wallace, and D.J. Wheeler. 1992. *Human Resources Management In Canada*. Scarborough, Ont.: Prentice-Hall Canada, Inc.

Menyasz, P. 1993. "Job Creation, Training: Priorities for HR Minister." *Canadian HR Reporter* (November).

Overman, S. 1992. "Retraining Puts Workers Back on Track." *HR Magazine* (July/August) 8, no. 7.

Premiers Council Report. 1989. "People and Skills in the New Global Economy." Toronto: Government of Ontario.

Simpson, W. 1988. "Can Government-Sponsored Training Reduce Unemployment in Canada?" *Entrepreneurship and Higher Education: Lessons for Colleges and Universities.* Washington, D.C.: Association for the Study of Higher Education.

Southerst, J. 1993. "If You Can't Beat 'Em..." *Canadian Business* (March): 66, no. 3.

Statistics Canada. 1991. *Adult Education and Training Survey.* Ottawa: Government of Canada.

4

Needs Analysis: Approaches and Methods

♦ ♦ ♦

INTRODUCTION

Most problems at work involve people. Difficulties with computers, workloads, and supplies appear relatively simple compared with personnel problems. One reason for this is that individuals are incredibly complex and relatively unique. Another reason is our failure to take the time to analyze the causes of poor performance. We search for simple solutions such as "he has a poor attitude," or "she lacks motivation." These explanations of human behaviour do not provide us with any useful information.

A proper analysis of poor performance would include a description of the performance that is ineffective (not the psychological label for the behaviour) and an assessment of the environment in which this behaviour is occurring. Thus, the employee with the "poor attitude" may be handing in assignments late (the behaviour) because there are positive consequences for doing so (such as more time for analysis or even coffee breaks, etc.). Sending this employee to a "motivation" course would result in no change in performance. Thus, an effective analysis of performance problems must include both the employees and their environment.

A review of the literature suggests that academics and practitioners are united on the definition of needs analysis as an investigative procedure designed to identify gaps or deficiencies in employee or organizational performance. (For a review of various models, consult Moore and Dutton [1987]; Sleezer [1992]; and Lewis and Bjorkquist [1992]).

Geroy (1986) effectively summarized needs analysis as a series of planned activities designed to deal with skills, knowledge, cultural realities, system characteristics, and internal and external environmental characteristics in order to affect organizational performance. The goal of needs analysis is to identify the differences between "what is" and "what is desired or required." The way to do this is to solicit information from all those who will be impacted by the process.

A needs analyst collects information from key people within an organization about the organization, the jobs, and the employees in order to determine the nature of the deficiencies (Pace et al., 1991). This information identifies the problem, which is simply the difference between the way the work is being done and the most cost-effective way of doing it. As Kaufmann (1991) stated, required results – current results = need.

Frameworks of analysis are important, but these are not readily available for most managers. Theories such Maslow's hierarchy of needs (Maslow 1954) do little to help managers identify causes of problem behaviour. This chapter attempts to provide multiple frameworks for the analysis of performance and subsequent training needs.

◆ ◆ ◆
RATIONALE FOR NEEDS ANALYSIS

There are three good reasons that organizations should take a proactive stance in the diagnosis of training needs.

BASE LINE

The first of these is to establish a base line of performance against which improvement can be measured. This base-line information allows trainers to:

◆ determine what the trainee already knows;

◆ estimate the cost of the present performance;

◆ design a program so that the trainee is trained in deficient areas only;

◆ test for improvements; and

◆ conduct cost-benefit analysis of the program.

Needs analysis is the cornerstone of the process of training and development (Okey, 1990). To quote Hobbs (1990), "an ounce of analysis is worth a pound of programming."

LEGAL

Employers also have a legal responsibility to assess worker knowledge and skills in areas regulated by the government. Ledvinak and Scarpello (1991) describe the nature of regulations imposed by government agencies that have responsibility for either the industry or issues across industries. In Canada, an example of a vertical (by industry) regulatory agency is that of the Ministry of Transportation, which regulates the standards and certification of public-transportation workers. A horizontal agency that regulates issues across organizations would be the Ontario Workplace Health and Safety Agency, which is concerned with occupational health and safety. Employers are legally bound to ensure that certain employees are certified. These regulatory agencies must be provided with evidence that designated employees have been pre-tested, or trained and tested, to meet certain regulations. The data provided by a good needs analysis would meet these requirements.

MORAL

Some argue that employers have a moral obligation to assess the needs of employees in order to reduce the impact of skill obsolescence (Wexley and Latham, 1991). A recent trend in employee relations suggests that large companies have a responsibility to their employees, even to the point of assisting them to find jobs in the event of layoffs and providing them with training to ensure their employability. Unions are demanding that workers have the right to be part of a needs-identification program in order to determine if the skills being taught are really necessary to do the job. These factors are strong arguments for conducting regular and objective assessments of training needs.

◆ ◆ ◆

THE DIAGNOSTIC PROCESS

This section suggests a number of approaches to assist in the identification of performance problems and potential training needs. The reading of this chapter will be facilitated by referring to Figure 4.1.

A CONCERN

The process of identifying training needs originates slowly and informally with a concern. This concern might be as subtle as noticing that employees are treating customers in an abrupt manner, or observing that employees are spending a lot of time asking one another for help with a new system. Others spot concerns by recognizing a shift in regular activities, such as an increase in defective parts, accidents, or complaints (Mills et al., 1989). At IBM, one needs-identification program began with the CEO's comment that about 10

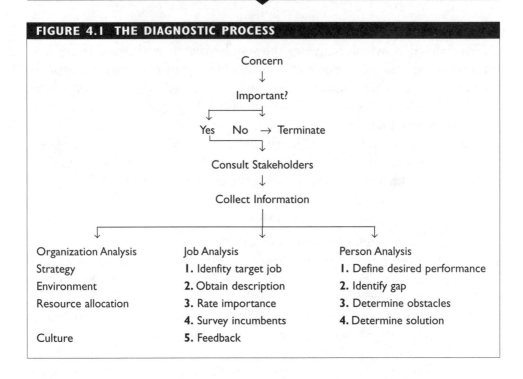

FIGURE 4.1 THE DIAGNOSTIC PROCESS

percent of all complaints addressed to him involved client dissatisfaction with IBM's handling of telephone calls (Estabrooke and Foy, 1992).

ITS IMPORTANCE

After a concern has been raised, the next step is to determine if the concern is central to the effectiveness of the organization. The training manager must be aware of the strategic orientation of the organization. The goals, plans, introduction of products and services, changes in technology, practices, and regulations should be clear. Human resource (HR) policies must be linked with the strategic directions of the company. The training strategy should boost the organization's competence to achieve its goals (Carr, 1992). In IBM's case, one strategic goal was customer satisfaction, and further analysis revealed that 70 percent of all customer contact was by telephone (Estabrooke and Foy, 1992). The complaints about telephone calls had to be taken seriously because the concern was central to the effectiveness of the organization.

THE STAKEHOLDERS

The next step in the needs-analysis process is to include the principals who have a vested interest in the process and outcome (Geroy et al., 1989). Interventions in organization systems have the same ripple effect as throwing a stone in a pond. Therefore, the designers of needs analyses must recognize that development programs operate within organizations consisting of individuals with their own beliefs and attitudes. Support from key players in the organization is necessary from the beginning of the needs-analysis process.

At a minimum, top management should understand the rationale for the needs analyses. Training analysts must obtain agreement on why the needs assessment is being done and who will be involved. Managerial expectations must be clarified (Goldstein, 1993). Likewise, other stakeholders, such as employees and/or their collective representatives, should be consulted. At IBM, interviews with employees revealed that they believed they treated customers courteously, and that the managers were antagonistic about learning telephone skills (Estabrooke and Foy, 1992). The attitude was "Just train the secretaries and switchboard operators," even though managers and even financial analysts were receiving calls from customers. The trainers at IBM worked hard to obtain agreement and support from employee needs for a full analysis. Management sent out a strongly worded message to employees that there was a problem, and, together, they were going to fix it. Indeed, the manager of U.S. operations made telephone effectiveness one of five key measures of effectiveness. (The others included profit and revenue measures.)

Cooperation, communication, and trust are critical variables in the success of any intervention (Glaser and Taylor, 1973). All stakeholders must buy into the diagnostic phase to ensure that the data collection will result in accurate information, and that they have a vested interest in the success of the program. The linking of the training plans to business strategy and the involvement of key stakeholders resulted in dramatic improvements in customer satisfaction at IBM.

DATA COLLECTION

The next stage in the determination of needs involves the documentation of the concern through the collection of information from a variety of sources. Three sources of information are the organization, the job, and the

FIGURE 4.2 MACRO- AND MICROTRAINING NEEDS

Macro- and Microtraining Analysis: The identification of macrotraining needs occurs when the entire organization, a whole department, or substantial numbers of employees need training. The example of IBM, cited earlier, would be considered a macrotraining needs analysis because 150 000 employees were affected. By comparison, a microtraining need exists for just one person, or a very small group of people. A personnel analyst who needs to know a software package in HR planning would be considered a case of a microtraining need. Similarly, a group of 10 sales representatives who needed to master a computerized reporting system would be regarded as a case of microtraining. Training for just a few people could be accomplished by a self-study program, an external course, or individual coaching.

employee. The next section includes a definition of each and procedures for conducting a needs analysis within each sector. This segment is followed by a presentation of data-collection methods, which are generic to any analysis of organizational or human performance. These analyses lead to the identification of macro- and microtraining needs. (See Figure 4.2 for an explanation of these terms.)

◆ ◆ ◆
ORGANIZATIONAL ANALYSIS

Organizational analysis is the study of the entire organization: its strategy, its environment, its resource allocation, its culture. An understanding of each of these components will provide information useful not only to the identification of training needs but also to the probability of the successful transfer of the training to the workplace.

STRATEGY

Most organizations have broad objectives. These may be stated as visions ("uncompromised dedication to quality"); goals ("the number one software business in Canada"); or competitive advantages ("40 percent of market share through the introduction of new products"). These broad statements trickle down to specific goals and objectives for each department or unit. These plans reflect an organization's plan for survival, growth, adaptation, profitability, etc. Because the business environment constantly changes, this is an ongoing planning process.

The process of relating training needs to corporate strategies can be understood by a concrete example. Pepsi Cola had a strategic objective of the development of talented people (Schuler, 1992). The goals generated from this objective included empowering employees, developing the necessary broad skills, and building career opportunities. The training programs resulting from these goals included changing the corporate culture (empowerment); detailed HR planning, which resulted in specific training programs; and a four-week leadership program.

Corporate strategies are intertwined with the environment of the organization.

ENVIRONMENT

Organizations exist within societies, with their complex mores, laws, and regulations that influence the operation of businesses and public agencies. Training programs are often a direct result of government regulations (as seen in the earlier example of safety regulations), or attitudes (e.g., managers need to understand the nature and effects of sexual harassment). Large organizations such as Ontario Hydro, which are foremost in the public eye, are often the leaders in the development of programs to meet both public expectations and government regulations.

Besides this regulatory influence, organizations are conscious of the strategies of competitors. The nature of the training program can be a direct result of an organization's attempt to establish a new market niche.

The environment is also dynamic and uncertain. New technologies, inventions, recessions, and trade agreements may profoundly affect not only the content of the training but the employees' receptivity to being trained.

RESOURCE ALLOCATION

Managers are always monitoring organizational information, such as number of units produced, percentage of defective products, accidents, complaints, scrap levels, etc. Any variance in these ratios from the expectations or the standards of the company could be the basis for an analysis. Obviously, inefficiencies could be the result of many factors, and the solutions could even exclude training. A thorough analysis will help in identifying causes and resolutions.

The monitoring of the flow of HR also provides much information for training purposes. Increases in turnover, hiring, transfers, and promotions often precipitate training programs. HR planning is the process of anticipating the need for employees with particular skills for anticipated jobs. By linking training plans with HR plans, organizations can prepare employees for new assignments, promotions, etc. to meet the organization's needs.

Organizational resources, including profitability and viability, will affect the organization's reaction to the introduction of change programs.

CULTURE

Organizations consist of more than buildings, equipment, and paper. They are social entities. The people within the buildings have feelings, attitudes, and values. The culture of an organization refers to the collective attitudes of its employees toward work, supervision, company goals, policies, and procedures (Bass and Vaughn, 1966). Employees also have opinions about such intangible systems as communication and decision-making. These attitudes are learned, affected by the experiences of the employee within the organization. Socialization agents and trainers must first be aware of these attitudes before attempting to change them.

Pace et al. (1991) suggest that the perceptions of employees can be measured along two dimensions or levels. The first level of assessment deals with attitudes of employees toward organizational systems, such as communication and decision-making. This analysis, termed "functional analysis," focuses on the processes used to achieve organizational goals. The achievement of these goals is measured, and, by correlation, the processes are evaluated. The implication is that outputs can be increased by changing process inputs. For example, if communication patterns can be changed from closed to open, then turnover or client complaints might be reduced.

The second dimension is that culture can be interpreted by the analyst in a highly subjective way. This interpretive analysis relies heavily on the abilities of the analyst and uses talk as the primary data-collection method. Organization talk centres on three types of messages: accounts, stories, and metaphors. The explanations people give for their behaviour are accounts. The answer to the query about the poor sales record provides analysts with useful information about both the individual and the corporate practices and milieu.

Stories are the equivalent of legends or parables in modern society. The verbal recreation of an event allows employees to learn the organization's norms and practices. For example, that a top executive made a favourable (and unexpected) decision on a proposal as he headed out to a golf game becomes translated by employees into an insight about how decisions are really made in the company.

Metaphors allow the employees to project a picture of their real feelings about work. Statements such as "this place is like a zoo" provides the analyst with a snapshot of overwork, chaos, lack of structure and control, etc. During coffee breaks, employees may complain that the organization is like riding an elevator: lots of ups and downs; someone is always pushing your buttons; sometimes you get the shaft, but what really bothers you are the jerks! (Pace et al., 1991) These metaphors, stories, and accounts are a rich source of employees' real perceptions.

Mining these attitudes, either through a functional or interpretive analysis, provides extremely valuable information. Asking employees what would help them make a stronger contribution to the organization, or what is preventing them from working to capacity, are questions that contribute rich data for organizational improvement. Air Canada conducted an organizational climate survey in 1991. They assessed 20 different climate dimensions including rewards and recognitions, management effectiveness, and job satisfaction (Dolan and Schuler, 1994). This perceptual information is critical because employee performance may be deficient as a result of culture, not ability.

Once the strategy, environment, resources, and culture of the organization have been assessed, the information gathered could be used to design a change program. Further information can be collected by examining jobs and employees.

◆ ◆ ◆
JOB ANALYSIS

A *job description* lists the specific duties carried out through the completion of several tasks. A task is the smallest unit of behaviour studied by the analyst and describes the specific sequence of events necessary to complete a unit of work. A *job analysis* results in a list of the activities or work operations performed on the job, and the conditions under which these activities are performed (Goldstein, 1993). Therefore, a job analysis reveals the steps required for a person to perform a job in the most effective way.

The steps involved in a job analysis are as follows:

1. Identify the target jobs. After an examination of records of production and organizational culture, determine which jobs have a performance gap. More than a job title is required here. For example, the term analyst often describes quite different types of jobs, depending upon the department or level within any organization. These target jobs may be identified by managers.

2. Obtain a job description. In large organizations, most positions have a description of the tasks and minimum qualifications required to do the job. If this description has not been updated within the last year, consult with both the manager and several incumbents in the position (subject-matter experts) to obtain a current listing of tasks and qualifications. The job description should contain a summary of the major duties of the job, a listing of these duties, and the conditions under which they are performed. All tools and specialized knowledge should be listed.

An example of a job description for a manager is contained in Figure 4.3 After preparing a job description, review the list of duties with subject-matter experts, managers, or job incumbents in interviews or focus groups.

3. Rate the importance of each dimension and the frequency of the performance of each task. The group interviews suggested in the previous step could be used to generate these rankings.

4. Survey a sample of job incumbents. Using the position description, develop a questionnaire or structured interview asking the managers and employees in the specific jobs to rate the importance of tasks and the competency with

---

FIGURE 4.3 JOB DESCRIPTION: MANAGER

◆ Administers, directs, and coordinates all activities needed for the department to carry out its objectives.

◆ Coaches, directs, and assists employees in the performance of their duties.

◆ Prepares written reports regarding activities of the department; acts as a lobbyist for organizational resources; provides feedback to upper management and employees on progress toward goals.

◆ Prepares departmental budgets; monitors financial performance of the department.

FIGURE 4.4 SAMPLE JOB-ANALYSIS SURVEY

For each of the following areas of skill, knowledge, and ability, please make two ratings. Looking at your own job, assess the importance of the task by circling a number from 1 (not important) to 5 (very important). Then, consider your own level of competence in that task and rate it from 1 (not at all competent) to 5 (extremely competent).

Job Task	Importance	Competence
Knowledge: ability to explain technical information to co-workers.	1 2 3 4 5	1 2 3 4 5
Control: ability to develop procedures to monitor and evaluate activities.	1 2 3 4 5	1 2 3 4 5
Planning: ability to schedule time, tasks, and activities efficiently.	1 2 3 4 5	1 2 3 4 5
Coaching: ability to provide verbal feedback to assist in the development of more effective ways of handling situations.	1 2 3 4 5	1 2 3 4 5

which they are performed. Two additional sections should be included in the survey (Nowack, 1991). The first includes demographic information such as tenure in the job, location, etc. The second section assesses the organization's climate by asking questions about attitudes regarding barriers to productivity and change, job satisfaction, work motivation, perceptions of managers, etc. An example of the nature of this survey is given in Figure 4.4. A supervisor could complete the survey for each employee—as an additional check on validity.

5. *Analyze and interpret the information.* Quantify the information by conducting some elementary statistical analyses. Identify those tasks that are important, frequently performed, and rated as low in ability. Statistical software packages can assist in this task and can even perform more complex analyses. Comparisons between groups may reveal additional important information. Job incumbents may rate their own performance highly, while their managers may feel that the employees are not working up to standard. New employees may feel that there are no barriers to optimum performance,

while those with several years of service may perceive problems. Landey and Vasey (1991) found that experienced police officers spent less time in traffic activities, and more in noncrime-related tasks than recent recruits, thus validating the need to collect background information on respondents. Conducting a training course without understanding the participants and the environment may result in less-effective learning and transfer of skills to the workplace.

6. *Feedback on results.* One route to prepare the organization for change is to provide small groups of managers and employees with feedback about responses to the survey. This feedback encourages employees to talk about areas of strengths and weaknesses and to propose solutions to problems. By "owning" the problem and generating the solution, employees may be more willing to change their behaviours.

◆ ◆ ◆
PERSONNEL ANALYSIS

A third focus of analysis is on the person performing the work. Although overlaps between the three areas of analysis occur, each plays a distinctive role. The analysis of the organization has provided information about its strategies and culture, about its norms and standards. The job analysis has contributed details about the tasks and the relevant knowledge, skills, and abilities needed to perform selected jobs.

In personnel or person analysis, the competencies of individual employees are assessed. Person analysis answers these questions: How well does the employee perform? Who, within the organization, needs training? What kind of training do they need?

A step-by-step process should help answer these questions:

1. *Define desired performance.* The first step is to establish measures of performance. These norms will be important in the needs analysis, during training, and in evaluating effectiveness after training.

Performance analysis is the process of studying employee or work-group behaviour in order to determine if the performance meets the work standards. A standard is the desired level of performance—ideally the quantifiable output of a specific job (Hobbs, 1990).

Defining standards of performance differs from describing tasks, which was a step in the analysis of jobs. A task might read "to process incoming mail." The standard would be to sort 500 pieces of mail within one hour, with less than a 0.05 percent error rate. Standards are expressed in terms of time, units, dollars, completions, etc.

One way to determine standards of performance is to study those employees who perform exceptionally well. A star or exemplary performer is an employee who consistently performs above the standard (Hobbs, 1990). Bell Labs studied both stars and average performers (Froiland, 1993). They developed a checklist of 60 to 80 work strategies, compared the two groups of performers, and determined that the stellar performance was due to nine strategies. Bell Labs then developed objective descriptions of these strategies and trained the average performers.

Another way to determine the most efficient way of working is to conduct studies, such as time–motion studies. The analyst could also assist the manager to determine the standards by asking questions such as: "When you envision the work being done properly, what does the worker do? When you praise or correct an employee's work, what specific tasks are you discussing? What would you like them to be doing that they are not doing?" (Laird, 1985). Standards can be generated by asking a series of questions about extremely effective and ineffective performance, a process similar to the development of a Behaviourally Anchored Rating Scale (BARS) appraisal form. (See Table 4.1.)

2. Identify the gap between desired and actual performance. Sources of data on gaps include performance appraisals, managerial requests for training, work samples, observations, self-assessments of competencies, and formal tests. More objective sources might be found in records of output, complaints, accidents, rejects, lost time, maintenance hours, and equipment efficiency. The employee's performance can be compared with industry norms or with that of other workers.

The "thinking" work of executives is much harder to measure than the "psychomotor" work of lower-level employees. Managerial measurements include organizational goals such as return on equity or increase in customers. Another approach is to measure the processes managers use to achieve goals, rather than the goals themselves. Goals such as market share may be influenced by factors such as the recession or competitor actions, which are beyond the control of the manager. Therefore, managerial processes such as delegation and control (see job description) are assumed to be a good substitute.

Wexley and Latham (1991) outline three types of measures used to assess employee performance: behaviourial measures, economic measures, and proficiency tests. *Behaviourial measures* are based on managerial or peer observations of performance. As such, they are subject to the biases inherent in human judgment:

◆ halo effect (the tendency to rate an employee highly on all characteristics because one characteristic, such as honesty, is rated highly);

◆ first impressions (the error of making snap judgments based on impressions received within a first meeting);

◆ similarity effect (the tendency to evaluate highly people similar to the rate in race or gender); and

◆ contrast effect (the tendency to compare workers against each other, rather than against standards).

TABLE 4.1 BEHAVIOURALLY ANCHORED RATING SCALES (BARS)
Key Competency: Service
5 *Excellent Performance* Incumbent will study customer-profile information cards; observe and greet customers with a smile; refer to interesting features of the merchandise related to customer-profile characteristics; ask specifically for a reaction, and offer a suggestion.
4 *High Performance* Incumbent will approach customers with a smile, inquire if they have noted a special feature, and offer assistance.
3 *Competent Performance* Incumbent will observe entering customers and offer assistance.
2 *Needs Improvement* Incumbent will observe entering customers and approach with a smile, if customer asks for assistance.
I *Ineffective Performance* Incumbent will engage in personal calls, lengthy breaks, or "busy" work to avoid customer contact.

There are techniques for training managers to overcome this subjectivity through the use of structured behaviourial rating scales. (See Table 4.1 for an example.)

Economic measures refer to the quantitative aspects of performance. Records of waste, sales, accidents, market share, etc. provide objective evidence of accomplishment. This source is useful for jobs such as factory worker or sales representative, but pose problems for the measurement of professional or managerial jobs where process is important.

Proficiency tests consist of sampling job performance through the use of formal tests (typing tests or safety knowledge exams) or simulated tests (managerial assessment centres or sales-calls role plays). These tests provide objective information that can be compared to norms. They may not reflect actual performance on the job, where every factor cannot be controlled. The ringing of telephones or the anger of a real customer may derail effective performance. However, these three measures usually provide better information than that provided by self-assessment.

Forecasting future needs is problematic. One approach is to compare the performance of recently hired workers to that of experienced workers, and to identify training needs of new employees.

3. Determine the obstacle to effective performance. Performance weakness may be the result of deficiencies in execution, not deficiencies in skill or knowledge. Sometimes, the gap is the result of the worker not knowing about the standard, not receiving adequate feedback about performance relative to the standard, and not being rewarded for meeting the standard.

A wide range of potential barriers to effective performance is presented in Table 4.2.

4. Determine a solution. If you consider all the barriers to performance cited in Table 4.2, only the first two (lack of skills and knowledge) suggest a training remedy.

The solution to poor performance is not always training. Saying "I've got a training problem" is like going to the doctor and saying you have an aspirin problem (Mager and Pipe, 1970). Training, like aspirin, is a solution, not a problem. Mager and Pipe have developed a decision tree to assist in determining if training is the solution. (See Figure 4.5.)

After the performance deficiency is noted, the manager must decide if the problem is worth spending either time or money to correct it. For

TABLE 4.2 BARRIERS TO EFFECTIVE PERFORMANCE	
Human	Lack of knowledge
	Lack of skills
	Lack of motivation
	Counterproductive reward systems
	Group norms
	Informal leaders
	Organizational political climate
Technical	Poor job design
	Lack of tools/equipment
	Lack of standardized procedures
	Rapid change in technology
Information	Ill-defined goals/objectives
	Lack of performance measurements
	Raw data, not normative or comparative data
	Resources suboptimized
	Ineffective feedback
Structural	Overlapping roles and responsibilities
	Lack of flexibility
	Lack of control systems

Source: Adapted from R.D. Chevalier, "Analyzing Performance Discrepancies with Line Managers," *Performance and Instruction* (November–December 1990). Reprinted by permission.

example, a manager may be irritated by employees who wear shoulder-length hair, but having short hair will make absolutely no difference to productivity or other measures of effectiveness. The exception might be in a manufacturing environment, where long hair would pose a safety problem (solved easily by wearing a head covering).

If, however, the performance deficiency is considered important, then the true analysis begins. Is it a skill deficiency? Mager's most important contribution to the training field was his posing of the questions: Could the

FIGURE 4.5 Mager and Pipe's Flow Diagram for Determining Solutions to Performance Problems

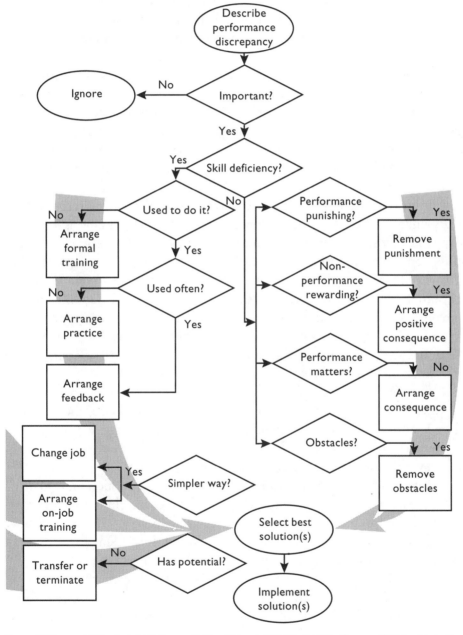

Source: R.F. Mager and P. Pipe, *Analyzing Performance Problems* (Belmont, Calif.: Lake Publishing Company, 1984). Reprinted with the permission of the publisher. Copyright © 1984 by Lake Publishing Company.

employee perform the task if his life depended on it? Could your teenager clean his or her room, if his or her life depended on it? Could your employees produce six units per hour if their lives depended on it? If the answer is yes, then the solution is not to teach them something they already know how to do; the solution is to provide the environment that allows or encourages them to do it.

Moving to the right of the flow chart in Figure 4.5, the analyst attempts to determine the cause of poor performance by asking a number of questions. Is the person punished for performing? While this question seems odd, organizational life is full of anecdotes of penalties for performance. The secretary who works twice as hard as another is punished by being given more work. The manager who does make decisions is berated for the occasional wrong decision.

The next consideration is the determination of rewards for effective performance. Are there positive consequences for performing as desired? Many times, when an employee does something good, the manager says nothing, on the assumption that the employee is being paid to work properly. However, positive behaviour that is not reinforced tends to deteriorate.

Sometimes, employees assume that their performance does not matter to anyone. When managers sit in their offices and fume over sloppy work but give no feedback to employees, or arrange no consequences for poor performance, the sloppy work will continue. Working with HR developers, managers can set up contingency management programs.

Contingency management is grounded in the belief that every act has a consequence, and if the consequence is perceived as a reward, then the act will be repeated. If there is no consequence or the consequence is negative or punishing, the action will not be repeated or will be concealed. By analyzing rewards and punishments, managers may see that they are asking for safe procedures but castigating those who slow down production. "Quality" may be the all-important word on the sign in the factory, but employees may be praised for production records. The determination of what constitutes effective performance, and the management of reinforcement for achieving it, is a far more powerful instrument of change than a training course.

Training is ineffective when the environment is the cause of the poor performance. Obstacles to effective performance may involve lack of authority, inadequate tools or technology, conflicting responsibilities, work overload, etc.

To restate the critical question asked earlier: Could the employee perform this task if his or her life depended on it? If the answer is yes, say no to training. If the employee couldn't do the work if his or her life depended on it, consider other changes before training.

Following the left side of the flow chart in Figure 4.5, consider if the employee ever performed the task and now needs some practice. Is the employee aware of the standards and receiving feedback on his or her performance against that standard? Dramatic results have been achieved by having employees measure their own performance against the standard.

Instead of training, can the work be rearranged, the employee transferred or terminated, or the job redesigned? For example, one task for a trainer might be to operate a software package that controls the administration of training courses. If the trainer is a "technopeasant," it might be easier to redesign the job so that a senior clerk operates the system and the trainer does what he or she does best: trains.

Training is one remedy for handling performance problems, but there are others that are more effective and less costly. Training is probably the most expensive solution. The costs of data collection and analysis, program design, salaries of training staff and trainees, travel, audiovisual support, etc. are tremendous. A further problem is that even the best-designed training course doesn't always work because the environment does not support the changed performance.

Training works best under the following conditions: tasks are performed frequently; the task is difficult; and correct performance is critical (Hobbs, 1990). If the needs analysis reveals that tasks are not frequently executed, that they are not critical, and that perfection is not required, then performance-improvement solutions such as job aids and coaching are more appropriate. More radical solutions may even be appropriate. Nadler (1990) suggests changing the people through firing and hiring, re-engineering the job, changing the equipment, or changing the organizational structure. See Chapter 6 (Supplements to Training) for other suggestions.

Even if training is determined to be the best solution, the costs and benefits of training must first be estimated. Trainers must ask questions such as "What is the cost of not doing the training?" "What are the monetary benefits to training?" (Chapter 11 on Costing Training discusses these questions.) Another consideration is the legal requirement to prove knowledge and skill levels for designated workers. A further point is the pressure exerted by top management to conduct the training. It is hoped that this pressure is a result of management objectives and priorities. These three elements are catalysts in the determination of priorities for training.

◆ ◆ ◆
DATA-COLLECTION METHODS

The identification of training needs can turn into a comprehensive research study. The cost, the time, and the rigor necessary for doing a perfect needs identification guarantee that most organizations will not do one. This section assumes that conducting some data collection and analysis, rather than having no objective measures, will result in a better training course. For readers interested in a purer form of research, the book *Research Methods in Human Resources Management* will be helpful (Schmitt and Klimoski, 1991).

The use of multiple methods helps analysts distinguish between perceived needs (what training courses employees feel they need), demand needs (what managers ask for), and normative needs (training needed to meet industry, unit, or job comparative standards) (Lee and Roadman, 1991). The following section describes some of the most common methods of needs identification.

◆ ◆ ◆
GENERAL METHODS OF DOCUMENTATION (HOW)

Steadham (1980) has developed a useful summary of nine basic assessment techniques, which are reproduced in Table 4.3.

Some software firms have developed workforce surveys that can be customized to include questions from broad climate issues to specific job standards. For example, a firm in Hampstead, Québec, has developed a software package that measures employee attitudes on a range of issues from communication ("Do you believe your manager listens to you?") to job benefits (Cornell, 1993). This technology allows HR personnel to develop customized surveys quickly, and to analyze results by region, unit, etc. A training manager at Rio Algom in Toronto states that his HR system contains 200 000 pieces of information on 500 employees. This system taps every skill of every employee ranging from forklift and fuel-tank exchange procedures to probing abilities (Rockburn, 1991).

TABLE 4.3 ADVANTAGES AND DISADVANTAGES OF NINE BASIC NEEDS ASSESSMENT TECHNIQUES

Techniques	Advantages	Disadvantages
Observation • Can be as technical as time-motion studies or as functionally or behaviorally specific as observing a new board or staff member interacting during a meeting. • May be as unstructured as walking through an agency's offices on the lookout for evidence of communication barriers. • Can be used normatively to distinguish between effective and ineffective behaviours, organizational structures, and/or process.	• Minimizes interruption of routine work flow or group activity. • Generates in situ data, highly relevant to the situation where response to identified training needs/interests will impact. • (When combined with a feedback step) provides for important comparison checks between inferences of the observer and the respondent.	• Requires a highly skilled observer with both process and content knowledge (unlike an interviewer who needs, for the most part, only process skills). • Carries limitations that derive from being able to collect data only within the work setting (the other side of the first advantage listed in the preceding column). • Holds potential for respondents to perceive the observation activity as "spying."
Questionnaires • May be in the form of surveys or polls of a random or stratified sample of respondents, or an enumeration of an entire "population." • Can use a variety of question formats: open-ended, projective, forced-choice, priority-ranking. • Can take alternative forms such as Q-sorts, or slipsorts, rating scales, either predesigned or self-generated by respondent(s). • May be self-administered (by mail) under controlled or uncontrolled conditions, or may require the presence of an interpreter or assistant.	• Can reach a large number of people in a short time. • Are relatively inexpensive. • Give opportunity of expression without fear of embarrassment. • Yield data easily summarized and reported.	• Make little provision for free expression of unanticipated responses. • Require substantial time (and technical skills, especially in survey model) for development of effective instruments. • Are of limited utility in getting at causes of problems or possible solutions. • Suffer low return rates (mailed), grudging responses, or unintended and/or inappropriate respondents.
Key Consultation • Secures information from those persons who, by virtue of their formal or informal standing, are in a good position to know what the training needs of a particular group are: a. board chairman b. related service providers c. members of professional associations d. individuals from the service population	• Is relatively simple and inexpensive to conduct. • Permits input and interaction of a number of individuals, each with his or her own perspectives of the needs of the area, discipline, group, etc. • Establishes and strengthens lines of communication between participants in the process.	• Carries a built-in bias, since it is based on views of those who tend to see training needs from their own individual or organizational perspective. • May result in only a partial picture of training needs due to the typically nonrepresentative nature (in a statistical sense) of a key informant group.
Print Media • Can include professional journals, legislative news/notes, industry "rags," trade magazines, in-house publications.	• Is an excellent source of information for uncovering and clarifying normative needs. • Provides information that is current, if not forward-looking. • Is readily available and is apt to have already been reviewed by the client group.	• Can be a problem when it comes to the data analysis and synthesis into a useable form (use of clipping service or key consultants can make this type of data more useable).

continued

Techniques	Advantages	Disadvantages
Interviews • Can be formal or casual, structured or unstructured, or somewhere in between. • May be used with a sample of a particular group (board, staff, committee) or conducted with everyone concerned. • Can be done in person, by phone, at the work site, or away from it.	• Are adept at revealing feelings, causes of, and possible solutions to problems that the client is facing (or anticipates); provide maximum opportunity for the client to represent himself spontaneously on his own terms (especially when conducted in an open-ended, nondirective manner).	• Are usually time-consuming. • Can be difficult to analyze and quantify results (especially from unstructured formats). • Unless the interviewer is skilful, the client(s) can easily be made to feel self-conscious. • Rely for success on a skilful interviewer who can generate data without making client(s) feel self-conscious, suspicious, etc.
Group Discussion • Resembles face-to-face interview technique, e.g., structured or unstructured, formal or informal, or somewhere in between • Can be focused on job (role) analysis, group problem analysis, group goal setting, or any number of group tasks or themes, e.g., "leadership training needs of the board." • Uses one or several of the familiar group facilitating techniques: brainstorming, nominal group process, force-fields, consensus rankings, organizational mirroring, simulation, and sculpting.	• Permits on-the-spot synthesis of different viewpoints. • Builds support for the particular service response that is ultimately decided on. • Decreases client's "dependence response" toward the service provided since data analysis is (or can be) a shared function. • Helps participants to become better problem analysts, better listeners, etc.	• Is time-consuming (therefore initially expensive) both for the consultant and the agency. • Can produce data that are difficult to synthesize and quantify (more a problem with the less structured techniques).
Tests • Are a hybridized form of questionnaire. • Can be very functionally oriented (like observations) to test a board, staff, or committee member's proficiency. • May be used to sample learned ideas and facts. • Can be administered with or without the presence of an assistant.	• Can be especially helpful in determining whether the cause of a recognized problem is a deficiency in knowledge or skill, or by elimination, attitude. • Results are easily quantifiable and comparable.	• The availability of a relatively small number of tests that are validated for a specific situation. • Do not indicate if measured knowledge and skills are actually being used in the on-the-job or "back home group" situation.
Records, Reports • Can consist of organizational charts, planning documents, policy manuals, audits, and budget reports. • Employee records (grievance, turnover, accidents, etc.) • Includes minutes of meetings, weekly, monthly program reports, memoranda, agency service records, program evaluation studies.	• Provide excellent clues to trouble spots. • Provide objective evidence of the results of problems within the agency or group. • Can be collected with a minimum of effort and interruption of work flow since it already exists at the work site.	• Causes of problems or possible solutions often do not show up. • Carries perspective that generally reflects the past situation rather than the current one (or recent changes). • Need a skilled data analyst if clear patterns and trends are to emerge from such technical and diffuse raw data.
Work Samples • Are similar to observation but in written form. • Can be products generated in the course of the organization's work, e.g., ad layouts, program proposals, market analyses, letters, training designs. • Written responses to a hypothetical but relevant case study provided by the consultant.	• Carry most of the advantage of records and reports data. • Are the organization's data (its own output).	• Case study method will take time away from actual work of the organization. • Need specialized content analysts. • Analyst's assessment of strengths/weaknesses disclosed by samples can be challenged as "too subjective."

Source: From "Learning to Select a Needs Assessment Strategy," by S.V. Steadham. In *Training and Development Journal*, 30, January 1980, pp. 56–61. Copyright © 1980 by the American Society for Training and Development, Inc. Reprinted by permission. All rights reserved.

COMPARISON OF METHODS

A study by Preskill (1991) suggests that some methods of analysis are better than others in terms of response rate, quality, and usefulness of the data and cost. Preskill tested three assessment alternatives: closed-ended survey, open-ended survey, and focus groups. A combination of the closed-ended survey plus focus-group interviews provided the most practical, useful, and cost-effective information.

There are many other sources of information. Some retail stores assess the competence of their sales staff through the use of professional shoppers, who rate sales performance against established standards (Tritsch, 1991). A bank tests employee knowledge using a computer-based analysis, and then compares the results with supervisory rankings (Tritsch, 1991).

A complete list of sources of needs analysis would include:

- Informal interview
- Survey method
- Formal interview
- Examination of records
- Advisory committees
- Questionnaires
- Formal research
- Benchmarking
- Regular management reports
- New technology or equipment
- Human resource plans

- Observation
- Performance tests
- Reports from superiors
- Checklists
- Assessment centres
- Management requests
- Production records
- New policies
- New products
- New legislation
- Appraisals and promotions

The best method depends on the time and money available, the experience of the analyst, and the nature of the responses. The next section describes some of the issues surrounding sampling.

◆ ◆ ◆

SOURCES OF INFORMATION (WHO)

Information about organizational and job performance is only as good as the source. One critical question in needs analysis is determining the source of the information. There are several options for the needs analyst.

SAMPLE SIZE

While it may be tempting to survey everyone in the organization, data collection and analysis becomes costly as the sample size increases. Moreover, a small sample of 100 people may generate results identical to a survey of the entire population of 1500; thus, money and respondent time are saved. Therefore the sample size should above all be robust enough to enable statistical analyses but small enough to provide information in a cost-effective manner.

SAMPLE DEPTH

Surveying only job incumbents about their perceptions of their own abilities may not result in the most objective portrait of performance gaps. Managers, too, should be asked for their performance evaluations. Those in frequent interaction with job incumbents, such as customers or employees in other departments, should also be surveyed. These different perspectives result in valuable information.

CONFIDENTIALITY

Surveys must be voluntary and confidential. Employees are naturally wary about the analyses of their jobs or performance. Such assessments have been used to determine workload or compensation. Therefore, front-end support must be created by involving the stakeholders (managers, employee groups, unions, etc.) in the goals and structuring of the survey. Communication from management must reinforce the importance and rationale for the analysis. Employees should be given written assurance of the voluntary nature of the survey. In addition, questionnaires should be coded so that a specific employee cannot be identified. Feedback to employees should consist of group responses.

◆ ◆ ◆

DATA-COLLECTION ISSUES

When collecting information from employees, HR analysts should be cautious when relying on self-assessment data, and in the use and interpretation of the information. This section outlines some problems with data collection.

SELF-ASSESSMENT

Much of the data collected on performance requires job holders to rate their own performance. This technique has its benefits and its limitations. Employees may be more motivated to be trained if they perceive that their needs are being met by the training program. Employees who are forced to attend training may be reluctant to transfer this training to the job (Noe and Schmitt, 1986). But self-perceptions of need pose many problems for the analyst.

Expressions of need include feelings or desires, and may have no relation to performance (Latham, 1988). Several studies have found weak relationships between self-assessment of performance and managerial assessments (McEnery and McEnery, 1987; Staley and Shockley-Zalaback, 1986). More damning is the review of 55 studies that found no strong relationship between self-evaluation of ability and other measures of performance (Mabe and West, 1982). However, a study at IBM demonstrated that employees can be trained in self-assessment by learning to break down a job into its component parts and analyze skills (Bardsely, 1987). This had the added benefit of the employees' accepting ownership of their development plans.

EXTENT OF DATA COLLECTION

Sometimes time is a constraint in data collection. The new equipment may be arriving on Monday, and it is easier to train all employees on all procedures instead of determining who needs training on which aspects of the new equipment.

Sometimes, the constraint is the quality of information. Managers may have difficulty answering even the simplest question: What is the expected performance level? In some cases, different managers may perceive different standards as the key measures of performance.

USE OF INFORMATION

Employees responding to questions about effectiveness may fear that the information will be used against them. They may fear a change in compensation, a restructuring or elimination of their jobs, or a negative personnel evaluation, with attendant losses of promotion or pay. They may distrust the analyst's ability to keep the data safe from the eyes of their supervisors.

CAUSE AND EFFECT

Most analysts find it difficult to disentangle cause and effect. For example, a poor quality product may be the result of a lack of knowledge on the part of employees, poorly designed work procedures, or even rumours about a plant shutdown.

COST BENEFIT

One study has determined that a majority of firms do not use formal needs assessment (Saari et al., 1988). People who work in training and development claim that they are not rewarded for taking the time (and money) to conduct needs analysis. Managers seem to feel that they should use training resources to train. They may also feel that they can accurately identify training needs and that more analysis is a waste of time. Managers may even have their own agendas such as rewarding employees by sending them to exotic locations for training. These managers may resist interference by the "personnel department" in management decisions.

As HR practitioners become educated and certified in their profession, the importance and application of front-end analysis may increase.

◆ ◆ ◆

SUMMARY

This chapter has examined the process of determining training and development needs. The rationale and the methods for conducting needs analyses were presented. Problems associated with the process were discussed. There is not a perfect needs-assessment model, and trainers must combine a number of methods and sources to develop an effective process.

CASE STUDY

Mobile Communications Ltd.

The growth in cellular phones at Mobile Communications Ltd. had been spectacular over the last decade. The firm experienced rapid increases in sales, employees, profits, and even complaints. However, the president of the company predicted only moderate growth now that the market has been saturated with competitors. He wished to maintain profit levels and market share by providing superior service. He envisioned doing this with a motivated and skilled workforce, but he did not have a good picture of either the motivation levels of his employees or the nature of their skill deficiencies. He therefore instructed his manager of training to conduct a needs analysis to supply this information.

Sue Bretton, the training manager, decided to conduct a survey of the organization climate and to do both a job and person analysis. For the organizational climate survey, she purchased a standardized "Organization Culture Survey" software package. This package tapped factors such as leadership (competence and fairness); job satisfaction (relationships with co-workers, promotion opportunities, motivation, work itself); and human resource policies, such as training opportunities and compensation.

The job-analysis survey consisted of having managers identify the organization's key positions. The incumbents of these positions were formally interviewed, with their supervisors, to determine the key competencies required to perform the jobs effectively. Real work examples of very effective or stellar performance were solicited, as well as incidences of incompetence. Top man-

agement reviewed these to ensure that these core competencies reflected the strategic orientation (customer service) of the company.

Person or personnel analysis was the next step. Each employee was rated on the BARS scale, developed in the job analysis. In addition, developmental discussions were held with every employee to supplement the climate-survey information and to identify employee career aspirations.

All this information was integrated, and the results indicated that employees would be more motivated if given incentive pay and managers with more management skills. Additionally, hundreds of employees with specific skill deficiencies were identified.

EXERCISES

1. The manager of training purchased an organizational climate survey that asked employees to rate their satisfaction with a number of organizational practices and processes. However, two items that she wished to assess were not part of the vendor's package. These were the coaching abilities of managers and the physical office environment. Develop a scale for measuring employee satisfaction for these two dimensions.

2. What do you think are the core competencies of a sales manager's job (a key position in this organization)? Take two of these competencies and attempt to describe them in behavioural terms. Brainstorm with your group and construct a BARS-type scale, listing examples of effective and incompetent performance.

References

Bardsely, C.A. 1987. "Improving Employee Awareness of Opportunity at IBM." *Personnel* (April).

Bass, B.M., and J.A. Vaughn. 1966. *Training in Industry: The Management of Learning.* Belmont, CA: Wadsworth.

Carr. C. 1992. "The Three R's of Training." *Training* 29, no. 6 (June).

Chevalier, R.D. 1990. "Analyzing Performance Discrepancies with Line Managers." *Performance and Instruction* 29, no. 10 (November–December).

Cornell, C. 1993. "Disk Drive Consultants." *Human Resources Professional* 9, no. 2 (February).

Dolan, S.L., and R.S. Schuler. 1994. *Human Resource Management: The Canadian Dynamic.* Scarborough, Ont.: Nelson Canada.

Estabrooke, M., and Foy, N.F. 1992. "Answering the Call of Tailored Training." *Training* 29, no. 10 (October): 84–88.

Froiland, P. 1993. "Reproducing Star Performers." *Training* 30, no. 11 (September).

Geroy G.D. 1986. *Education for Work: An Integration of Vocational Education and Employer-Sponsored Training in Minnesota.* Research Report no. 13. University of Minnesota, Training and Research Center.

Geroy, G.D. 1990. *Education for Work: An Integration of Vocational Education and Employer-Sponsored Training in Minnesota.* St. Paul: Training and Development Research Center, University of Minnesota, Report #13 .

Geroy, G.D., P.C. Wright, and P.L. Caffrey. 1989. "Establishing a Multi-Craft Maintenance Operation." *Performance and Instruction* 28, no. 7.

Glaser, E.M., and S.H. Taylor. 1973. "Factors Influencing the Success of Applied Research." *American Psychologist* 28, no. 2, 579–84.

Goldstein, I.L. 1993. *Training in Organizations.* 3rd ed. Pacific Grove, Calif.: Brooks/Cole Publishing Company.

Hobbs, D.L. 1990. "A Training-Appropriation Process." *Training and Development Journal* 44, no. 4 (May).

Kaufman, R. 1991. *Strategic Planning Plus: An Organizational Guide.*

Glenview, Ill.: Scott Foreman Professional Books.

Laird, D. 1985. *Approaches to Training and Development*. Rev. ed. Reading, Mass.: Addison-Wesley Publishing Company.

Landey, F.J., and J. Vasey. 1991. "Job Analysis: The Composition of SME Samples." *Personnel Psychology* 44.

Latham, G.P. 1988. "Human Resource Training and Development." *Annual Review of Psychology* 39.

Lee, W.W., and K.H. Roadman. 1991. "Linking Needs Assessment to Performance Based Evaluation." *Performance and Instruction* 30, no. 7 (July).

Lewis, T., and D.C. Bjorkquist. 1992. "Needs Assessment—A Critical Reappraisal." *Performance Improvement Quarterly* 5, no. 4.

Maslow, A.H. 1954. *Motivation and Personality*. New York: Harper & Row Publishers, Inc.

McEnery, J., and J.M. McEnery. 1987. "Self-Rating in Management Training Needs Assessment: A Neglected Opportunity." *Journal of Occupational Psychology* 60, 49–60.

Mabe, P.A., and S.G. West. 1982. "Validity of Self-Evaluation of Ability. A Review and a Meta-analysis." *Journal of Applied Psychology* 67, 280–296.

Mager, R.F., and P. Pipe. 1970. *Analyzing Performance Problems or You Really Oughta Wanna*. Belmont, Calif.: Lear Siegler, Inc./Fearon Publishers.

Mills, G.R., W. Pace, and B. Peterson. 1989. *Analysis in Human Resource Training and Organization Development*. Reading, Mass.: Addison-Wesley.

Moore, M.L., and P. Dutton. 1987. "Training Needs Analysis: Preview and Critique." *Academy of Management Review* 3, no. 3.

Nadler, L. 1990. *Designing Training Programs: The Critical Events Model*. Reading, Mass.: Addison-Wesley Publishing.

Noe, R.A., and N. Schmitt. 1986. "The Influence of Trainer Attitudes on Training Effectiveness: Test of a Model." *Personnel Psychology* 39: 497–523.

Nowack, K.M. 1991. "A True Training Needs Analysis." Training and *Development Journal* 43, no. 4 (April).

Okey, J.R. 1990. "Tools of Analysis in Instructional Development." *Educational Technology* 30, no. 6.

Pace, R.W., P.C. Smith, and G.E. Mills. 1991. *Human Resource Development: The Field*. Englewood Cliffs, N.J.: Prentice-Hall.

Preskill, H. 1991. "A Comparison of Data Collection Methods for Assessing Training Needs." *Human Resource Development Quarterly* (Summer).

Rockburn, J. 1991. "Streamlining Human Resources." *The Globe and Mail* (15 October): B15.

Saari, L.M., T.R. Johnson, S.D. McLaughlin, and D.M. Zimmerle. 1988. "A Survey of Management Training and Education Practices in U.S. Companies." *Personnel Psychology* 41, no. 4: 731–44.

Schmitt, N.W., and R.J. Klimoski. 1991. *Research Methods in Human Resources Management*. Cincinnati: South-Western Publishing.

Schuler, R.S. 1992. "Linking the People with the Strategic Needs of the Business." *Organizational Dynamics* 21, no. 4 (Autumn).

Sleezer, C.M. 1992. "Needs Assessment: Perspectives from the Literature." *Performance Improvement Quarterly* 5, no. 2.

Staley, C.C., and P. Shockley-Zalaback. 1986. "Communication Proficiency and Future Training Needs of the Female Professional: Self-Assessment Versus Supervisors' Evaluations." *Human Relations* 39, 891–902.

Steadham, S.V. 1980. "Learning to Select a Needs Assessment Strategy." *Training and Development Journal* 34, no. 4 (January).

Tritsch, C. 1991. "Assessing your Training." *Human Resource Executive* (May).

Wexley, K.M., and G. Latham. 1991. *Developing and Training Human Resources in Organizations*. 2nd ed. New York: Harper Collins Publishers.

5

Setting
Objectives

INTRODUCTION

Training programs have goals, and these goals are usually described as objectives. Instructional or learning objectives and Management by Objectives (MBO) have a lot in common—they are both results-oriented, performance-based planning tools. Training and development can no longer be viewed only in terms of the content, but must be seen as resulting in performance improvement. Simply put, the critical question is "What should the trainee be able to do at the end of the training program?" This chapter provides a model and techniques for establishing training objectives.

The end result of training must be both measurable and observable (Donaldson and Scannell, 1986). The process of determining what is to be learned begins with someone in the organization perceiving a problem or deficiency. A formal needs analysis (described in Chapter 4) results in the identification of specific performance weaknesses, or opportunities for improving effectiveness. With these data in hand, the human resource (HR) developer can state specifically the behaviours that are to change. The most effective way to do this is through the preparation of objectives.

An objective is a statement of what participants are expected to be able to do after a training course or development program. (The distinctions between a program, course, session, etc. are not critical to this discussion. Generally, a course is a learning experience, usually off the job site, conducted over a specified period. A program might consist of several courses, include on-the-job work experience, and occur over a longer period. A session might be part of a course or a program.)

The emphasis in training is on performance, or behaviour on the job. Learning can be described as the process of acquiring new skills, knowledge, and attitudes, while performance is the use of these new skills, knowledge, and attitudes (Nadler, 1990). Therefore, the establishment of learning objectives focuses on performance on the job. This performance should be observable and measurable (Ribler, 1983).

◆ ◆ ◆
ADVANTAGES OF OBJECTIVES

As trainers and developers work with programs, they discover that there is a strong case to be made for knowing exactly what a course promises to achieve (or its objectives). The reasons for this include:

1. Trainees need to have a clear understanding of what is expected of them. Objectives allow them to focus their energies on achieving these goals, rather than waste energy on learning irrelevant tasks, or trying to figure out what is required of them. Several studies have demonstrated that, if instructors use objectives, students can be more efficient learners (Mager and McCann, 1961; McNeil, 1966; Miles et al., 1967). The clarity of the goal and the specific feedback toward its achievement is critical to training. Someone once said that baseball would die if it weren't for its emphasis on performance statistics. Such statistics suggest clear goals for future achievement.

2. Trainees can be assessed prior to instruction to determine if they have mastered any of the objectives. Depending on the results, students can either omit certain sections of a course or undertake other training in order to master the prerequisites.

3. The selection of content, teaching modes, and evaluation methods is simplified by objectives. Trainers will concentrate on methods that produce results, rather than use favourite or trendy training techniques.

4. Objectives communicate to supervisors, professional groups, assessors, and others what the student is expected to have learned by the end of the training program. Instructors who teach preceding and subsequent units of training also need this information.

5. Management and the training supervisors know exactly what is expected of trainees and can reinforce the new skills learned in the job situation.

6. Accountability for training results may make managers more likely to approve a course that specifies improvements to be achieved. This communicates to employees that training means business and that it is an integral part of the planning of the organization.

7. A precise, objective, and measurable statement of learning objectives enables evaluators to gauge the quantitative benefits of a program. Mager

(1975) said it best: "We need to know where we are going before we can get there."

◆ ◆ ◆
THE WRITING OF OBJECTIVES

The writing of objectives is a skill that can be learned. The skill in writing objectives does not lie in the amassing of behaviour verbs such as "recognize" and "evaluate" but in the ability to rework needs-analysis data into performance outcomes. An objective should state the desired behaviour, the conditions under which the behaviour is performed, and the standards of acceptable performance.

Five steps should be followed when writing objectives (Cranton, 1989).

1. List the goals of the instruction. An example would be: *The student will be able to describe the domains of learning.*

2. These goals should then be translated into observable or measurable items. The example cited above might then read: *The student will be able to define objectives, discuss five advantages and three limitations of objectives, list the domains of learning, and give an example of an objective within each domain.*

3. The degree of detail must be considered. This will vary with the level of learning within various contexts or institutions, and with the learner. We might take one of the above objectives and state: *The student will be able to list the domains of learning with 90 percent accuracy.*

4. The circumstances or conditions of evaluation must be stated. Will the student list the domains alone, or with an open book, within 15 minutes, etc.? The objective should include this information.

5. The next step would be to take the list of objectives and have them reviewed by other instructors and former and current trainees. The goal is to assess whether the objectives are measurable, clear, comprehensive, and achievable, and whether they adequately reflect course content. Adult learners, in particular, should be widely consulted on the learning objectives. This is practical and feasible in a training situation, less so in educational institutions where goals are predetermined.

Objectives should contain the following five elements:

1. Who is to perform the desired behaviour? Students and participants are the easiest to identify. In a training situation, where employees are not necessarily students in a classroom, more accurate descriptors might be "all first-level supervisors," "anyone conducting selection interviews," or "all employees with more than one month of experience." (The trainer is not the "who," although it is tempting for some students to write, for example, that the trainer will present five hours of information on communication. The goal of the instructor is to maximize the efficiency with which all students achieve the specified objectives, not just present information (Kibler et al., 1970).

2. What is the actual behaviour to be employed to demonstrate mastery of the training content or objective? Words like "type," "run," and "calculate" can be measured easily. Other mental activities such as comprehension and analysis can also be described in such a way as to be measurable, as shown at the end of this chapter.

3. and 4. Where and when is the behaviour to be demonstrated and evaluated, i.e., under what conditions? These could include "during a 60-minute typing test," "on the ski hill with icy conditions," "when presented with a diagram," or "when asked to design a training session." The tools, equipment, information, and other source materials for training should be specified. Included in this list may be things the trainee may not use, such as portable calculators.

5. What is the standard by which the behaviour will be judged? Is the trainee expected to type 60 words per minute with less than three errors? Can the student list five out of six categories?

The final written objective will contain three components:

a. Performance: what the trainee will be able to do after the session;

b. Condition: the tools, time, etc. under which the trainee is expected to perform;

c. Criterion: the level of acceptable performance.

A well-written objective would read as follows:

> *The sales representative (who) will be able to make 10 calls a*
> *day to new customers in the territory assigned (what, where,*

when), and will be able to generate three (30 percent) sales worth at least $500 from these calls (how, or the criterion).

The first attempts at writing objectives will be difficult. However, after some experience, a generalization of these planning skills will occur. Managers will start thinking in terms of management by objectives and performance appraisals using measurable results. People negotiating assignments and other work will evaluate the "contract" or objective in terms of its measurability.

Representative workers should be involved in the development of the learning objectives. A team consisting of the trainer, trainees, and their supervisors would be ideal (Laird, 1985). At some point, the objectives should be reviewed with, and approved by, the executives of the organization and the supervisors of the trainees. Nadler (1990) cites a case where a sales training program, based on a needs analysis of sales representatives, was rejected by senior management because management were secretly planning fundamental organizational changes.

At this stage, the learning objectives should closely resemble the task analysis (discussed in Chapter 4). For example, one task of the job of a receptionist could be: *The receptionist (who) sorts incoming mail by categories of complaints, requests for information, and invoices (what) within 60 minutes, with less than one percent processing errors (how).* This could easily become a training objective. A learning objective that reads like an actual job behaviour is more likely to be approved, learned, and used on the job.

In summary, a learning objective contains an observable action, with a measurable criterion outlining conditions of performance.

◆ ◆ ◆
TYPES OF OBJECTIVES

There is a tool to assist trainers in the development of objectives. Bloom (1956; 1964) compiled a list of specific learning objectives, which he named *Taxomony of Educational Objectives*. The Taxonomy divides the categories of objectives into three domains: cognitive (knowledge), affective (attitudes), and psychomotor (skills). Each of these domains contains a hierarchical listing of behaviours, on the assumption that each successive behaviour is more difficult than and depends upon learning of the previous behaviour. This categorization of behaviours is extremely helpful to course designers and will be discussed in some detail.

◆◆◆
DOMAINS OF LEARNING

As mentioned, learning is the process of acquiring some new skill, attitude, or knowledge. Performance describes the use of the skill, attitude, and knowledge. Later in the text, we will discuss techniques to ensure transfer of learning to performance on the job. For this chapter, we will concentrate on learning.

In any textbook on learning in psychology or education, the term "domains of learning" accurately portrays a fundamental concept, basically that there are areas and levels of learning. The three basic areas are cognitive, affective, and psychomotor. Most managers and employees would be more comfortable with the comparable terms of knowledge, attitudes, and skills— or simply: the head, the heart, and the hand.

◆◆◆
KNOWLEDGE

This first and largest area of learning includes all intellectual processes: recalling facts, understanding concepts, applying these concepts to practical situations and analyzing theories (Cranton, 1989). This area is what people generally think of as learning. Within this category, Bloom (1956) has identified levels of learning. These levels are arranged hierarchically, and, as mentioned, the assumption is that the first level must be mastered before the subsequent levels can be learned.

The levels within the cognitive domain are:

1. Knowledge. This simplest level of learning includes the recognition and recall of basic facts. Students call it rote learning.

> *Example: Apprentices will be able to list the six steps in machine assembly, with zero errors, within 10 minutes.*

Words that describe this function are: *define, outline, sort, recall, recount, match, record, list, cluster, name, repeat,* and *label.*

2. *Comprehension.* At this level, the student not only knows the information but can demonstrate that he or she understands the material.

> *Example: Managers will be able to describe in their own words the meaning of sexual harassment.*

Key defining words are: *locate, recognize, identify, paraphrase, tell, describe, report, explain, cite, support,* and *summarize.*

3. *Application.* As the label suggests, this step involves the use of knowledge and understanding. After learning rules, principles, or other basic knowledge, the learner attempts to apply this knowledge to problems or new situations.

> *Example: Building-code inspectors will be able to identify 99 out of 100 building-code infractions during a mock inspection lasting two hours.*

Cue words under this category are: *select, use, imitate, demonstrate, apply, frame, illustrate, solve, organize, sequence,* and *manipulate.*

4. *Analysis.* At a higher level, students are able to critically analyze a theory or a concept. By comparing and contrasting information, the student appraises information. (In some cases, the application stage is not a prerequisite for this level.)

> *Example: While observing a squash match, the trainee will be able to compare and contrast the strategies used by the two players.*

This type of learning is more complex and is dependent on understanding the various components of the subject area. Sometimes the application level is not necessary for the analysis level. This will vary by subject.

The descriptive verbs in this category are: *examine, distinguish, differentiate, outline, characterize, compare/contrast, research, interpret, debate/defend, conclude* and *analyze*.

5. *Synthesis.* At this level, students analyze information from a wide variety of sources and meld the facts and theories into a coherent concept or position. A student paper is the best example of synthesis. At work, the preparation of a proposal or plan is a good illustration of the concept of synthesis.

> *Example: The student will prepare a paper on a training method, in which the concept is defined, illustrated, analyzed, and a conclusion on its effectiveness is discussed.*

The critical verbs are: *propose, create, invent, plan, formulate, design, emulate, speculate,* and *construct*.

6. *Evaluation.* The highest level of cognitive learning—evaluation—refers to a student's ability to critique, for example, a performance or a research proposal. This evaluation is not based on an emotional response to the performance or material but is an intellectual process guided by information learned at previous levels. It implies that a set of criteria for judging has been learned and can be applied.

> *Examples: Managers will be able to evaluate a new product-development proposal using both internal and external market standards.*
>
> *After observing a tennis match, the learners will be able to rank the players on the basis of technical skill.*

Some cue verbs are: *judge, rate, criticize, justify, argue, persuade, value, assess,* and *evaluate*.

The outline of these levels of learning assists the instructor in the design of the training program. In general, knowledge of concepts precedes understanding. Application is aided by a thorough comprehension of the facts.

Synthesis, analysis, and evaluation are dependent on an orderly procession through the levels.

◆ ◆ ◆
ATTITUDES

A more precise label for this area of learning is the affective domain. Included in this category are attitudes, values, emotions, motivation, beliefs, and interests. These are emotional responses rather than intellectual ones. In most occupations, interest and motivation are critical to performance. In others, such as teaching and nursing, beliefs and values play a critical role in the style of work. In particular, organizations of the nineties appear more concerned with employee attitudes, such as being a team player and having concern for the customer. Given this climate, the discussion on the definition and measurement of attitudes is germane.

There are those, such as the behavioural theorists, who argue that attitudes cannot be observed and measured, and therefore cannot be learned (Skinner, 1968). (See page 141 for a description of the behaviourist school.) To change a person's behaviour, behaviourists would modify the incentives for desired performance, not the person's attitudes. For example, they would reward managers with praise and financial bonuses if managers promoted women into supervisory positions. Behaviourists would contend that the managerial attitude toward women was irrelevant and that results are the only variable of importance. (Some supervisors and parents embody this position when they state, "I don't care if you like it, just do it.")

Others argue that attitudes are the key components of performance (Rogers, 1969). They insist that attitudes must be modified before behaviour can change. Therefore, faced with the challenge of increasing the percentage of women supervisors, these psychologists would attempt to change the attitudes of managers through courses outlining the nature and effects of discrimination, and attempt to increase the sensitivity of managers to equity issues.

Both positions can be understood through the use of examples. We all know of people who were coerced into learning a new skill or attending classes in an area in which they were afraid or resistant, and these people then became converts. Examples abound of individuals who have completed courses designed to change their attitudes and have returned more sensitive and willing to change their behaviour.

However, examples can be cited of managers who attended sensitivity or leadership training and did not modify their practices, until management changed the rewards and punishments for inappropriate behaviour. Modifying attitudes is complex, and this controversy is not easily resolved.

Debate on the issue of changing attitudes also focuses on the reluctance of some employees to have their belief systems challenged. They would like to do the job, and not be forced into training courses on empowerment and team building. Does the employer have a right to try to change people's beliefs and values?

Some argue that beliefs play a fundamental role in the effective operation of an organization. These people claim that organizations have a right, and even a responsibility, to change the attitudes of managers who believe, for example, that women can never be good supervisors because women are too emotional. But employees argue that they are there to do a job, not to have trainers tamper with their minds. They feel that they have a right to certain beliefs.

Organizations usually resolve this dilemma by arguing that certain attitude-change programs are in compliance with laws, such as employment-equity legislation. People can believe whatever they like, as long as their attitudes result in behaviour and performance that comply with laws such as those concerning human rights.

Obviously, this solution works for practices that are legislated, but it does not resolve the issue for programs that seek to analyze and change attitudes to relationships or openness to change. Critics have argued that managers (and organizations) should be sued for malpractice when they play games with employees, such as those found in the rock-climbing exercises of outdoor training (Zemke, 1978). Any course touching on personal-growth matters could be open to charges ranging from wasting time to harming managerial effectiveness. Indeed, in Atlantic Canada, a group of employees charged their employer with a violation of their rights. In this case, attendance at a course on self-actualization was compulsory. Employees claimed that the beliefs presented about the power of the self interfered with and contradicted their religious beliefs. The employees won and were no longer forced to attend company courses.

In order to legitimize attitude-change programs, organizations must learn to specify the objectives of these programs. Specifying the agenda will facilitate employees buying in to the programs. In this chapter we assume that changing attitudes is a legitimate goal in some circumstances, and we provide a framework for the analysis of attitudinal objectives.

LEVELS OF AFFECTIVE LEARNING

1. Receiving. At this level, the learner is asked simply to participate in a learning experience. Remember the door-to-door sales representative who primes the customer by pleading "Just let me demonstrate the product" or your mother imploring "Just try the broccoli." Implied in these statements is that after a person listens to information or observes products or demonstrations, he or she might then be more willing to move to the next step.

> *Example: The employee will listen to the presentation on the
> need to automate parts of his or her job.*

At this level, the trainee is expected to pay attention but is not required to respond.

2. Responding. The next level requires a reaction of some kind. These responses could include the expression of an opinion (either positive or negative), or some demonstration of an emotional reaction ("Wow! Uchh").

> *Example: After watching a presentation on the need for robots
> in the workplace, the trainee will express an opinion
> about robots.*

There is no commitment on the part of participants beyond an affective reaction of interest, enjoyment, etc.

3. Valuing. This stage requires a trainee to express a commitment to the belief or activity. The person is asked to value the material learned and to act upon it.

> *Example: The employee will be able to identify obstacles and
> opportunities of automation.*

4. Organization. At this stage, the belief or value becomes part of a larger theory or system in the structuring of attitudes. The trainee does not simply believe in isolated values but is on the road to developing a comprehensive philosophy. The result is a complex value system.

> *Example: The employee will suggest three ways to improve other areas of his or her work through automation.*

The key characterization here is the interrelationship of different values.

5. *Characterization.* At this stage, the belief system or philosophy is absorbed into a person's fundamental life beliefs and becomes a principal value for meaning in life. All or most actions will be grounded by the belief. The person is characterized by the value, e.g., she is a feminist, he is a real leader, or they are liberals.

> *Example: The trainee understands the role of automation in improving work processes and facilitating his or her personal life.*

The reader should now perceive the development of measurable objectives as a fundamental planning tool, not just in training but in business and personal areas.

This last step represents a philosophy or world view. This is the stage employees might fear and resent, particularly if "characterization" involves rejecting previously held belief systems. The new belief system, introduced and mandated by the organization, may run counter to values expressed by significant groups or people in the worker's life, such as the church or the family. The controversy surrounding the intrusion and pressure on employees to adopt certain beliefs is valid.

◆ ◆ ◆
SKILLS

The third area of learning concerns skill objectives. This domain includes physical skills such as the gross motor skills used in operating a saw or the fine motor skills used in drawing. Movements in dance or crafts could be included here. The portraying of emotions through bodily movements, such as nonverbal communication found in social work or drama, would fall into this category. (Not all skills are in the physical, creative, or technical sectors. Managers need to learn physical skills such as the use of eye contact in negotiation and presentation skills.)

The subcategories in this area are:

1. Perception. The learner must first be aware of the tools or objects of learning, or the environment in which the psychomotor response is expected. The senses are alerted, and this forms the basis for the subsequent development of the skill.

> *Example: The apprentice chef will be able to select the 20 most important kitchen tools of a master chef.*

Note that no physical activity is involved but that this level requires the use of the senses and is a prerequisite for the next level.

2. Set. A mental or physical set, or preparedness, is required before action is initiated. A mental set may include a visualization of a tennis stroke or a mental listing of the steps involved in preparing a soufflé. Physical preparedness may include standing in the proper position to receive a tennis serve or arriving at the playing field in uniform.

> *Example: The apprentice chef will be able to assemble the necessary equipment needed to prepare a cheese soufflé.*

3. Guided Response. As its name suggests, this level of learning implies a dependency on the instructor to guide the learner through the motions required. The golf student may have the instructor demonstrate how to hold a golf club or even physically adjust the hands of the trainee on the club. The skill may be broken down into specific movements, which are practised independently while receiving appropriate feedback.

> *Example: The apprentice chef will model the steps used in making a soufflé, in the correct sequence, as demonstrated by the master chef.*

4. *Mechanism.* With repeated practice of the specific movements, the trainee will perform the task independently and proficiently. Through modelling, guidance, and feedback, the action becomes habitual.

> *Example: The apprentice chef will create a cheese soufflé.*

Usually, this is the degree of achievement required: the person will perform the task independently and proficiently.

5. *Complex Overt Response.* At this stage, the trainee can execute a series of skills, each one composed of specific movements. The result is a sequence or patterns of moves, usually associated with the craft or sport. The skill is done without hesitation, and the sequences of skills are done efficiently and effectively.

> *Example: The apprentice chef plans a menu, buys the ingredients, and prepares and serves a gourmet meal for six.*

6. *Adaptation.* Conditions under which a skill is performed often change. Those players or performers with advanced skills can adapt or adjust their performance immediately. (Once, while the author was watching a play in London, England, the actor's dramatic knifing of an orange miscarried. The actor made up a line to accommodate the blunder, and the show went on.) In sports, movements by opponents make adaptation a valuable level of learning.

> *Example: The apprentice chef will be able adapt a menu designed for four in order to serve ten, and will be able to substitute at least three ingredients that are not available.*

Varying a response according to changing conditions is the desired characteristic at this level.

7. *Origination.* The most creative skill level compels the trainee to generate new movements or actions. This level would include the writing of a play, the creation of a new style of negotiation, or the development of a new technique for teaching presentation skills.

Example: The apprentice chef will create an original recipe.

These categories of learning objectives should cover most conditions in training and development, thus enabling the program developer to more accurately pinpoint the results expected.

◆ ◆ ◆
CAUTIONS ABOUT LEARNING OBJECTIVES

New trainers might be tempted to write easily measurable objectives such as "the sales representative will be able to recall the six steps to closing a sale." The trainer can quite easily choose both a method and an evaluation system that guarantee that all students obtain 100 percent on a test. But, obviously, this is not what the sales manager wants. She wants the sales representatives to close sales or generate profits. Therefore, the objective should be stated as a skills objective along the lines of: "In the field, the sales reps will be able to close sales 30 percent of the time, by the second call. This will represent an improvement of 20 percent over present success rates." We can then calculate the costs and benefits of the training.

The presentation of objectives in specific steps creates the impression that objectives can be isolated by domain and category. In real life, there is much overlap. For example, a trainer can be expected to learn "to present a workshop on negotiation, using a negotiation video and role plays, so that all students participate." In this example, cognitive skills (negotiation principles); attitudinal skills (encouraging participation); and motor skills (operating a VCR) are all required. From a practical viewpoint, it is not necessary to isolate the categories in every instance.

◆ ◆ ◆
OBJECTIONS TO THE USE OF OBJECTIVES

TIME

The development of measurable objectives takes time. This time could be spent convincing managers to buy into the training, or in actually doing the training. Obviously, there is the hope that the use of objectives will save time. By stating clearly what we are hoping to accomplish, we will not waste time on other activities.

The amount of time involved in developing objectives is highly dependent on the level of detail required. Little time is required to think about and write: "list the three domains of learning." But a considerable amount of time is required in the writing of objectives for a training session for a mentally challenged person learning to clean stores, for example. The activities of cleaning would have to be broken down into small and specific steps to accommodate the ability of the trainee. At the other end of the continuum, the difficulty of writing objectives for leadership training occurs because leadership effectiveness has never been usefully defined and measured. Therefore, the trainer must spend a considerable amount of time defining leadership effectiveness at his or her company.

RIGIDITY

Critics of objectives argue that once goals are written, they are written in stone. This allows for no flexibility in the program to include unexpected learner interests or relevant current issues.

In the program design, however, time can be built in for discussion of student interests and current issues. Trainers should also be alert to unexpected outcomes. Students may learn statistics and learn to hate statistics. If this is seen as an undesirable outcome, what aspects of the program can be changed?

STIFLING THE LEARNER

"Students are told what to learn, and they memorize it and regurgitate it" is the thrust of this argument. But as we have seen, the higher levels within the domains of learning encourage creativity and independent thinking on the part of the learner. Surely, the evaluation of a research proposal or the creation of a new method to teach tennis represent highly creative and individual acts.

Some critics have obviously misunderstood the nature of objectives. It is true that you can give students easily accomplished objectives, such as to define role play and to name three circumstances for which role play is effective. But you can also solicit three novel ways to use role plays, or the preparation of a role play, using information from a recent work experience; this is not spoon-feeding students information.

SOME JOBS DON'T HAVE STANDARDS

If some jobs don't have standards of performance, then how are performance appraisals conducted? How do managers know if an employee is doing well? Does it matter if performance is done well? Does it matter if the job exists? The first step is to define the job; from this, deficiencies in performance can be more accurately determined.

For example, in real life, professors mark original essays and managers rate performance without written standards. These standards exist in their minds; behaviourial objectives simply make them explicit. We would argue that all jobs do indeed have standards.

TRIVIAL LEARNER BEHAVIOURS

This criticism is related to the objection cited above. Critics contend that minor and insignificant objectives are easiest to operationalize, with the result that really meaningful outcomes of education may be underemphasized (Popham, 1968).

However, the truth is that explicit objectives (with significant educational learner behaviours) make it far easier for educators and trainers to attend to important instructional outcomes. A trainer of managers might say that his or her goal is to make people better communicators, but in fact what he or she is asking them to do is to memorize key words like "active listening," without being able to be active listeners.

DEHUMANIZING

Behaviour can be objectively, mechanistically measured; hence there must be something dehumanizing about the measurement approach. Adults resist being measured in some way, and associate this with exams and tests. But there are sophisticated ways of measuring quality as well as quantity of learning. The process need not be dehumanizing, like true–false tests, but can be liberating and creative, such as making a presentation before one's colleagues.

UNDEMOCRATIC

Specifying in advance what we expect the learner to learn runs counter to a tradition of freedom of expression and democracy. In reply to this concern, we suggest that the trainer negotiate the objectives with the students, after a process of consultation. A needs analysis is an important part of this consultation.

Related to this democracy argument is the one that individual trainees should not have to conform to a group standard. Critics argue that adults are capable of self-diagnosis and are capable of assessing their own needs. Miller (1983) counters that trainees should negotiate with the program developers to ensure that the objectives do meet their needs. Involving the trainees at the needs-analysis stage is important. Furthermore, the success of a training event increases when everyone agrees upon, or contracts for, the intended outcomes.

More importantly, however, education and training are not entirely, or even largely, open to negotiation. Neither governments nor corporations would want university students or new supervisors to define their goals entirely independent of the "authorities." Trainers and managers will always define what they want the learner to learn, more or less efficiently.

A related argument contends that rigid adherence to objectives eliminates the possibility of learning opportunities in the classroom. There is nothing preventing these kinds of spontaneous discussions from contributing to student learning; objectives merely inform the instructor about whether these opportunities are diversions or irrelevant entertainment for the class (Popham, 1968).

THIS AIN'T LIFE

Trainers rarely specify their goals in terms of measurable learner behaviours, so let's be realistic. But there is a distinction between recognizing the status quo and applauding it.

Performance-based objectives may not be relevant to all types of training. Programs that develop leaders or creative thinkers may require broad objectives that are individualized and flexible. These objectives differ from performance-based objectives in that they can be customized to the individual, they may take a long time to show results, and the process is emphasized over the results (Stonehall, 1992).

ACCOUNTABILITY

With measurable objectives, trainers might be judged on their ability to produce results in learners rather than on the many other bases of competence. It doesn't take a genius to realize that objectives (and therefore trainers) can be measured, and that trainers will be judged on their ability to attain these objectives. They should be.

Trainers should be judged on ends, not means. Some current indices of trainer effectiveness include: emotional reaction of audiences (jokes and stories help); the comfort level of the room; and the amount of free time during training. Trainers may even be judged on method: some trainees favour case studies or games and may dislike a trainer who uses computer-assisted instruction. Results should be the principal criteria of evaluation.

After reading this chapter, it is hoped that you will be able to list the levels of learning, be motivated to use them, and have the skills to do so.

You should be able to:

♦ Prepare a learning objective from each of the domains of learning.

♦ Describe the advantages and limitations of learning objectives.

♦ Apply this knowledge in the context of a real training situation.

♦ ♦ ♦
SUMMARY

This chapter has described the advantages of objectives, detailed a method for preparing objectives, and discussed concerns about the use of objectives.

EXERCISES

1. Identify a skill that your roommate, partner, or parent would like to acquire. Some examples might be: to use a particular software package for the computer, to use the cleaning cycle on the oven, or to gain a better understanding of existentialism. Study the task and develop learning objectives in each of the three categories: knowledge, skills, and attitude. Exchange these with a student partner, who will assess them in terms of the criteria outlined within this chapter (measurable performance, using who, when, where, how criteria).

2. Obtain a job description from an organization. If necessary, rewrite the task descriptions so that they become objective and measurable. Use these to write learning objectives for that job. Include the key components of who, what, where, when, and how well.

References

Bloom, B., ed. 1956. *Taxonomy of Educational Objectives: The Cognitive Domain.* New York: David McKay.

_____. 1964. *Taxonomy of Education Objectives: The Affective Domain.* New York: David McKay.

Cranton, P. 1989. *Planning Instruction for Adult Learners.* Toronto: Wall and Thompson.

Donaldson, L., and E. Scannell. 1986. *Human Resource Development: The New Trainer's Guide.* 2nd ed. Reading, Mass.: Addison-Wesley Publishing Company, Inc.

Kibler, R.J., L.L. Barker, and D.T. Miles. 1970. *Behavioral Objectives and Instruction.* Boston: Allyn and Bacon, Inc.

Laird, D. 1985. *Approaches to Training and Development.* 2nd ed. Reading, Mass.: Addison-Wesley Publishing Company.

McNeil, J.D. 1966. "Concomitant of Using Behaviourial Objectives in Assessment of Teacher Effectiveness." Paper presented at the American Educational Research Association Convention, Chicago.

Mager, R.F. 1975. *Preparing Instructional Objectives.* 2nd ed. Belmont, Calif.: Fearon.

Mager, R.F., and J. McCann. 1961. *Learner Controlled Instruction.* Palo Alto, Calif.: Varian and Associates.

Miles, D.T., R.J. Kibler, and L.E. Pettigrew. 1967. "The Effects of Study Questions on College Students' Test Performance." *Psychology in the Schools,* no. 4, 25–26.

Miller, G.V. 1983. "Individualizing Learning Objectives." In L.S. Baird, C.E. Schneider, and D.E. Laird, eds. *The Training and Development Sourcebook.* Amherst, Mass.: Human Resource Development Press.

Nadler, L. 1990. *Designing Training Programs: The Critical Events Model.* Reading, Mass.: Addison-Wesley Publishing Company.

Popham, W.J. 1968. "Probing the Validity of Arguments against Behaviourial Goals." Paper presented at the annual American Educational Research Association Conference, Chicago.

Ribler, R.I. 1983. *Training Development Guide.* Reston, Va.: Reston Publishing Co., Inc.

Rogers, C.R. 1969. *Freedom to Learn.* Columbus, Ohio: Charles E. Merrill.

Skinner, B.F. 1968. *The Technology of Teaching.* New York: Appleton Century-Crofts.

_____. 1974. *About Behaviourism.* New York: Alfred A. Knopf.

Stonehall, L. 1992. "The Case for More Flexible Objectives." *Training and Development* (August).

Wigley, R.R. 1991. *Learning Objectives ... and Beyond.* Calabasas, Calif.: Practical Management, Incorporated.

Zemke, R. 1978. "Personal Growth Training." *Training Magazine* 15, 5 (May).

6

Alternatives
and
Supplements

◆ ◆ ◆

INTRODUCTION

Now that needs have been identified (Chapter 4) and objectives set (Chapter 5), we must determine when and if a training program is appropriate. The business or career problem(s) that must be solved may not succumb to training, e.g., the problem may not be "trainable"—other remedies may give better results. The key issue, then, is not to lean automatically on training to solve business problems but to consider all the alternatives and to supplement training, where needed, with other shorter- and longer-term activities.

This chapter outlines some of the major methods that both replace and support the formal training function. The trainer will find that they are necessary ingredients to the development of a whole range of vocational skills and knowledge.

◆ ◆ ◆

SELF-DEVELOPMENT

Self-development is a process that occurs when individuals (sometimes groups) seek out the necessary resources to engage in learning that enhances their careers and personal growth. The concept has become increasingly popular because traditional training methods lack the flexibility to respond quickly to dramatic and constant organizational change.

Organizations that support self-development will invest in both people and technical resources, promote the concept through word and deed, and regard all business activities as learning opportunities. Only then will the conditions for self-learning be created, ultimately enhancing workplace creativity and commitment (Phillips, 1993).

THE PROGRAM

Although employers are increasingly moving toward developing their human resources (HR) through self-development, their people need a process by which to increase capabilities and skills. One model, suggested by Huntly (1991), outlines a five-step approach:

1. the senior manager evaluates him- or herself on specific skills, probably based on a needs analysis;

2. the subordinate evaluates his or her superior on identical characteristics;

3. they meet, compare evaluations, and work out appropriate goals;

4. then together, they develop a skills and behaviours listing;

5. finally, a gap analysis is performed by matching the skills profile with the work requirements and objectives.

To be successful, this process requires constant dialogue and trust between the various levels of management.

Similarly, Frayne developed a more individual-based approach, founded on "systematic data gathering about one's own behaviour" (1989, 47), combined with goal setting, self-monitoring, and self-evaluation. This process is supported by written contracts (with one's self) in which goals are set, actions delineated, and self-imposed rewards and punishments administered. As with other types of training, maintenance strategies are developed to prevent "relapse" and to avoid "high risk" situations. Like other experts, however, Frayne recognizes that the environment is an "essential key to the individual's ability to maintain self-managing behaviors" (1989, 49).

This belief is shared by Tucker, Moravec, and Ideus (1992). For self-development to flourish, they feel that diverse contributions need to be valued by management. Another necessity is for employer and employee goals to be in harmony. An effective self-development program, therefore, results in increased innovation and strengthened commitment.

SELF-DEVELOPMENT, NOT ABANDONMENT

Despite the rhetoric, there appears to be one issue constantly overlooked: employees need help with "self" development. Indeed, it is suggested that German and Heath's (1994) work in the career-development field also holds true for the self-development process:

> *Employee-initiated career development does involve self-responsibility, although the irony is that most of us need help*

*with it. There are elements of partnership not only between the
individual and the organization as first thought, but also with
fellow employees through peer mentoring. There is integration
at the individual level in addition to the individual/organiza-
tion interface (1994, 14).*

Self-development, therefore, is a function that must be carefully planned,
monitored, and nurtured, otherwise, self-responsibility can become a syn-
onym for neglect.

♦ ♦ ♦
COACHING

Although coaching has evolved into a motivational technique that is seen as
a prelude to progressive discipline, and as a method for dealing with performance problems, it will be discussed here as a vehicle for self-development
in the more positive sense. Closely related to self-development, the coaching
function can be defined as the planned use of opportunities in the work environment to improve or to enhance employee strengths or potential.
Weaknesses are considered only if they prevent the employee from functioning, or if they are below the manager's tolerance level (Lovin and
Casstevens, 1971; Frankel and Otazo, 1992).

The key elements in this definition of coaching are: "planned," "opportunities in the work environment," and "strengths." First, the process revolves
around an agreed-upon plan or set of objectives developed mutually by
employee and manager. Development does not occur haphazardly or by
chance; the process proceeds in a logical agreed-upon fashion. Second, the
work environment is the training laboratory (sometimes expanded to include
the community) as transfers, special assignments, assigned responsibility,
vacation replacements, conference speaking engagements, and the like are
used as learning tools. Therefore, the necessary formal infrastructure, perhaps
attached to the firm's appraisal or evaluation system, must be in place for the
system to work (Blakesley, 1992).

PREPARING THE COACH

Most managers want to influence their employees' performance. How (or if)
they go about this task determines in large part the characteristics of the

superior/subordinate relationship and whether the organization is effective. Employees react to these attempts to influence them according to their desire for variety or challenge, their ability to cope with pressure or stress, and the rate at which they can deal with change. A manager must realize that each individual is unique and must value this uniqueness; only then will he or she take the time to help the employee develop through coaching strategies (Hopkins and Kleiner, 1993; Jacobs, 1989).

As well, much of the literature deals with employee *weaknesses*. The manager must fight this tendency, concentrating instead on improving strengths. If, for example, an employee is shy, with poor public-speaking skills, it makes little sense to "coach" that employee by allowing him or her to attend departmental-level meetings as the manager's representative. Not only will his or her performance likely be poor (a reflection on the coach), but the employee's inadequacies will be accentuated and made known to a larger group. Conversely, an employee who excels at public speaking might be asked, as part of a planned developmental strategy, to help present the unit's annual report to senior management, further improving upon a considerable strength (Rosenberg, 1990, 1992; Blakesley, 1992; Finn, 1991; Howell, 1991; Burdett, 1991; Minor, 1989; Beh, 1993).

PREPARING THE EMPLOYEE

To make coaching work, the employee and the coach must trust each other; otherwise development will be seen by the employee as "extra" work. Indeed, perhaps the most important aspect of the coaching process is ongoing dialogue and feedback. It is only under these conditions that employees participate willingly in a two-way process that often requires extra effort and risk taking (Barry, 1992; Hutzel and Varney, 1992; Kruse, 1993).

THE COACHING PROCESS

The coaching process begins with a dialogue between coach and employee, during which a set of objectives is defined. Then, coaching opportunities are identified by a mutual examination of the environment. A long-term plan is struck, along with an evaluation or measurement procedure. As well, the process is fitted into the employee's career-development goals and usually made part of the organization's long-term strategies. The term "usually" is used to cover the situation in which an employee is leaving an organization by mutual consent, perhaps because he or she has outgrown a job and wishes to move on. Here, the employer can help the individual leave on amiable terms by continuing the coaching activity.

The employee performs the agreed-upon task (see below) and then reports to the supervisor both informally and formally during the annual or semi-annual evaluation. They discuss and agree, or maybe disagree, on the results of the current program and then plan the next round of activity, as coaching is an ongoing process (Kroeger, 1991). With practice, this approach develops into a continual transfer of skills (Whittaker, 1993; Azar, 1993).

Several devices can be used as coaching tools. For example, a special-project assignment that will enhance a specific skill is a useful approach, as there is no need to reorganize other work or to hire additional staff. Conversely, job rotation often requires extensive preparation, in that employees exchange entire jobs on a long-term basis.

Although vacation replacement has long been used as an upgrading technique, its usefulness has been questioned. The replacement position rarely carries real authority. Most employees play only a caretaker role, then return to their original jobs without having accomplished or learned much.

A more useful coaching technique is to design a method or schedule of representation, either at meetings or as committee members. Depending upon the skill or knowledge to be developed, the benefits can be significant, as this long-term exposure to more senior colleagues benefits the employee, while freeing the coach for other tasks. Unfortunately, expediency, not planned development, is often the governing factor when choosing individuals for these assignments (Lovin and Casstevens, 1971).

In large retail organizations, for example, a management trainee may be rotated through several departments before choosing one in which to specialize. Hence, transfers have been used as an effective coaching device for many years. While these internal transfers may be reasonably easy to arrange, however, the two-income family is a major impediment to coaching decisions that require relocation, as the spouse will need to find work in the new location. Thus, external transfers are of limited utility, unless the move is part of a long-term career-development strategy, e.g., an overseas posting that will last two years or more.

Where transfers are impractical, job redesign or restructuring may be used. Here, some portion of the job is changed so that new skills must be used. The restructuring of one job may, of course, affect the work of others.

Thus, job redesign should be part of an overall work strategy that embraces an entire work unit.

There may be situations in which even job restructuring is impossible. The coach may then have no choice but to suggest job enlargement—the employee taking on more work. Although often not a popular alternative, it may be necessary that an employee perform certain new tasks in order to grow professionally. A "larger" job may be the only answer. This approach will work best with individuals who have been on the job for some time and are mature to the task. A less-experienced person might panic when faced with more work.

As the last three coaching activities to be mentioned here—conference attendance, professional memberships, and teaching/publishing—take place outside the firm, the coach must be concerned with control over the process. Conferences, in particular, can be treated as social events rather than as serious opportunities to learn. Although there may be spinoff benefits (e.g., exposure to leading experts or networking), coaching is the planned acquisition of skills or knowledge; thus conferences must be chosen where attendance will meet a clearly defined purpose.

Similarly, professional societies can be used for a number of reasons— networking, publicity, leadership development, training, updating, and group-participation enhancement. Again, these functions need to serve a planned purpose. If, for example, an employee's job provides little opportunity to manage others, the coach might suggest a term as chairperson of the annual conference committee. Likewise, an employee who shows promise as a speaker might be coaxed into volunteering as Master of Ceremonies for a fundraiser, thus gaining more experience in public speaking.

The old adage, "the best way to learn something is to teach it," is true only if the task is approached with enthusiasm and if the teaching is done at the right level. Undoubtedly, the preparation process and the necessity of explaining oneself to others helps to fine-tune one's knowledge. An employee, however, will need to possess high-level skills and knowledge before obtaining the teaching position. More important from a coaching perspective, therefore, might be the opportunity to help an employee to become at ease and to relax in front of people.

Undoubtedly, many more ideas for coaching could be found. The key is to constantly remind oneself that coaching is the *planned* acquisition of skills and knowledge through the use of existing, or carefully modified, opportunities in the work or professional environments. This focus will prevent both the squandering of developmental opportunities on those who won't benefit and the loss of many potential training activities.

◆ ◆ ◆
MENTORING

Similar to coaching, but even more intense, mentoring is a process during which a senior person within an organization takes a personal interest in guiding and helping a more junior employee to obtain career and salary advancement. Although common during the late 1970s and 1980s, few of these programs were successful because HR professionals did not understand the intensely personal nature of the relationships. Indeed, these early experiments were fraught with sexual attraction, broken marriages, and career-damaging rumours (Burke and McKeen, 1990; Hinch, 1993; Metthes, 1991).

The last five years, however, has seen a resurgence of mentoring activity, not only in male mentor–female protégé relationships, but in female-to-female relationships as well. In fact, as women reach positions of power, more and more are being thrust into the mentoring role.

There are significant challenges to overcome, however, in getting female mentor-female protégé arrangements to work effectively. The mother/daughter concept, the search for self-identify, and the "ideal" mentor, when combined with organizational barriers like promotion of females as tokenism, the glass ceiling, and direct hostility from men when women network with one another, make some women reluctant to take on the mentoring role (Gallege, 1993; Parker and Cram, 1993).

Nevertheless, mentoring cannot be ignored, as both professional and academic research consistently have suggested that intensively mentored professionals have greater career prospects and higher incomes than other similar groups. For example, Chao et al. (1992) found "clear differences" between what were termed "mentored individuals" and "non-mentored" individuals, while Scandura (1992) suggested that protégés' promotion records and wage levels were related directly to career and social-support systems provided through mentoring. These findings are supported by previous work. Dreher and Ash (1990), for example, found a positive relationship between mentoring, promotion, and income, as well as enhanced satisfaction with wages and benefits.

Mentoring, therefore, is a critical element in enhancing the career prospects of all identifiable groups within an organization: women, the physically and mentally challenged, minorities, and men. It should be noted, however, that mentoring is not a panacea. Early career progress still seems dependent upon socioeconomic background, in that the mentoring process helps people from higher socioeconomic backgrounds more than others, perhaps because those with higher socioeconomic backgrounds gravitate toward higher-level, more powerful mentors (Whitely et al., 1991).

Still, mentoring is becoming one of the primary human resource development (HRD) tools of our time. In practical terms, one must not only differentiate between formal and informal mentoring programs but begin by preparing the organization for such programs, starting at the highest levels. Indeed, a formal mentoring initiative will not be successful unless the organization's culture is prepared to receive it. While commitment must be made at all levels, it is at the individual level that the process can most easily break down. Signals sent by derailed mentoring schemes include delay between assignment and first meeting with protégé, poor meeting locations (e.g., the cafeteria), and infrequent contacts (Jackson, 1990).

Jackson's (1993) later work highlighted several areas of concern to managers wishing to implement formal mentoring programs:

1. *Confidentiality.* It is important that the relationship remain confidential and for the protégé to believe that it will be confidential. Therefore, the right mentor must be chosen. The protégé is unlikely to feel comfortable, for example, if the mentor is his or her boss.

2. *Choice of mentors.* Mentors must be motivated to participate in the program and to make sufficient time available to their protégé. They also need to be knowledgeable about how the organization really works.

3. *Training.* Mentors and protégés both need training. This process should entail more than giving mentors a book to read about mentoring. It should, for example, involve the opportunity to share experiences about mentoring. Training protégés, usually as part of the induction process, is partly concerned with demonstrating the organization's commitment to mentoring, but also involves setting appropriate expectations for the mentoring relationship.

4. *Matching mentors and protégé(s).* Matching is an important process that needs to be handled with care. Inevitably, some assigned relationships will

not work out. A procedure needs to be in place to allow either party to cancel the arrangement without too much loss of face.

5. *Not everyone needs a mentor.* Formal programs will assign people to mentors, but it should also be recognized that some protégés will make few demands on their mentors (Jackson, 1993, 14).

As an HRD technique, then, mentoring has advantages in both the short term and the long term. First, the protégé learns the social graces necessary for survival within the firm. The story is told of a young MBA, who, during a presentation by a vice-president, spotted an error in some figures. She pointed out the mistake during the seminar in very forthright terms. The VP didn't mind, but the resulting backlash from the middle manager responsible for preparing the data caused her to leave the job. A mentor would have coached this young person in the art of seminar participation (particularly in those conducted by vice-presidents) and/or protected her from the wrath of an ego-bruised senior colleague.

Similarly, the mentoring function can be a major factor in long-term career development. Every individual needs to learn about career options—both internal and external. Often, such information is known only to insiders, e.g., mentors. As well, strengths, weaknesses, skills, and even interests often are best assessed by an objective outsider, e.g., the mentor. Finally, career-development action plans are best assessed in concert with a more seasoned individual, one able to spot pitfalls and omissions. As an HRD intervention, then, mentoring can be one of the most useful tools to help meet what Jackson (1993) calls the "career development challenge."

◆ ◆ ◆
PERFORMANCE AIDS

While self-development, coaching, and mentoring are alternatives to training, the three methods that follow are supplements. Performance aids and electronic support systems affect the individual and the job in a direct manner. Conversely, organizational development initiatives require an organization-wide commitment.

Employees who are placed in positions where they must react very quickly may not be able to rely on memory. A panel operator in a nuclear power plant, for example, may have 15 seconds (or less) to perform a series of safety sequences. In the less hectic world of insurance sales, one manager found that a potentially sound sales trainee constantly neglected to complete the entire sales sequence and paper work. Both these employees, despite their vastly different work environments, were helped by performance aids.

In the first instance, an indexed manual containing various operating sequences was developed and placed on a wheeled trolley within easy reach of all the operators' positions. The sales problem was solved by creating a checklist containing all the steps or tasks to be completed each time the salesperson visited a prospective client. Each step completed was "checked off" by the employee and the sheet was signed and dated. The manager then reviewed each call with the trainee. In this case, the checklist was discarded after about three weeks, as the sales trainee was performing to the standards set by management (Arajis, 1991).

A performance aid, then, is *any* device that helps an employee do the job. Aids can be signs or prompts ("Have you turned off the computer?"); trouble-shooting aids ("If the red light goes on, the machine needs oil"); instructions in sequence ("To empty the machine, follow the next five steps"); a special tool or gauge (even a long stick to measure how much gas is in an underground tank); flash cards to help counsel clients; or pictures (of a perfectly set table, for example) (Ukens, 1993; Meyers, 1991).

The philosophy behind the use of performance aids suggests that requiring the memorization of sequences and tasks sometimes takes too much training time, especially if the task is not repeated daily. As well, new employees can be on the job more quickly if armed with a series of temporary performance aids. Finally, routine (and not so routine) trouble-shooting and repair responses can be performed much more quickly and with less frustration.

When designing visual performance aids that help employees remember key information, all the skills of the graphic artist's craft should be utilized. Ease in reading, space between letters, colour, boldness, symbols, and graphic language ("Pull Here!") are all used to communicate (Cowen, 1992; King, 1994; Arajis, 1991). Audio aids also must clearly communicate intent. A buzzer alarm, for example, may be useless, but a taped warning ("Connect your safety harness!") is hard to ignore.

The designers of every training program, then, should consider how performance aids might save money and time. With ingenuity, the trainee's work life not only can be made easier but significant improvements in both performance, downtime, and safety records can result.

◆ ◆ ◆
ELECTRONIC PERFORMANCE-SUPPORT SYSTEMS

An electronic performance-support system (EPSS) is a computer-based system that improves employee productivity by providing on-the-job access to integrated information, advice, and learning experiences (Raybould, 1990). More simply, they are computer programs that incorporate at least two support systems to help solve work-related problems. They are job aids. All of us who have pressed the "HELP" key on a computer and received instructions on how to file or design a pie chart have experienced EPSS. The goal of an EPSS is to provide whatever is necessary to generate performance, and learning, at the time it is needed. This brings training back full cycle to its origins. People learning about work first learned on the job site with "master" craftsmen, using observation, explanation, questions, and coaching. With large numbers of employees to train, training moved out of the workplace and into formal classrooms. This resulted in moving training out of the job context. Subject-matter experts, not job experts, taught. With computers, we can return to the advantages of having "someone" constantly on the job to assist with questions and problems.

EPSS offers even more advantages than computer-based training. With EPSS, information is accessed only when it is needed. Only the information that is needed is given; there is no information overload. It is ridiculous to expect that enough information can be crammed into everyone's memory during training, then "banked" for access later. EPSS is particularly useful for training in high-turnover jobs, like bank tellers (Gebber, 1991), and tasks that are difficult, are performed infrequently, and must be performed perfectly (Ruyle, 1991). As increasing number of employees use personal computers, EPSS will become the norm in training employees such as cashiers, bank tellers, insurance agents, etc.

Resistance to computer-based training stems from a hesitation on the part of the organization to commit to rapidly changing hardware. At this point in time, companies are investing in only a limited number of learning "stations," where trainees go to work on "courseware." The high cost and rapid obsolescence of the hardware necessary to run the courseware make managers reluctant to invest in it. Until every employee is provided with a personal computer that can handle multimedia applications, the many advantages of training technology are reduced.

A second inhibiting factor is the instructors themselves. Some traditional trainers are not computer-literate, and rightly fear the change to computer-based training. Others recognize that they can be replaced by the technology. A low-threat opportunity to allow trainers to test the multimedia approach is to place the learning stations in the classroom (O'Keefe, 1991).

Most industry analysts perceive these two barriers as temporary problems. Computer-based training will become a standard way of supplying information, particularly for current generations who are not computer-phobic.

◆ ◆ ◆
ORGANIZATIONAL DEVELOPMENT

This final training methodology often leads to workplace redesign. Hence, its application may result in training, retraining, or the use of any alternative or supplement to training.

Organizational development (OD) is a process that uses our knowledge of the social sciences to plan, design, and implement changes in the work culture and procedures, in order to make the work setting more palatable and to increase organizational effectiveness and/or profitability. The steps include: information gathering, problem identification, action or intervention planning, intervention, or implementation, and evaluation (White and Bednor, 1991).

The OD approach to changing the way an organization operates works best when:

1. an outside, trained change agent is hired;

2. senior managers recognize that there are problems and want real change;

3. senior managers strongly support the change initiative and are willing to seek out and listen to opinion leaders at all organizational levels;

4. there are early successes that encourage further interest and participation from all levels;

5. there is respect for the management talents of those in whose unit or function the change is occurring;

6. both line and staff personnel cooperate in the change effort;

7. there is effective coordination, communication, and control of the change process;

8. there is an evaluation procedure that measures the results, and these results (both successes and failures) are communicated widely (Vecchio, 1988);

9. change is viewed by all employees as a long-term necessity to remain competitive;

10. reward systems reinforce change (Cherrington, 1994).

Thus, proponents of OD try to mobilize the organization's entire HR pool toward achieving the employer's mission, while simultaneously creating a viable, growing organization of people whose personal needs for self-worth, growth, and satisfaction are significantly met at work (Hersey and Blanchard, 1988).

Remembering that culture, systems, and ultimately behaviour must be changed, there are numerous techniques the OD specialist can use. Cherrington (1994), for example, divides interventions into five categories: interpersonal, group, intergroup, organizational, and cultural. Under "interpersonal," he places coaching/counselling, sensitivity training, and process consultation (problem diagnosis and alternative solution evaluation).

Group interventions consist of group problem-solving meetings, team-building meetings, analysis of roles (to reduce role confusion), and responsibility charting—an intervention that clarifies responsibilities concerning decision-making and taking action.

Interventions that focus on intergroup relationships include:

◆ identification of the common foe, e.g., focusing attention on an enemy that threatens both groups;

◆ working together: groups are forced to interact, communicate, and solve common problems or reach common goals;

◆ membership interchange, during which group members are rotated among or between groups;

◆ conflict confrontation sessions, in which groups are brought together to air differences, while solving common problems.

Organizational interventions are comprehensive, affecting an entire work group or firm. Structural change, for example, can have significant and lasting impact on both the individual and the way an organization operates. Similarly, sociotechnical system design, involving the creation of work teams and the systems that allow them to function effectively, is typically concerned with developing the skills and attitudes necessary for employees to work autonomously.

Total Quality Management (TQM) is also part of OD, but better research is needed on the implementation process. Finally, the most difficult area in which to work, cultural intervention, refers to the systematic change or clarification of collective corporate or organizational identity, e.g., what it is really like to work here.

As these techniques are concerned with the effectiveness of the entire organization, they are often combined into "a consideration in general of how work is done, what the people who carry out the work believe and feel about their efficiency and effectiveness, rather than a specific, concrete, step-by-step linear procedure for accomplishing something" (Burke, 1994).

The entire OD movement has its critics. Hersey and Blanchard (1988), for example, suggest there are more OD intervention failures than successes. A different focus was taken by McKendall (1993), who argued that OD intervention, in the drive to encourage cooperation, increases the power of management. Further, she accuses OD practitioners of "self-deception," in the creation of a discipline (OD) that has (wrongly) been given the label "scientific," when the major aim is the qualitative institution of social and environmental reforms (Van Eynde et al., 1992).

Despite these criticisms, however, OD remains a major method for increasing employee effectiveness. The technique cannot be discounted as long as the movement continues toward democratic, participative management.

◆ ◆ ◆
SUMMARY

As the theme of this text is to manage performance, not performers, this chapter has outlined some necessary alternatives to training. The idea that self-development is a method of coping with continual change fits well with our view that formal learning can be too inflexible to meet individual needs. Similarly, we stress that coaching must not be seen as a method for dealing with performance problems but for self-development in a more positive sense. Planned utilization of learning opportunities in the workplace, therefore, can be used to help employees to achieve their long-term career goals.

A process similar to coaching, mentoring places junior employees in contact with senior people who take a personal interest in their career advancement. To make mentoring programs successful, it is important that the relationship remain confidential, that both mentor and protégé be trained appropriately, and that the participants be properly matched.

The three supplements to training—performance aids, electronic support systems, and organizational development (OD)—each affect performance quite differently. The first two help an employee to perform sequences without memorization or prompt proper behaviour in some way, while OD is a complex intervention technique that uses social science principles to improve work environments.

E X E R C I S E S

Why Carl Left: A Workplace Dilemma*

John Webster was head of the tool-and-die section at Keswick and Sons Ltd. A hard taskmaster who had learned his trade in Great Britain, he had trained almost 100 apprentices, only to watch as a large portion left for other companies as soon as they obtained their journeyman's papers. The company had invested hundreds of thousands of dollars in the apprenticeship program over the last dozen years and John sensed that management was reluctant to support the plan much further. John was watching this year's crop of four apprentices, therefore, with a particularly anxious eye.

Carl Vox was one of the best apprentices Keswick and Sons had attracted in a long time. Not only was he brighter than most and quick to learn, but he was a hard worker who disliked making mistakes. John felt Carl had the ability to become a master tradesman. He hoped that Carl would continue his studies, as the company desperately needed skilled people of Carl's calibre.

John's hopes, however, were not to be realized. On the day Carl graduated, after accepting congratulations, receiving a gift, and being taken out to a sumptuous dinner, he confided to John that he had been offered a job as a sales representative by a large German specialized machinery firm. Nothing John said could make Carl change his mind. Carl talked of the freedom sales would offer him and how he felt that his future did not lie in a "dingy old factory."

Feeling more depressed than he had felt in a long time, John returned to the plant to find a note from Mr. Keswick: "See me when you return." John went immediately to the president's office to be told that unless retention rates for the apprenticeship program showed marked

*Reproduced here with permission from MCB University Press: originally published in P. Wright (1988) *The Trainer's Case Compendium*. Bradford: MCB University Press.

improvements next year, Keswick and Sons would be abandoning that type of training in favour of direct recruitment of skilled tradesmen from overseas.

John's next stop was the personnel department. "Maybe," he thought, "I can get help in developing some sort of program to keep these young people here once they graduate."

Question

1. Play the role of an OD specialist. How would you apply the principles of OD in attempting to find a solution to decrease the number of apprentices that leave as soon as they graduate?

NOTE: *This storyline is a fictional version of a real-life situation that existed at Canadian General Electric many years ago.*

A Case of Confusion and Bewilderment

When TPK, a manufacturer of small appliances—electric kettles, toasters, and irons—automated its warehouse, the warehouse crew was reduced from 14 to 4. Every one of the displaced stockmen was assigned to another department, as TPK had a history of providing stable employment.

Jacob Peters, a stockman with over 15 years of service, was transferred to the toaster assembly line, to be retrained as a small-parts assembler. When he arrived to begin his new job, the foreman said, "I have a job for you, but I'm worried about your lack of experience. You'll be working on the old thermostat welder-assembler machine. It may take you a while to get a handle on it ... and I really can't afford the time to get you up to speed."

Although Jacob was eager to learn his new job, he knew the pressure was on, and that the foreman would be watching him closely. There were a bunch of manuals describing the machine, but they didn't seem to make much sense.

The job seemed terribly complicated. There were eight steps to learn and four lights—red for too hot; blue for too cold; green for O.K., and amber for caution, change in progress. As Jacob worked the thermostats through the various sequences, he had to keep an eye on the lights and two pressure gauges. After several attempts, Jacob kept spoiling material. All day he tried, with the foreman constantly reminding him of a missed sequence, an unread gauge, an amber light—"get ready now, it will either turn red or blue ... make adjustments accordingly! Hurry!"

At the end of the day, the foreman had to arrange for an experienced operator to work overtime, or lack of thermostats would have shut the whole line down.

As Jacob was leaving, frustrated and tired, the foreman hauled him into his office: "Listen chum ... you have to get the hang of this job. We make seven different thermostats. If you can't learn the steps for the simple ones you're making now, what will happen next week when we're doing kettles?...Now those are really complicated!"

The next day Jacob booked off sick.

Question

1. Change Jacob's training program and/or work environment to make it possible for him to perform efficiently within a short time period.

References

"Angry, Agreeable, Quiet, and Chronic Offenders." *Training and Development* 47, no. 5, 22.

Appell, A. 1989. *A Practical Approach to Human Behaviour in Business.* Columbus: Charles E. Merrill.

Arajis, B. 1991. "Getting Your Sales Staff in Shape." *Graphic Arts Monthly* 63, no. 5: 125–27.

Azar, B. 1993. "Striking a Balance." *Sales and Marketing Management* 145, no. 2, 34–35.

Barry, T. 1992. "The Manager as Coach." *Industrial and Commercial Training* 24, no. 2, 14–16.

Beh, H. 1993. "Mentoring the Young Manager." *Asian Business* 29, no. 7, 63.

Blakesley, S. 1992. "Your Agency ... Leave It Better Than You Found It." *Managers Magazine* 67, no. 4, 20–22.

Broadwell, M. 1969. *The Supervisor and On-The-Job Training.* Reading, Mass.: Addison-Wesley.

Burdett, J. 1991. "To Coach, or Not to Coach—That is the Question." *Industrial and Commercial Training* 23, no. 5, 10–16.

Burke, R., and C. McKeen. 1990. "Mentoring in Organizations: Implications for Women." *Journal of Business Ethics* 9, no. 4, 317–32.

Burke, W. 1994. *Organization Development.* 2nd ed. Reading, Mass.: Addison-Wesley.

Chao, G., P. Walz, and P. Gardner. 1992. "Formal and Informal Mentorships." *Personnel Psychology* 45, no. 3: 619–36.

Cherrington, D. 1994. *Organizational Behaviour.* Boston: Allyn and Bacon.

Costley, D., and R. Todd. 1983. *Human Relations in Organizations.* New York: West Publishing Co.

Cowen, W. 1992. "Visual Control Boards Are a Key Management Tool." *Office Systems* 9, no. 10, 70–72.

Deegan, A. 1982. *Coaching.* Reading, Mass.: Addison-Wesley.

Dreher, G., and R. Ash. 1990. "A Comparative Study of Mentoring Among Men and Women in Managerial, Professional, and Technical Positions." *Journal of Applied Psychology* 75, no. 5, 539–46.

Finn, W. 1991. "One-on-One Coaching." *Successful Meetings* 40, no. 8, 102–04.

Frankel, L., and K. Otazo. 1992. "Employee Coaching: The Way to Gain Commitment." *Employment Relations Today* 19, no. 3, 311–20.

Frayne, C. 1989. "Improving Employee Performance Through Self-management Training." *Business Quarterly* 54, no. 1, 46–50.

Gallege, L. 1993. "Do Women Make Poor Mentors?" *Across the Board* 30, no. 6, 23–26.

Gebber, B. 1991. "Help! The Rise of Performance Support Systems." *Training Magazine* 28, no. 12, (December): 23–29.

German, C., and C. Heath. 1994. "Career Development 2000." *Training and Development* 12, no. 5,12–14.

Gold, L. 1981. "Job Instruction: Four Steps to Success." *Training and Development Journal* 35, no. 9, 28–32.

Hersey, P., and K. Blanchard. 1988. *Management of Organizational Behaviour*. 5th ed. Englewood Cliffs: Prentice Hall.

Hinch, G.E. 1993. "Mentoring: Everyone Needs a Helping Hand." *Public Manager* 22, no. 1, 31.

Hopkins, R., and B. Kleiner. 1993. "How to Be an Effective Coach in Business." *Agency Sales Magazine* 23, no. 6: 57–61.

Howell, A. 1991. "Coach Your Way to Improvement." *Training and Development* 32, no. 8, 12–16.

Huntly, S. 1991. "Management Development—Considerations and Implementation." *Industrial and Commercial Training* 23, no. 2, 20–25.

Hutzel, T., and G. Varney. 1992. "The Supervisor's Role in Self-directed Workteams." *Journal for Quality and Participation* 15, no. 7, 36–41.

Jackson, C. 1990. *Careers Counselling in Organizations: The Way Forward*. IMS Report 198, Institute of Manpower Studies, University of Sussex.

_____. 1993. "Mentoring: Choices for Individuals and Organizations." *The International Journal of Career Management* 5, no. 1, 10–16.

Jacobs, D. 1989. "Coaching Employees to Perform Better." *Management World* 18, no. 4, 6–9.

King, W. 1994. "Training by Design." *Training and Development* 48, no. 1, 52–54.

Koehler, K.G. 1992. "Orientation: Key to Employee Performance and Morale." *CMA Magazine* 66, no. 6, 6.

Kroeger, L. 1991. "Your Team Can't Win the Game Without Solid Coaching." *Corporate Controller* 3, no. 5, 62–64.

Kruse, A. 1993. "Getting Top Value for Your Payroll Dollar." *Low Practice Management* 19, no. 3, 52–57.

Laird, D. 1985. *Approaches to Training and Development*: 2nd ed. Reading, Mass.: Addison-Wesley.

Lovin, B., and E. Casstevens. 1971. *Coaching, Learning, and Action*. New York: American Management Association.

McKendall, M. 1993. "The Tyranny of Change: Organizational Development Revisited." *Journal of Business Ethics* 12, no. 2, 93–104.

Metthes, K. 1991."Corporate Mentoring: Beyond the Blind Date." *HR Focus* 68, no. 11, 23.

Meyers, D. 1991. "Restaurant Service: Making Memorable Presentations." *Cornell Hotel and Restaurant Administration Quarterly* 32, no. 1, 69–73.

Minor, M. 1989. *Coaching and Counselling*. Los Altos: Crisp Publications, Inc.

Mumford, A. 1993. "How Managers Can Become Developers." *Personnel Management* 25, no. 6, 42–45.

Nadler, L. 1982. *Designing Training Programs*. Reading, Mass.: Addison-Wesley.

Odiorne, G.S. 1970. *Training by Objectives*. London: Collier-Macmillan.

O'Keefe, B. 1991. "Adopting Multimedia on a Global Scale." *Instruction Delivery Systems* (September/October): 6–11.

The Ontario Training and Adjustment Board. 1991. *Skills to Meet the Challenge: A Training Partnership for Ontario*. Pamphlet.

Parker, V., and K. Cram. 1993. "Women Mentoring Women: Creating Conditions for Connection." *Business Horizons* 36, no. 2, 42–51.

Phillips, K. 1993. "Self-development in Organizations: Issues and Actions." *Journal of European Industrial Training* 17, no. 5: 3–5.

Raybould, B. 1990. "Solving Human Performance Problems with Computers: A Case Study: Building an Electronic Performance Support System." *Performance and Instruction* (November–December): 4–14.

Renner, P.F. 1989. *The Instructor's Survival Kit*. Vancouver: Training Associates Ltd.

Rosenberg, A. 1992. "Coaching Without Criticizing." *Executive Excellence* 9, no. 8, 14–15.

Rosenberg, D. 1990. "The Key to Retraining Professionals." *Security Management* 34, no. 8, 116–22.

Ruyle, K. 1991."Developing Intelligent Job Aids." *Technical and Skills Training* (February/March): 9–14.

Scandura, T. 1992. "Mentorship and Career Mobility: An Empirical Investigation." *Journal of Organizational Behaviour* 13, no. 2, 169–74.

Stern, S., and H. Muta. 1990. "The Japanese Difference." *Training and Development Journal* 44, no. 3, 74–82.

Tench, A. 1992. "Following Joe Around: Should This Be Our Approach to On-the-job Training?" *Plant Engineering* 46, no. 17, 88–92.

Tucker, R., M. Moravec, and K. Ideus. 1992. "Designing a Dual Career-track System." *Training and Development* 46, no. 6, 55–58.

Ukens, C. 1993. "Cards Help Pharmacists Counsel Patients In a Flash." *Drug Topics* 137, no. 1: 24–27.

Van Eynde, D., A. Church, R. Hurley, and W. Burke. 1992. "What OD Practitioners Believe." *Training and Development* 46, no. 4: 41–46.

Vecchio, R. 1988. *Organizational Behaviour*. Chicago: The Dryden Press.

White, D., and D. Bednor. 1991. *Organizational Behaviour*. Needham Heights: Allyn and Bacon.

Whitely, W., T. Dougherty, and G. Dreher. 1991. "Relationship of Career Mentoring and Socio-economic Origin to Managers' and Professionals' Early Career Progress." *Academy of Management Journal* 34, no. 2, 331–51.

Whittaker, B. 1993. "Shaping the Competitive Organization." *CMA Magazine* 67, no. 3, 5.

7

Transfer of
Training
and
Development

INTRODUCTION

Training is an investment. However, several studies have estimated that only 10 percent of training dollars invested result in actual change on the job (Georgenson, 1982). The loss to organizations is significant. In Canada, the annual amount invested in training is estimated to be $4 billion. In the United States, the annual figure is estimated to be more than $100 billion (Gist, 1990). If employees are seen as resources, then money spent on training must be viewed as investments in human capital development. This chapter outlines methods for optimizing this training investment.

Organizations concerned about their training investment are concerned with more than just the effectiveness of the training course. The course itself is just the "acquisition" phase; trainers can easily prove that trainees leave the programs having acquired new skills. But if trainees do not apply these newly acquired skills on the job, then most of the resources spent in designing and conducting training courses are wasted.

Organizations are increasingly focusing their attention on implementation and maintenance; they are concerned with the *transfer* of training. "Transfer" refers to the implementation in the work environment of the skills acquired during the training program, and the maintenance of these acquired skills over time (Baldwin and Ford, 1988).

This chapter examines the factors that facilitate the transfer of training. These factors are derived from research on learning, which will be described briefly in order to ground the discussion. The transfer factors are then grouped by time: before, during, and after training. Research that focuses on adult learning principles is integrated within the chapter, where appropriate. Indeed, we use here one of the main principles of adult learning: start with a problem (transfer of training), not a body of knowledge (learning theory).

Reading of this chapter will be made easier by consulting the analytical framework presented in Table 7.1.

Descriptions of the two main schools of learning follow.

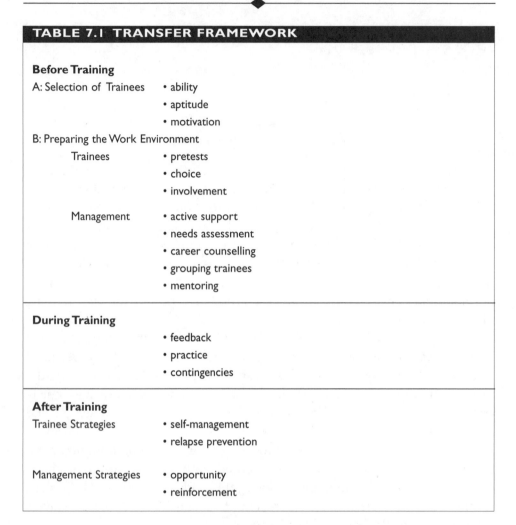

TABLE 7.1 TRANSFER FRAMEWORK

Before Training

A: Selection of Trainees
- ability
- aptitude
- motivation

B: Preparing the Work Environment

Trainees
- pretests
- choice
- involvement

Management
- active support
- needs assessment
- career counselling
- grouping trainees
- mentoring

During Training
- feedback
- practice
- contingencies

After Training

Trainee Strategies
- self-management
- relapse prevention

Management Strategies
- opportunity
- reinforcement

◆ ◆ ◆
LEARNING THEORIES

For years, researchers have deplored the lack of integration of learning theories into training design (Goldstein, 1991; This and Lippet, 1983). This chapter seeks to redress this complaint by demonstrating the association between learning theory and transfer prescriptions, although the link between a suggestion for transfer and the underlying learning precept that guides it is not always apparent.

Intuitively, most trainers use some guidelines, derived from learning theories. For example, those charged with influencing behaviour or performance recognize the value of rewarding good performance. This "intuition" is substantiated by numerous experiments conducted under the auspices of the behaviourist school of learning.

In order to validate many of the recommendations contained here, an overview of the two major streams of learning theory is presented: the conditioning perspective and the cognitive perspective. The conditioning perspective or behaviourist school describes events surrounding performance. The cognitive school describes the role of mental processes in learning.

◆ ◆ ◆
THE CONDITIONING PERSPECTIVE

Researchers such as Pavlov, Thorndike, Skinner, and Hull all approached learning as a process of association. B.F. Skinner (1953) defined learning as a relatively permanent change in behaviour in response to a particular stimulus or set of stimuli. The behaviourist school believes that learning is a result of rewards or punishments, which follow a response to a stimulus. In this trial-and-error approach, a stimulus or cue would be followed by a response, which is then reinforced and strengthens the likelihood that the response will occur again. For example, behaviourists would argue that similar principles are at work when an adult submits an innovative proposal and is praised, as would occur when a pigeon pecks a red dot and is given a pellet of food. When a response is reinforced through food, money, attention, or anything pleasurable, then the response is more likely to be repeated. If there is no reinforcement, then, over time, the response will cease. If the response is punished, then it will not be repeated. The conditioning framework is illustrated in the following diagram:

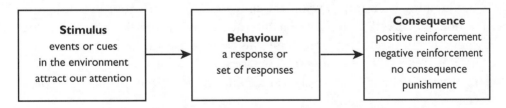

Negative reinforcement is the removal of a negatively valued outcome after an act. To illustrate this concept, think of an alarm clock ringing. When you turn it off, the noise stops (the negative consequence is removed).

Managers and trainers use conditioning principles as they attempt to influence employee behaviour. Much of this chapter discusses the appropriate uses of reinforcers. Linking desired complex behaviour to pleasurable consequences is based on three connected concepts: *shaping, generalization,* and *chaining.*

Shaping is extremely important for learning complex behaviour. Imagine trying to train a dog to fetch the newspaper from the front gate every morning. You could wait forever for this response to occur naturally so that you could then reinforce it with a dog biscuit. A more efficient method for teaching this behaviour is to reward the dog in small steps (give food as the dog moves toward the gate, then as he approaches the exact spot, then sniffing the paper, etc.). Shaping refers to the reinforcement of each step in the process, until it is mastered, and then withdrawing the reinforcer until the next step is mastered. Role plays and behaviour modelling make extensive use of this concept, rewarding trainees for the acquisition of separate skills, performed sequentially.

The second important concept is that of generalization: the conditioned response occurs in circumstances different from those during acquisition (Pearce, 1987). The learning process in a classroom is kept deliberately simple. All extraneous factors are removed so the trainee can concentrate on learning a skill such as negotiation. The trainer then structures the learning environment to better reflect reality, for example, by having one negotiator play-act being very angry or delivering a memo from the president with new instructions. Thus, the trainee learns to generalize the skill from a simple, controlled environment to a different, more difficult one. This is the goal of trainers—that learning acquired during training will be imported into the work environment and used.

Chaining is another important concept. In the previous example, the dog does not need to be given a biscuit for every correct act. Most dog owners give a biscuit and praise at the same time, until the biscuit is no longer necessary. The dog learns to associate and value secondary reinforcements. Humans obviously value reinforcers at much more complex levels.

Expectancy theory (Vroom, 1964), while based on studies of motivation, is a more cognitive approach to conditioning and has implications for training. This theory proposed that the energy that a person directs toward an activity is a direct result of:

1. the individual's expectancy (subjective probability) that the effort will lead to the achievement of the goal or activity;

2. the instrumentality (subjective likelihood) of the activity to attain consequences or reinforcers; and

3. the valence (subjective values) of the consequences to the individual along a positive to negative continuum. Thus:

$$\text{Effort} = \text{Expectancy} \times S \text{ (Instrumentality} \times \text{Valence).}$$

The implications of this equation are that potential trainees must believe that they are capable of achieving the training objective and that these training goals will result in more desirable outcomes for attendance and learning than nonattendance.

The conditioning perspective is not strictly a behaviourist view, in the sense that cognition does play a role. As described, Vroom's (1964) expectancy theory can be easily incorporated into a conditioning perspective. Nor is it primarily an animal view, in that much research on verbal learning and memory has been done with human subjects (Weiss, 1991). Many of the recommendations contained here for reinforcement, feedback, and practice are founded on the principles of the conditioning perspective.

◆ ◆ ◆
THE COGNITIVE PERSPECTIVE

The cognitive perspective is not completely different from the conditioning perspective. The principles of both build upon precepts of acquisition and consequences. The cognitive theorists believe that cognitive processes (thoughts, feelings, observations) play an important role in learning. They argue that learning would be a slow, error-prone business if everyone had to attend to cues, act, and then be reinforced. Learning to drive a car or deal with a violent client might be activities too dangerous to even begin. Instead, much learning occurs through imitation or modelling. We observe the actions of others, paying attention to the reinforcing or punishing outcomes of their behaviour. We are conscious of copying the modelled behaviour. Considerable research has demonstrated that people observe and reproduce the actions and attitudes of models (Luthans and Davis, 1983).

Expectancy plays an important mediating role in this process (Tolman, 1959). Expectancy refers to knowledge about the relationship between an act and its outcomes. Administrative trainees will observe and model a senior executive in the belief that if they act in the same way, they will be rewarded in some distant future. Cognitive theorists define learning in terms of changes in cognition (internal brain activity) that may or may not be reflected in behaviour.

An emerging theory of learning states that cognition plays a role not only in imitating behaviour but in initiating and controlling it. People can defer immediate rewards for more powerful ones, can set more challenging goals, can control both stimuli and consequences. In other words, people can manage their own behaviour in a very active sense (Luthans and Davis, 1983). The application of this theory can be found in the section on self-management and relapse prevention later in this chapter.

The theoretical underpinnings of the prescriptions contained in the following sections will be apparent.

◆ ◆ ◆
BEFORE TRAINING STARTS

This section focuses on the prework necessary in the selection of candidates for training, and the preparation of the work environment for the return of the trainee with new knowledge, skills, and attitudes. (The authors recognize that the implementation of all the ideas presented in these three phases is not possible in every organization. However, the implementation of some is imperative in order to ensure transfer).

◆ ◆ ◆
SELECTION OF TRAINEES

Trainability. The first question that must be answered before an employee undertakes a change program is: Can this individual be trained? An examination of three characteristics (ability, aptitude, and personality) of potential participants may provide answers to the question.

Ability refers to the knowledge and skills the individual already possesses, and may include cognitive skills and psychomotor skills. Examples of cognitive skills include basic numeracy and literacy knowledge, the intelligence to learn complex rules and procedures, etc. Psychomotor abilities could include the eye-hand coordination necessary to operate machines or the visual acuity needed to detect defects. The potential trainee must have certain basic skills in order to undertake training leading to more advanced skills.

Aptitude refers to the potential of the employee. For example, an employee may not know how to program software, but given his or her superior intelligence and capacity for logical problem-solving, one could conclude that he or she will succeed in a programming course.

Both abilities and aptitudes can be measured by cognitive tests and by work-sample tests. Cognitive tests, such as intelligence tests, will include subtests of specific abilities such as numerical reasoning, spatial aptitude, deductive reasoning, and verbal ability. The subtests provide important information about the ability of a potential trainee to learn the material.

Work-sample tests consist of a sample of the skills or abilities needed for job performance. Thus, a person who is interested in becoming an assembler of electrical components might be given the chance to observe a skilled assembler perform a series of simple tasks. The candidate would then be asked to perform the task and would be rated against a standardized checklist. Research on the effectiveness of job-sample tests has proven that they predict not only later training performance but also attendance and dropout rates (Robertson and Downs, 1989).

Although most work-sample tests involve the demonstration of psychomotor skills, they are equally effective with knowledge-based tests (Reilly and Israelski, 1988). Trainers can use a sample of the course material in order to test the degree to which trainees can learn information in a fixed time period. A candidate for a programming course could be given a written test that required solving a problem using logic. If the trainee did well against a standardized appraisal form, then the trainer could be reasonably certain that the candidate would do well in the course.

The use of these tests provides significant savings for employers. Some courses in electronics may cost an employer $30 000 per trainee and last six months. An hour-long test that could predict training performance is obviously a prudent investment.

These tests are particularly useful if the results are fed back to the employee. People are generally unaware when their behaviour is ineffective or inappropriate, and so have little incentive to change. Most change programs are built on the concept that change must be preceded by "unfreezing" (Lewin, 1958). "Unfreezing" means that trainees must recognize or be aware of the disadvantages of their current way of doing things, and must unlearn this style. To facilitate "unfreezing," trainers could provide proof that present knowledge or skills are inadequate. Tests provide this kind of objective feedback. After present deficiencies are revealed, new information is more likely to be absorbed, integrated (refrozen), and transferred. When training is presented without unfreezing, trainees may distort information or only perceive information that is consistent with their current beliefs (Hastie and Kumar, 1979). Tests or work samples are important, therefore, not only as predictors of performance but also for receptiveness and transfer of training.

Personality Traits. Researchers have isolated several personality factors that help to predict success in training courses. Indeed, these traits seem to predict success in other endeavours as well. The most commonly cited success traits are need for achievement (Baumgartel et al., 1984) and internal locus of control (Noe, 1986). (A person with a high need for achievement likes to accomplish something difficult as rapidly and as independently as possible. A person with an internal locus of control believes that he or she can manipulate the environment and control his or her fate.) These traits can be measured by personality tests, which are usually not available to trainers who are not psychologists. However, there are other traits that trainers can measure by means of simple questionnaires.

Motivation is one of these. "Motivation" refers to the trainee's effort, persistence, and choices. Motivation can be influenced by internal factors, such as one's innate need for achievement, and by external factors, to be discussed later in this chapter.

One motivational component that is gaining increasing attention is the trait of self-efficacy. Self-efficacy is the belief in one's capability to perform a task (Bandura, 1986). It refers not to the actual skills one has but to judgments about what one can do with those skills (Mager, 1992). This is a critical factor in understanding learning, because it is possible that trainees can actually learn the required knowledge and skills but believe that they cannot do the job. Studies of managers learning to use software programs show that those with high self-efficacy do better and have a higher motivation to learn than those with low self-efficacy (Gist, 1989; Gist et al., 1989). Motivation to learn is in turn related to learning achievement (Tannenbaum et al., 1991).

Trainers can maximize the acquisition and ultimate transfer of new skills and knowledge by assessing applicants' readiness (abilities, aptitudes, and motivation to learn). These are mostly intrinsic characteristics of the trainees, over which the organization has little control. If everyone in the group needs to be trained, regardless of personal traits, there are several methods human resource developers can use to prepare the trainees and their work environments to maximize transfer.

PREPARING THE WORK ENVIRONMENT

Before the course begins, trainers should work actively with both trainees and their managers to facilitate the ultimate transfer of newly acquired behaviour to the job situation.

Involvement of the Trainee. Consider the learning environment most of us have experienced. As students in school, we were told what to learn, when, and how. Learning was supposed to pay off in some unknown way in the distant future.

As adults, employees need to know why they are learning material. They are concerned with its immediate and practical application, and with its relevance to their problems or needs. Adults tend to be problem-centred in their approach to learning. Using this basic insight, McMaster University in Hamilton, Ontario, redesigned its medical degree program. Instead of teaching medicine by subject matter (chemistry, physiology), they created a problem-centred curriculum. After identifying about 200 of the most common problems faced by a physician, they developed learning modules containing everything a doctor needed to know about anatomy, pharmacology, etc. in order to solve the problem. (For a thorough discussion on the needs of adult learners, consult *The Adult Learner: A Neglected Species* by Malcolm Knowles [Houston, Texas: Gulf Publishing Co., 1990].

Other contrasts between the school experiences of children and the training experiences of adults are highlighted in Table 7.2. The factors listed in this table have powerful implications for trainers, at every stage of the transfer cycle. Before training starts, trainees must be involved in needs assessment, identification of real job problems, career planning, precourse assignments, and goal setting.

Pre-tests. Chapter 4, on needs assessment, demonstrated that pre-tests are useful in determining the entry-level skills of employees so that courses can be designed appropriate to the trainees' skill levels. Chapter 12, on evaluation, will explain how these pre-tests serve as data useful for measuring change in performance as a result of the training course. But pre-tests are

TABLE 7.2 TEACHING CHILDREN AND ADULTS

Factor	Children	Adults
Personality	Dependent	Independent
Motivation	Extrinsic	Intrinsic
Roles	Student	Employee,
	Child	Parent, Volunteer, Spouse, Citizen
Openness to change	Keen	Ingrained habits and attitudes
Barriers to change	Few	Negative self-concept
		Limited opportunities
		Time
		Inappropriate teaching methods
Experience	Limited	Vast
Orientation to learning	Subject-centred	Problem-centred

equally important in designing courses that motivate trainees. Pre-tests allow trainers to design individual and tailor-made paths of learning for adults.

As previously discussed, the information from pre-tests allows trainers to demonstrate in an objective manner that training is needed. This information can also serve as course material from the real world of the trainee. The motivation of adult learners is increased by the demonstration of the need to learn new skills, and by relating the new skills to the problems or work situations of the trainees. Research has documented that trainees who believed in the results of the needs assessment achieved more in training (Noe, 1986) and found the training more useful (Noe and Schmitt, 1986) than those who did not.

Choice. Another variable that must be considered when dealing with adults is choice. Children have no choice in attendance. Adults may have some choice in company programs, but here opinion is divided. Some argue that by making attendance mandatory, managers communicate the importance of training and ensure that all employees are using the same skills, thus providing powerful reinforcements (Broad and Newstrom, 1992). In one study, researchers found that a mandatory course resulted in higher intentions by engineers in the course to transfer training to the workplace (Baldwin and Magjuka, 1991). A study by Hicks and Klimoski (1987), however, found that managers who could choose to attend a performance-appraisal workshop achieved more from the workshop than those who were forced to attend. Providing detailed information about the workshop, which was designed to facilitate the managers' attendance decision, rather than just providing the typical positive overview, also resulted in greater achievement (Hicks and Klimoski, 1987).

Involvement. Trainees must be involved in the development of their change experiences. The person in the boat with you seldom bores a hole in it (Broad and Newstrom, 1992). Involvement in the design and planning of the learning experience is one way to get trainees to jump aboard. Precourse work or assignments may also serve as means to involve participants.

INVOLVEMENT OF MANAGEMENT

The need for management support, reiterated throughout text, is beginning to sound like the background noise of a tap dripping. In this section, we present concrete suggestions that move beyond verbal pleas for "support, please."

Active Support. Before an employee is sent to a training program, managers should have to complete a questionnaire and respond to interview questions ascertaining the need for, and potential application of, the course material. CIBC requires its managers who have requested training to answer questions such as: What is the training need? What are the employees doing now and what should they be doing? Why do you feel that training will solve the problem? What would you want them to be able to do after the training?

Needs Assessment. Managers should be part of the needs-assessment phase, for both microcourses (individual) and macrotraining (group development programs). If there is a match between the content of the program and departmental/trainee needs, then the manager must move beyond support to involvement and commitment.

Broad and Newstrom (1992) suggest having managers complete a form that commits them to support. Such a form is presented in Figure 7.1.

Career Counselling. Another useful role for managers to play before a training course is that of career counsellor. Trainees who have had discussions regarding their careers, and who have established career goals or plans, are more likely to benefit from training than others (Williams et al., 1991). Where possible, trainees should be told of the benefits of learning the new skills. These advantages could range from fewer client problems and

---

FIGURE 7.1 TRAINING SUPPORT CONTRACT—SUPERVISOR

I,............................, agree to:

1. Provide time for the employee to complete precourse assignments.
2. Provide release time for attendance, and ensure that the employee's workload is undertaken by others to eliminate interruptions.
3. Review the course outline with the employee, and discuss situations in which the newly acquired knowledge and skills can be used.
4. Upon the return of the trainee, provide timely opportunities to implement the skills, and reinforce new behaviours.

Signature...

Title..

---

increased speed in processing orders to more personal incentives such as increases in pay or promotion.

Groups of Trainees. Training transfer is also facilitated by sending several or all members of a department to the training course. Experience has shown that peers not only provide technical support for the transfer of training but also moral encouragement through the development of a transfer culture, using catch phrases and anecdotes jointly encountered in training.

Course Mentor. Another useful precourse suggestion is to pair the trainee with an alumnus of the program, who can identify the benefits and barriers to implementation. This mentor might also serve to alleviate the anxiety of the adult learner, who may lack self-confidence in his or her ability to master new material.

The implementation of these suggestions before training begins will result in a heightened attention to learning and a focus by the trainee on the importance of learning to transfer.

◆ ◆ ◆

DURING THE TRAINING

Previous chapters discussed the functions of needs assessment, learning objectives, and methods in the acquisition of knowledge and skills. This section examines the acquisition of content during a training course, using principles derived from adult learning.

When designing a course (see Chapter 8), the trainer should include feedback, practice, and contingencies that will optimize employee learning and transfer.

Feedback. The most fundamental step in improving performance is to provide knowledge about present performance. This was seen, in the previous section, as a first step in unfreezing present behaviour. Unless adults have evidence that their present performance is not as effective as it could be, there is little motivation to change.

If the trainee has not received this feedback before the course begins, then a first stage in the design process is to develop an exercise, role play, or questionnaire that provides relatively objective feedback on present knowledge, skills, or attitudes. Many commercial training establishments supply assessment inventories that measure conflict styles, leadership styles, knowledge about sexual harassment, attitudes toward conflict, etc.* These "tests" allow adults, whose attitudes and habits may be ingrained and difficult to change, to realize the nature of their present behaviours, and provide impetus to change. These tests build on Lewin's (1958) theory that trainers must unfreeze behaviour, teach new skills, and refreeze the new behaviour before any change will occur.

During training, feedback can be provided to guide trainees as they attempt new behaviours. This feedback should be designed to correct performance. When incorrect responses are given, the feedback should include the correct response. Negative feedback ("you failed to acknowledge the client's problem") will not be perceived as punishing if the source is knowledgeable, friendly, trustworthy, and powerful enough to affect outcomes like promotions (Ilgen et al., 1979).

Feedback in some learning situations consists of the results of tests. Tests are usually graded by some combination of measurements against an objective standard (criterion) and a group standard (normative). Criterion reference measures are designed to compare an individual with a given performance requirement or standard, regardless of how others perform (Nadler and Nadler, 1990). This approach is used for knowledge tests, such as theories of electricity, in training in industry.

---

* Companies such as Pfeiffer & Company Publishing in Toronto and Human Resource Development Press in New York provide catalogues listing training tools, exercises, instruments, games, role plays, etc.

The normative approach compares learners with one another for the purpose of ranking (as is done in university classrooms). Adults should be evaluated against the attainment of specific criteria, not compared publicly to their peers. In other words, evaluations such as final tests and exams should be criterion-related, not normative. Adults should not be graded on a curve (Bass and Vaughn, 1969).

Feedback is most effective when it is immediate (i.e., it occurs directly after response is given). Feedback works when it is specific ("The head is tilted back at this angle," not "You moved the head wrong," or "Good, you have the right 25-degree angle," not just "good"). In a study of the effect of feedback on the performance of hourly workers, Miller (1965) concluded that the relevance, specificity, timing, and accuracy of the feedback are the critical factors in mastery of learning. Trainees receiving this type of feedback are more likely to adjust their responses toward the correct behaviour, more likely to be motivated to change, and more likely to set goals for improving or maintaining performance (Locke and Latham, 1990).

Training methods such as computer-assisted instruction and structured behaviour modelling have feedback as an integral, and imbedded, focus.

PRACTICE

Learning is often defined as a relatively permanent change in behaviour occurring as a result of reinforced practice or experience (Wexley and Latham, 1991). Practice is defined as repetition or rehearsal, so that responses or behaviour can be improved. Practice can be a physical activity (learning to type) or a mental activity (memorizing the categories of learning objectives). Obviously, feedback is an essential prelude to practice.

A demonstration of the correct response or behaviour is a good start for practising a response. After a demonstration, trainees should begin with practice that is coached and guided by the trainer, moving through each of the critical tasks that form the whole (Yelon and Berge, 1992). The next step is practice with coaching from peers. The final stage is independent practice. At this point, the trainer could vary conditions so that the skill is executed in different situations. In this way, the trainee is more likely to use the skill on the job.

Another approach to transfer through practice is to start with an explanation of the theory or general principles, provide a demonstration of these, arrange employee participation in a simulation, arrange practice on the job with feedback and coaching, and then guide the employee with a mentor (Anthony et al., 1993).

Practice does not suggest that there can be no theory in training. There is evidence that trainees learn better when a theoretical framework, general principles, or key elements of the content to be learned are given (Goldstein, 1993).

In practising mental skills, the strategies trainees use to aid memory include the use of mnemonics or organizers. Mnemonics is a learning tool that helps us memorize, for example, the names of the Great Lakes, by using a simple word, such as HOMES (Huron, Ontario, Michigan, Erie, and Superior). Organizers are cues that may be verbal, quantitative, or graphic, already understood by trainees, and used to incorporate new knowledge. For example, the icons or symbols of a file cabinet or wastebasket used in software writing programs aid the new user in identifying ways to save or trash information. Trainees can use these mental models to improve learning by focusing on important components and relationships, organizing new material, and linking these to current knowledge (Mayer, 1989).

Building on similarities encourages transfer. Human resource developers should ensure that the training situation reflects the job to some degree. The identical-elements theory states that positive transfer will occur only if identical elements are present in both the old (training course) and new situations (Bass and Vaughn, 1969). But even if identical elements don't exist, the trainee's work environment should be somewhat similar to enhance generalization. Above all, the trainees should perceive the training as relevant (Elangovan and Karkowsky, 1992).

Practice is more effective when practice periods are spread over time, rather than massed together (Baldwin and Ford, 1988). Massed practice, or cramming, is practice with virtually no rest periods. Students might argue that they can succeed on an exam for which they have crammed, but research shows that memory loss after cramming is greater than if a student had studied over several weeks (Goldstein, 1993). Furthermore, organizations would prefer that trainees retain material over many months, rather than just know it for the course test or simulation. Therefore, trainers teaching a new skill such as performance-appraisal interviewing could increase learning by spacing the training and practices over a week of two-hour sessions, rather than cramming it into an eight-hour day.

Active practice is more effective than passive learning. A student who writes out possible exam questions and responses learns more than another who just reads the book. A manager would learn more by actually conducting a mock interview than by listening to a lecture on interviewing. In general, both adults and children learn by doing.

Practising complex material in parts or stages is more effective than practising the whole activity at once. For example, piano students often learn complex pieces one hand at a time.

Overlearning, i.e., learning something until the behaviour becomes automatic, is an effective way to train people for emergency responses or for complex skills in which there is little time to think in a job situation. Automaticity refers to the performance of a skill to the point at which little attention from the brain is required in order to respond correctly (Yelon and Berge, 1992). Typing is the most common example of automaticity. Overlearning is an effective method in both cognitive and physical tasks. The greater the degree of overlearning, the longer the resulting retention (Driskell, 1992).

CONTINGENCIES

The learning principle with the most powerful influence is that of contingency theory. Contingency theory states that behaviour that is reinforced by desirable consequences tends to strengthen and occur more frequently in response to similar stimuli. Reinforcers or rewards can be psychological, such as praise, recognition, and attention. They can also be more tangible, such as gold stars, marks, bonuses, or promotions.

Contingencies, or consequences, may be the only possible motivation tool in some training situations. A clerk who has to memorize hundreds of regulations, with little meaningfulness to his or her personal life, may respond only to extrinsic rewards or even punishments.

This leads to the question: Is punishment effective? Overall, the answer has to be "no." Punishment, while appearing to produce instant results in the stopping of bad behaviour, has serious consequences. Punishment tells the individual to stop, but does not tell the individual the correct thing to do. This creates anxiety. Punishment works only when the enforcer is present. The teenager still smokes when there are no authority figures present; the worker arrives late when the boss is away. Punishment produces anger and retaliatory behaviour against the one administering the punishment. In summary, punishment is not a good idea.

Rewards have none of these side effects. Rewards tell the employee what is being done correctly and encourages its repetition. Rewards feel good—workers will continue the good behaviour and provide proof of this even when the reward giver is absent, and workers feel positively about people who reward them.

Effectiveness of reinforcers can be increased by managing the strength and timing of the reinforcer. Success can be seen as a reward, while failure feels like a punishment. Therefore, trainers should construct the learning experience in manageable chunks in which the trainee experiences success. (However, if the task is too easy, trainees will not perceive it as a success.)

The timing of reinforcers can shape behaviour. For example, instead of waiting until a manager conducted a perfect appraisal interview (and waiting forever!), trainers would praise the specific, isolated behaviours of good interviewing as they occurred. Over time, the accumulation of isolated behaviours would result in good appraisal behaviour. In this way, response patterns are shaped.

When learning new tasks, continuous reinforcement is ideal. However, after some self-efficacy is achieved, partial reinforcements are as effective and much more similar to the real world. Back on the job, it is unlikely that the trainee will be praised every time he or she does something correctly.

Although in a training situation the trainer can easily use reinforcers such as praise, these rewards are being given by an external agent. The ideal situation is to create an atmosphere in which the reinforcers become intrinsic or internal. Workers may do things the right way because the right way gives them pleasure, or saves time, or solves their problems.

The trainer can increase the trainee's intrinsic motivation to learn. Some approaches would be to emphasize the future value of the skill and to relate the content to interesting, meaningful materials outside the training program (Bass and Vaughn, 1969). Trainees learn and remember meaningful material more easily than material unrelated to their lives (McGehee and Thayer, 1961). Trainers can refer to information, problems, and anecdotes collected from the needs analysis to provide the link between classroom material and work situations. New material should be introduced using terms and examples familiar to employees. Providing an overview of the course and presenting it logically, and from the least to the most complex material, also aid memory. The inclusion of managers as leaders of program components also increases the meaningfulness of the material (Nadler, 1982).

Another reason for moving toward intrinsic reinforcement is that reinforcements are highly personal. Some people may be encouraged by public praise, others may find this embarrassing.

In summary, during a training program, trainers should incorporate active feedback, practice, and contingencies into the program.

◆ ◆ ◆
AFTER THE TRAINING PROGRAM

After a training course, most participants are motivated to try to use their new skills. But only 50 to 90 percent are able to do so. Some quit trying because they receive no support for their attempts. Others give up after initial attempts because they encounter problems in the application and the old technique seems to work better and faster. The trainer, aware of these universal problems of transfer, can devise strategies to manage the transfer and to prevent a relapse to precourse behaviours. There are two components to these postcourse strategies: the trainees and their managers.

◆ ◆ ◆
TRAINEE STRATEGIES

SELF-MANAGEMENT

Employees can be trained to manage their own postcourse behaviour (Latham and Frayne, 1989). By self-management we mean that trainees set goals, formulate written behavioural contracts, and administer their own contingencies.

Numerous research studies have demonstrated that people who have set specific, difficult goals achieve the best performance (Locke and Latham, 1990). Trainers should incorporate goal setting as an essential part of the training program. One method of goal setting is to prepare a performance contract.

A performance contract is a statement, mutually drafted by the trainee and the trainer near the end of the course, that outlines which of the newly acquired skills are seen as beneficial and which will be applied to the job. A copy can then be given to the trainer, a peer, or the supervisor who will then monitor progress toward these goals. The more specific the goals, the more likely they are to be attained. An example of a specific goal might read: "Identify five new customers within 30 days." Trainees could submit progress reports to both the human resources developer and their manager. A variation on the timing, i.e., signing the contract jointly before the course, alerts the trainee to the critical elements of the program and commits the supervisor to monitoring progress (Leifer and Newstrom, 1980).

The importance of goal setting must be emphasized. Considerable research demonstrates that setting goals results in superior performance (Goldstein, 1993). From these studies, we know that trainees should agree to the goals; that the goals must be specific, not vague; that the goals should be hard and challenging but matched to the ability of the trainee; and that there must be a feedback mechanism to allow for the measurement of progress.

Besides goals, there is another simple technique for assuring effective transfer. Job aids can increase the transfer of material learned to the job (Thiagarajan, 1990). Job aids include checklists, posters, instructions embedded into software, and easily referenced instructions. For example, employees learning about hazardous-waste management can be provided with a checklist that summarizes the major steps in handling radioactive material. This checklist, if prepared as a colourful poster, will increase the chances of employee application. Job aids are useful when performance is difficult, is executed infrequently, can be done slowly, and when the consequences of poor performance are serious (Ruyle, 1990).

RELAPSE PREVENTION

Relapse prevention utilizes behavioural principles to sensitize trainees to the possibilities of skills erosion and "immunizes" them against factors in the environment that cause the erosion (Tziner and Haccoun, 1991). The technique was adapted from programs for treating addictive behaviours such as smoking and drinking (Wexley and Latham, 1991). Relapse in the work context means reverting to using the old skills or pretraining behaviour on the job.

Relapse prevention consists of making trainees aware that relapse will occur and that temporary slips are normal. They are asked to identify those barriers to implementation and those situations in which relapse is likely to occur. For each of the new skill areas, the trainees are asked to develop a coping strategy. For example, if workers think they will abandon the new ways when there is too much work, time-management techniques could be discussed.

Relapse-prevention programs work. Trainees who received training in relapse prevention showed higher levels of course knowledge and used the knowledge more (as rated by their supervisors) than those who did not receive this training (Tziner and Haccoun, 1991).

Behavioural checklists are another method used to prevent relapses (Wexley and Nemeroff, 1975). In one study, a group of participants were given checklists derived from the behaviours learned on the course, and received training in monitoring and recording their behaviour. This group was better at applying the new skills than another that did not receive the checklists.

Learners should expect a follow-up report to training from the training department (Nadler and Nadler, 1990). They should know what will be expected and that these results will be shared with their supervisors. Trainers could even consider a followup assignment.

The training can be reinforced by scheduling alumni days (Parry, 1990). About five weeks after the course, participants reunite to discuss successes and barriers to implementation. This time should be considered the real "graduation day." This alumni network can be further strengthened by forming a group of graduates who meet monthly. For macrodevelopment (or organization-wide) projects, this alumni association could develop newsletters and arrange for guest speakers. Indeed, Buller and Cragun (1991) argue that networking is the most important outcome of training. A study conducted with managers who had attended a training course demonstrated that the training broadened their network of relationships within the company and that this, in turn, enabled them to get work done more effectively across organization lines (Buller and Cragun, 1991).

Through the use of goal setting and relapse-prevention programs, trainees are more likely to apply what they have learned. If these strategies are coupled with support from the organizational environment, the likelihood of transfer of new skills to the job is increased.

◆ ◆ ◆

MANAGEMENT MAINTENANCE STRATEGIES

Training alone is rarely successful in achieving long-term performance improvement. Indeed, as noted earlier, perhaps as few as 20 percent of performance problems are caused by lack of knowledge or skills (Spitzer, 1990).

The work environment must be managed to provide opportunities for optimum performance and to reinforce this performance when it occurs.

OPPORTUNITY

Training transfer can be inhibited by the "bubble" syndrome, in which the trainee is expected to use the new skills without support from the environment (Hatcher and Schriver, 1991). Management can burst the bubble by ensuring that time between training and on-the-job application is minimal. Assignments, or opportunities, to try the new skills should be given as soon as the trainee returns from the course.

Managers can also help by allowing the trainee time to try out or even experiment with new behaviours without adverse consequences. An organizational climate characterized by high appreciation for performance and innovation has a positive impact on the transfer of skills (Baumgartel et al., 1984). In organizations that place a high value on learning, the cultural norm is developed in which the acquisition and application of new knowledge and skills is institutionalized (Zucker, 1987).

REINFORCEMENT

The problem with reinforcement during a training course is that it may be too frequent. The problem after the course is that reinforcement is infrequent or nonexistent. Behaviour that is not reinforced is not repeated. If the sales representative dutifully submits the reports as taught but no one even notices they are filed, then the rep will waste no further energy doing this task. A Xerox study showed that only 13 percent of trainees were using their new skills six months after training when management did not coach and support their use (Zucker, 1987). Supervisors of trainees should be trained themselves to observe and reinforce the new skills, while being patient and tolerant of errors.

A second problem with reinforcement of skills or behaviours in the work environment is the possibility of reinforcing behaviour that conflicts with the newly acquired skill (Baird et al., 1983). For example, managers may be praising the practice of safety, while the organization's incentive system rewards faster and greater production of units. Sometimes the problem is not this obvious. For example, shop floor supervisors were taught active listening skills in order to resolve grievances at the first stage of resolution. However, they quickly learned that they could save time and trouble with aggrieved employees by passing the grievance to the next level of management. Therefore, before the trainee returns from training, an appraisal of the real and hidden contingencies in the job setting should be done. (If this is done early enough, at the needs-analysis stage, there may be no need for training. Employees may already know what to do; the environment may just not support it. See Chapter 4 on needs analysis.)

Sometimes, trainees may not perform in the "new" way because they do not see any benefit for doing so. Outcome expectancies influence behaviour. If a trainee believes that a pay increase or a promotion will result from the application of certain skills, then he or she is more likely to apply them (Bandura, 1977). If the new skills are incorporated into merit-pay plans, then the probability increases that employees will use them (Wexley and Latham, 1991). Conversely, employees who apply the new skills and receive no rewards are very disappointed and are more likely to withdraw (emotionally or physically) from the job (Caplow, 1983). Those employees who returned to school to get a degree and then received no recognition or promotion for all that hard work understand this phenomenon.

Reinforcement should be used because it works. A Motorola Inc. study found that in plants where management reinforced quality-improvement training, those plants received an additional $33 return on every dollar invested (Clemmer, 1992).

Supervisors are more likely to reinforce newly learned skills if they themselves have been trained or have participated as trainers in the course (Wexley and Latham, 1991). In this way, they can both model the behaviour and observe its occurrence. Senior executives at Vancouver-based Finning Ltd., the world's largest Caterpillar dealer, are the first to attend training and are among the people delivering training (Clemmer, 1992). This cascading effect tells employees that management is serious about the learning and application of new skills. In addition, when managers are required to teach the new skills, they learn them very well. They are also aware that their employees are watching them to see if they practise what they preach.

There are dozens of other, easy-to-do methods a manager can use to help a returning trainee. These include transfer discussions, reducing job pressures initially, arranging for co-workers to be briefed by the trainee, arranging practice sessions, publicizing successes, and giving promotional preference of those trained (Broad and Newstrom, 1992). Western Gas

Marketing, Ltd. of Calgary rates their managers on the application of new skills on their performance-appraisal form (Clemmer, 1992).

The conclusion to be drawn from all this research is that training cannot be seen as an isolated event—just the course. The course, or development program, should be one activity among dozens in a carefully designed effort to improve performance. The target should be performance.

◆ ◆ ◆
SUMMARY

This chapter examined the factors, based on research on adult learning, that facilitate the transfer of learning to the job. These methods include preparatory steps before the training course and reinforcement procedures after the course. The role of the trainer in maximizing the learning during the course and its ultimate transfer to the work environment was discussed.

E X E R C I S E

The School Board

Carlos daSilva was sitting at his desk in the training office, thinking about his meeting scheduled at 2:00 p.m. He was looking forward to the meeting with the superintendent of the school board, knowing that he would be praised for the multimedia interactive-communications program he had designed. For years, parents, students, and teachers had been complaining that nobody listened, that decisions were made without participation, and that good ideas went unacknowledged. A needs analysis had confirmed that these problems were widespread.

As a recently appointed trainer with a strong background in teaching, Carlos tackled the communications problem as his first assignment. He designed what he immodestly considered to be the finest three-day communications program in any school board. He had spent months on the design: finding videos, CD-ROMS, exercises, and games that taught active listening, upward communication, brainstorming, and other areas identified in the survey.

However, the meeting with the superintendent went poorly. Although some teachers loved playing with the latest "teaching" technology in the communications course, most did not change their behaviour at work. A second analysis showed that the old problems persisted.

As an experienced trainer, you realize that Carlos had made a classic training mistake. He had spent most of his time and energy on developing the program and had failed to consider the transfer of the newly acquired knowledge and skills of the work environment.

Describe in detail what Carlos could have done (before, during, and after the course) to ensure that the problems identified in the survey would not have persisted.

References

Anthony, W.P., P.L. Perrewe, and K.M. Kacmar. 1993. *Strategic Human Resource Management*. Fort Worth: The Dryden Press.

Baird, L., C.E. Schneier, and D. Laird. 1983. *The Training and Development Sourcebook*. Amherst, Mass.: Human Resource Development Press.

Baldwin, T.T., and J.K. Ford. 1988. "Transfer of Training: A Review and Directions for Future Research." *Personnel Psychology* 41, 63–105.

Baldwin, T.T., and R.J. Magjuka. 1991. "Organizational Training and Signals of Importance: Linking Pretraining Perceptions to Intentions to Transfer." *Human Resource Development Quarterly* (Spring): 25–36.

Bandura, A. 1977. *Social Learning Theory*. Englewood-Cliffs, N.J.: Prentice-Hall.

_____. 1982. "Self-Efficacy Mechanism in Human Agency." *American Psychologist* 37, 122–47.

_____. 1986. *Social Foundations of Thought and Action: A Social Cognitive Theory*. Englewood Cliffs, N.J:. Prentice-Hall.

Bass, B.M., and J.A. Vaughn. 1969. *Training in Industry: The Management of Learning*. Belmont, Calif., Wadsworth Publishing Company.

Baumgartel, H., M. Reynolds, and R. Pathan. 1984. "How Personality and Organizational Climate Variables Moderate the Effectiveness of Management Development Programs: A Review and Some Recent Research Findings." *Management and Labour Studies* 9, 1–16.

Broad, M.L., and J.W. Newstrom. 1992. *Transfer of Training*. Reading, Mass.: Addison-Wesley Publishing Company.

Buller, P.F., and J.R. Cragun. 1991. "Networking: The Overlooked Benefit of Training." *Training and Development* 45, no. 7 (July): 41–44, .

Camp, R.R., P.N. Blanchard, and G.E. Huszczo. 1986. *Toward a More Organizationally Effective Training Strategy and Practice*. Englewood Cliffs, N.J.: Prentice-Hall, .

Caplow, T. 1983. *Managing an Organization*. New York: Holt.

Clemmer, J. 1992. "Why Most Training Fails." *The Globe and Mail* (15 September): B26.

Driskell, J.E. 1992. "Effects of Overlearning on Retention." *Journal of Applied Psychology* 7, no. 5, 615–22.

Elangovan, A.R., and L. Karakowsky. 1992. "The Role of Trainee and Environmental Factors in Transfer of Training: A Framework for Research." *Annual Proceedings of The Administrative Sciences Association of Canada* 13, no. 7.

Georgenson, D.L. 1982. "The Problem of Transfer Calls for Partnership." *Training and Development Journal* 36, no. 10, 75–85.

Gist, M.E. 1989. "The Influence of Training Method on Self-efficacy and Idea Generation Among Managers." *Personnel Psychology* 42, 787–805.

_____. 1990. "Transfer Training Method: Its Influence on Skill Generalization, Skill Repetition, and Performance Level" *Personnel Psychology* 43, (Autumn): 501–23.

Gist, N.E., Schwoerer, and B. Rosen. 1989. "Effects of Alternative Training Methods on Self-efficacy and Performance in Computer Software Training." *Journal of Applied Psychology* 74, 884–91.

Goldstein, I.L. 1991. "Training in Work Organizations." In M.D. Dunnette and L. Hough, eds., *Handbook of Industrial and Organizational Psychology.* 2nd ed., Vol. 2. Palo Alto, Calif.: Consulting Psychologists Press.

_____. 1993. *Training in Organizations: Needs Assessment, Development and Evaluation.* 3rd ed. Pacific Grove, Calif.: Brooks/Cole Publishing Company.

Hastie, R., and P.A. Kumar. 1979. "Person Memory: Personality Traits as Organizing Principles in Memory for Behaviour." *Journal of Personality and Social Psychology* 37, 25–38.

Hatcher, T., and R. Schriver. 1991. "Bursting the Bubble that Blocks Training Transfer." *Technical and Skills Training* (November–December):12–15.

Hicks, W.D., and R.J. Klimoski. 1987. "Entry into Training Programs and its Effects on Training Outcomes: A Field Experiment." *Academy of Management Journal* 30, 542–52.

Ilgen, D.R., C.D. Fisher, and M.S. Taylor. 1979. "Consequences of Individual Feedback on Behaviour in Organizations." *Journal of Applied Psychology* 64, 349–71.

Knowles, M. 1990. *The Adult Learner: A Neglected Species.* Houston, Texas: Gulf Publishing Company.

Latham, G.P., and C.A. Frayne. 1989. "Increasing Job Attendance Through Training in Self-Management: A Review of Two Studies." *Journal of Applied Psychology* 74, 411–16.

Leifer, M.S., and J.W. Newstrom. 1980. "Solving the Transfer of Training

Problems." *Training and Development Journal* (August): 34–46.

Lewin, K. 1958. "Group Decision and Social Change." In E.E. Maccoby, T.M. Newcomb, and E.L. Hartley, eds., *Readings in Social Psychology*. New York, NY: Holt.

Locke, E.A., and G. P.Latham. 1990. *A Theory of Goal Setting and Task Performance*. Englewood Cliffs, N.J.: Prentice-Hall.

Luthans, F., and T. Davis. 1983. "Beyond Modelling: Managing Social Learning Processes in Human Resource Training and Development." In Baird, C.E. Schneier, and D. Laird, eds., *The Training and Development Sourcebook*. Amherst, Mass.: Human Resource Development Press.

McGehee, W., and P.W. Thayer. 1961. *Training in Business and Industry*. New York: Wiley.

Mager, R.F. 1992. "No Self-efficacy, No Performance." *Training* 29, no. 4 (April): 32–36.

Mayer, R.E. 1989. "Models for Understanding." *Review of Educational Research* 59, 43–64.

Miller, L. 1965. *The Use of Knowledge of Results in Improving the Performance of Hourly Operators*. General Electric Company, Behavioral Research Service.

Nadler, L. 1982. *Designing Training Programs: The Critical Events Model*.

Reading, Mass.: Addison-Wesley Publishing Company.

Nadler, L., and Z. Nadler. 1990. *The Handbook of Human Resource Development*. 2nd ed. New York: John Wiley & Sons.

Noe, R.A. 1986. "Trainee Attributes and Attitudes: Neglected Influences on Training Effectiveness." *Academy of Management Review* 4, 736–49.

Noe, R.A., and N. Schmitt. 1986. "The Inflence of Trainer Attitudes on Training Effectiveness: Test of a Model." *Personnel Psychology* 39, 497–523.

Parry, S. 1990. "But Will They Use It?" *Training and Development Journal* (December): 15–17.

Pearce, J.M. 1987. "A Model of Stimulus Generalization in Pavlovian Conditioning." *Psychological Review* 94, 61–73.

Reilly, R.R., and E.W. Israelski. 1988. "Development and Validation of Minicourses in the Telecommunications Industry." *Journal of Applied Psychology* 73, 721–26,

Robertson, I., and S. Downs. 1989. "Work Sample Tests of Trainability: A Meta-analysis." *Journal of Applied Psychology* 74, 402–10.

Ruyle, K.E. 1990. "Developing Great Job Aids." *Technical and Skills Training* (July): 27–31.

Skinner, B.F. 1953. *Science and Human Behaviour*. New York: McMillan.

Spitzer, D. 1990. "Confessions of a Performance Technologist." *Educational Technology* (May): 12–15.

Tannenbaum, S.I., J.E. Mathieu, E. Salas, and J.A. Cannon-Bowers. 1991. "Meeting Trainee's Expectations: The Influence of Training Fulfilment on the Development of Commitment, Self-efficacy and Motivation." *Journal of Applied Psychology* 76, 750–69.

Thiagarajan, S. 1990. "ID Basics: 1, 2, 3...7." *Performance and Instruction* (November/December): 1579.

This, L., and G. Lippet. 1983. "Learning Theories and Training." In L.S. Baird, C.E. Schneier, and D. Laird, eds., *The Training and Development Sourcebook*. Amherst, Mass.: Human Resource Development Press.

Tolman, E.D. 1959. "Principles of Purposive Behaviour." In *Psychology: A Study of Science*, edited by S. Koch. New York: McGraw-Hill.

Tziner, A., and R.R. Haccoun. 1991. "Personal and Situational Characteristics Influencing the Effectiveness of Transfer of Training Improvement Strategies." *Journal of Occupational Psychology* 64, no. 2, 167–77.

Vroom, V. 1964. *Work and Motivation*. New York: Wiley and Sons.

Weiss, H.M. 1991. "Learning Theory in Industrial and Organizational Psychology." In M.D. Dunnette and L.M. Hough, eds., *Handbook of Industrial and Organizational Psychology*. 2nd ed., Vol. 1. Palo Alto, Calif.: Consulting Psychologists Press.

Wexley, K.N., and G.P. Latham. 1991. *Developing and Training Human Resources in Organizations*. 2nd ed. New York: Harper Collins Publishers.

Wexley, K.N., W.F. Nemeroff. 1975. "Effectiveness of Positive Reinforcement and Goal Setting as Methods of Management Development." *Journal of Applied Psychology* 60, 446–50.

William, T.C., P.W. Thayer, and S.B. Pond. 1991. "Test of a Model of Motivational Influences on Reactions to Training and Learning." Paper presented at Society for Industrial and Organizational Psychology, St. Louis (October).

Yelon, S., and Z. Berge. 1992. "Practice-Centred Training." *Performance and Instruction* (September): 8–12.

Zucker, L. 1987. "Institutional Theories of Organization." *Annual Review of Sociology* 13, 443–64.

8

Program
Design

◆ ◆ ◆
INTRODUCTION

The development of a program to change knowledge, skills, and attitudes can be approached from various levels of intervention. At the first level, individuals may undertake self-development by choosing courses from universities, colleges, private training organizations, or even a corporation's own catalogue of courses. At the next level, managers may recommend employees for specific courses with the goal of improving performance or meeting certification norms. A third level of intervention occurs when an organization attempts to increase its capacity to learn by focusing on continuous improvement, with the corresponding need for training in related skills such as literacy, team-building, and coaching.

The perspective of this chapter is the actual course or program used to support any of the preceding levels of interventions. The chapter answers basic questions in program design dealing with participants, content, and methods. The prescriptions in program design are applied to a specific case, developed within the chapter.

Having considered the various methods of reinforcing training in Chapter 7, we turn now to the design of training programs. Proper program design is important for four reasons. First, a competently prepared training plan will make the task of competing for funding easier. Second, a good plan will enable training activity to be directed toward real training problems, not symptoms of problems. Third, the planning document will ensure that the problems under consideration can be solved by training and not some other intervention method. Fourth, good planning leads to enhanced credibility with line managers. All of these factors combined will help the training department become a respected part of the organizational culture rather than existing as an inconsequential secondary activity on the margins of corporate power.

In Chapter 4, needs-analysis methods were outlined, followed by the task of writing training objectives. This chapter incorporates data from both these activities to produce a blueprint for the design of the program or course.

◆ ◆ ◆
THE PROGRAM DESIGN BLUEPRINT

There are several phases involved in the actual design of a training program. These phases are sequential, with the output of one phase becoming the input to the next.

The first two of these phases—needs analysis and setting objectives—have been carefully outlined already. They are as important to program design as is a foundation to a house. The following case study will assist in the explanation of the subsequent steps.

CASE STUDY: THE HANWELL CORPORATION

The Hanwell Corporation is a wholesale office-supply distribution company that has been in business for more than 20 years. The staff source more than 2000 products from many parts of the world, process orders, and distribute them by mail or courier all across Canada.

Only 5 percent of Hanwell's business is outside of Canada. The president, however, wants to take advantage of the low Canadian dollar, the U.S./Canada Free Trade Agreement, and her firm's core expertise in finding products at costs lower than the competition to increase exports to 50 percent of sales by the year 2000.

She knows that her internal systems are incapable of handling more business. Accurate access to data is not possible. The status of individual customer orders cannot be determined, inventory control and purchasing are not linked, accounts and sales misinformation result in problems such as bankrupt customers being shipped products, etc. Despite these problems, the lower costs of Hanwell products result in increasing orders.

Furthermore, the president knows that Americans expect superior service so that an export thrust into this much more competitive market would be pointless until sales and service standards are improved.

A needs analysis accurately reflected these perceived gaps in information and service. Two levels of analysis (organization and positional) resulted in the specification of objectives to be accomplished. With the installation of a comprehensive information-systems package, the following objectives represent some of the learning goals that must be achieved:

1. All warehouse personnel must be able to access product information within five minutes of receiving an order; if product is out of stock, then

warehouse personnel must be able to place a purchase order after completing a customer financial analysis.

2. Order processing time will be reduced by 50 percent within three months, 100 percent of late penalties on accounts payable will be eliminated within six months, dollar volume of inventory will be reduced by 25 percent, items on back order will be reduced by 35 percent within nine months, etc.

3. All sales clerks must be able to complete a customer order form with less than 1 percent error, within one day of receipt of call. No phone should ring more than three times. All customer problems must be resolved to customer satisfaction 90 percent of the time, while following company practices within 48 hours of a complaint.

4. Customer-survey results must show that customers are exceptionally happy with customer service 90 percent of the time.

After reviewing the objectives, the trainer asked the key management team questions (discussed in Chapter 4) such as:

◆ Are these goals important? Yes

◆ Is there a skill deficiency? Could the employees meet these standards if their lives depended on it? The answer would be that they could not; they do not have the knowledge or skills to accomplish these objectives.

◆ Are there organizational obstacles to performing as desired? No, just the lack of knowledge and skills. The environment would be very supportive.

◆ Do employees have the mental/physical capacity to achieve these objectives? Yes. They have learned other similar skills. (If the answer was "No, the employees are not literate or do not wish to learn these skills," there are resources available to the trainer. The reader might want to consult Chapter 3 on stakeholders, which outlines government programs to assist with literacy training or outplacement counselling.)

IS TRAINING THE SOLUTION?

The next step is to determine if training is the solution to the problem or if it is the most appropriate way to achieve these objectives. A quick scan of Chapter 6, "Alternatives to Training," reveals that some of these methods (such as coaching and mentoring) would be too slow and "fuzzy" to accomplish these specific objectives. Technology might be considered as part of the solution. For example, an electronic performance-support system (EPPS) might assist employees with detailed information about accessing the computer system. However, it is probably not the best method of introducing people to computers or of motivating them to use computers and provide superior customer service. In Hanwell's case, a training program seems like an appropriate solution to their problems.

But before the trainees step into a classroom, a number of questions still need to be answered.

IS THE ENVIRONMENT PREPARED FOR THE RE-ENTRY OF TRAINED WORKERS?

A review of Chapter 7 would suggest that Hanwell managers need to be involved in the process of training by completing questionnaires regarding competencies, career counselling, allowing employees time for prework, and pledging to support changes in skills or ways of doing things. As indicated in Chapter 7, adults need to know why they are being trained. Effective transfer of new skills to the job situation depends on tapping their motivations to learn and to apply this learning to the job.

WHO NEEDS TO BE TRAINED?

The training situation is now analyzed at three levels:

- What positions (not people) will be affected by the systems change?

- What core responsibilities will be affected in each case?

- How and to what degree will the proposed changes affect each job?

The adoption of a software system will directly affect (i.e., change the duties) of the sales representatives, sales clerks, purchasing agents, accounts clerks, and shippers. For example, the shippers maintain inventory records, pack and ship orders, receive incoming goods, determine the most economical shipping methods, manage storage and retrieval systems, etc. Some aspects of their job will obviously be directly affected by the new software.

From this analysis, the positions that will be changed by the president's initiatives have been identified. Now, the competency levels of the holders or incumbents of these positions must be assessed.

WHAT KNOWLEDGE/SKILLS MUST BE ACQUIRED?

Chapter 7 refers to the need to select trainees carefully based on their abilities, aptitudes, and motivation. The employees must be assessed or tested to determine current knowledge and skill levels. Performance tests or interviews could be conducted to develop a base line of competencies. These tests also act as motivators in the sense that they indicate the need for change, a necessary step in the unfreezing process, discussed earlier. These tests may also demonstrate that some employees already know some of the material to be taught. These knowledgeable employees can either bypass certain learning modules or can act as coaches during the training process.

For several decades, psychologists have been interested in the manner in which skills and knowledge are acquired (Weiss, 1990). Numerous research studies have suggested that the acquisition of skills and knowledge can be approached sequentially (behaviour or skills are chained together on a restricted path) and hierarchically (simpler skills must be acquired before the acquisition of more complex ones). In this case, the clerks must be able to guide a customer sequentially through a complaint (from asking about product type to negotiating a settlement), and hierarchically (from asking fact-based questions to using active listening skills and mediation techniques). Within the sequencing process (the order in which content is presented), Nadler (1990) has suggested two approaches:

1. the general to the specific—This approach suggests that the learner is given an overview of the material before learning specific skills. This holistic approach works particularly well with adults.

2. the specific to the general—This approach, based on behaviourist principles, develops first-order skills before combining these into a complete sequence of skills.

The choice of approach depends both on the content of training and the needs of learners.

Not all deficiencies in knowledge must be addressed by the training course alone. Enough information could be provided in a course to get people started in using the new procedures; then more detailed information could be transferred through other means such as an EPPS or coaching. Basic information, such as how to turn on a computer or keyboarding, must precede the development of advanced systems handling. How much of the advanced information must be communicated through training and embedded in trainee memory? There are situations, such as the rare order from a customer in Alaska, that are best handled by coaching, a job aid, or reference to a supervisor. Training for every contingency is not cost-effective. We cannot assume, for instance, that employees are motivated to change. Must the trainer develop methods to deal with computer phobia or resistance? Informal discussions, rather than detailed task analysis, should provide this kind of information. Listening carefully to the "talk," as defined in Chapter 4, may provide some insights about motivational levels.

Employees' current levels of knowledge and skills can be compared to the organization's desired levels as outlined in the performance goals or objectives. The gap between the two represents the organization's training needs and determines the precise content of the training course.

WHAT METHOD SHOULD BE USED TO TRAIN?

A variety of training methods are described in Chapter 9. Obviously, there are an enormous number of methods from which to choose. The choice of method will be constrained by time, money, or tradition. For example, trainees may be more comfortable with small-group training than with computer-assisted training.

A re-examination of the levels of learning will assist the trainer at this stage. Although the "expert" trainer will be very familiar with the content to be learned, he or she must determine the depth or extent of that content. For example, do trainees need only theory (i.e., to know only the definitions of a software package) or do they need to critique the software (such as might occur in the evaluation stage of knowledge)? (See Chapter 5 on objectives.) Most likely, the employees will be at the application stage of the knowledge area. The trainer should develop content areas that correspond to the knowledge needed to perform the desired skills. A list of objectives for each segment of the program would be helpful in determining methods.

If the trainee's motivation to learn is weak, a review of the steps used to determine attitude levels (Chapter 5), adult learning principles (Chapter 7), and methods for changing attitudes (Chapter 9) would reveal solutions.

"Application" levels are best learned using simulations, coaching, etc. (See Chapter 9.) High levels of feedback, practice, and reinforcement during the training process should ensure not only the employees' ability to transfer the skills learned to the job but the motivation to do so. (The employees should be highly motivated to learn because the old system will cease to exist say on a Friday, and the new system will be up and running on the Monday.)

After reviewing the information from these chapters, the training developer now faces a "make or buy" decision. There are many private training companies and consultants in Canada that offer an extensive array of courses on general topics such as computer training and customer service. In most cases, it is more economical for an organization to purchase (buy) these materials, packaged in professional formats, than to develop (make) the materials themselves, which in many cases will be used only once or twice. The advantages of packaged programs are high quality, immediate delivery, ancillary services (tests, videos), the potential to customize the package to the organization, benefits from others' implementation experience, extensive testing, and often less expense than internally developed programs (Nadler and Nadler, 1990).

The advantages of internally developed programs are security and confidentiality, use of the organization's language, incorporation of the organization's values, use of internal content expertise, understanding of the specific target audience and organization, and the pride and credibility of having a customized program (Nadler and Nadler, 1990). A cost-benefit analysis would be necessary to determine the best option.

◆ ◆ ◆
THE COURSE

Based on analysis of all the information suggested above, the curriculum (i.e., the content and the method) and the schedule can be developed.

Pace et al. (1991) have suggested one approach that is particularly effective for teaching skills. The training sequence should consist of four basic activities:

1. *Experience*—Present an experience or situation that demonstrates a problem that participants would be experiencing at work, such as having to deal with an irate client. This allows trainees to "feel" the problem.

2. *Information*—Present theoretical information, concepts, or "mental models" that explain why the problem occurred and that lead to discussion of alternative approaches.

3. *Analysis*—Analyze the demonstrated situation to illustrate the effectiveness of the concepts or material to be taught.

4. *Practice*—Practise the new concepts in order to solve the problem. While performance chunked into bits of small skills will seem slow and awkward at first, the smoothness and speed of the response will increase with feedback and practice (Logan, 1985). Picture the new piano student playing the same piece as a skilled pianist. The effects of training, feedback, and practice become apparent. Early performance is dependent on thinking through the steps (cognitive skills), while later performance is more habitual (requiring less thought). Therefore, skills and knowledge must be broken into small steps, with lots of opportunity built in for feedback and practice.

Experienced trainers will suggest that the training schedule be flexible (with outside limits) to allow for participation; that the dullest or hardest material be built in at peak energy times; that methods be varied; and that the underlying objective is that the *trainees learn*, not that the *trainer teaches*.

Chapter 10, which discusses the fair treatment of people in the classroom, provides suggestions to increase participation of trainees. These techniques should be built into the design and delivery of the course. An example of one module of the training course is presented in Figure 8.1.

The training plan or design is an important management tool. It allows for both the approval and the smooth operation of workplace learning activity. It enables expenditures to be budgeted for and monitored. The development of a training plan is a signal to other members of the organization that training is to be conducted in a professional manner.

Returning to our case study at Hanwell, it appears that the content necessary to have the employees trained and operational by Monday morning can be taught in two days. The training at Hanwell will consist of a two-day weekend session (to minimize disruptions to regular business). The trainer will be an individual from the company who sold Hanwell the software package. (He or she will continue to act as an on-site advisor during the first two weeks of operations.)

FIGURE 8.1 SAMPLE MODULE DESIGN

Objective: All customer complaints must be resolved to customer satisfaction.

Program: Trainees will be able to employ active listening skills to identify the exact nature of the complaint and to empathize with the customer's viewpoint.

Time: Day 2, 9:00 a.m.–12 p.m.

Course Outline:

9:00	Show video of customer-service representative demonstrating a negative (ineffective) method of handling a customer complaint.
9:20	Discuss video, asking participants to highlight errors in complaint handling and the consequences of these errors.
9:35	Present concepts and advantages of active listening. Outline techniques. Distribute handout, which summarizes key points and allows room for notes.
10:00	Break.
10:15	Show video of effective resolution of customer complaint, using techniques of active listening.
10:30	Practice. In groups of three, assign participants the roles of customer, service representative, and observer. Give each a script and instruct them to demonstrate two specific skills (which have been modelled in the presentation and video). Have observer provide feedback using feedback guidelines contained in the script.
11:00	Regroup. Discuss barriers and problems in implementation.
11:15	Distribute new role plays and assign new roles to participants. Practise skills.
11:40	Summarize key points. Discuss barriers to transfer and methods to overcome these barriers. Prepare implementation goals with participants.

WHAT TRAINING SUPPLIES AND EQUIPMENT ARE NEEDED?

With the determination of the supplies necessary for training, such as manuals or equipment such as VCRs, the training budget is more easily developed, the program more accurately costed, and the actual training session more likely to run smoothly. Commonly ordered supplies include overhead projectors, material on transparencies or acetates, VCRs and tapes, and workbooks or manuals.

Neophyte trainers will often purchase or rent videos or films to make the course more entertaining. While it is important that trainee attention be maintained, videos should have an instructional objective directly related to course content. Videos must be introduced by asking participants to identify information and elements related to that part of the course. The students are then prepared to discuss these at the conclusion of the video.

Hanwell probably needs a manual for each employee, 10 computers in a classroom, software for each computer, note pads, pens, flip charts, etc.

COSTING AND EVALUATION

Chapters 11 and 12 will explore these topics in detail. In general, any training activity should be evaluated to determine if the objectives have been met and if the training was a good investment.

The president of Hanwell, for example, will need to be reassured that the new software is functioning according to plan. (The vendor has a stake in the training process, too, as a smoothly operating system may lead to work in other companies.) Finally, the employees (at all levels) will want their work life to return to normal as soon as possible. A fast, efficient system changeover, characterized by a minimum of confusion and frustration, is therefore essential for both employees and the organization.

◆ ◆ ◆
AFTER THE COURSE

There are at least two strong reasons that trainees at Hanwell will use the skills they have learned in the course. The first is that the system demands it. The trainees must use the new system to do their jobs. The second is that the trainer will be there to act as a source of information and inspiration. As a resident coach, he or she will know who needs help and the level of help needed. Reinforcement and encouragement by both the coach and the managers for the meeting of new standards will ensure that employees progress toward the desired goal. Consult Chapter 7 for other suggestions for ensuring that the newly acquired skills are applied on the work site.

◆ ◆ ◆
SUMMARY

This chapter outlined basic steps in the preparation of a training course. Through the careful development of objectives (resulting from the needs analysis), the trainer can identify the current gaps in knowledge and skills, the precise program objectives, the most appropriate training methods, and the methods of evaluation. The design of the curriculum is based on all of this information, adult learning principles, and concepts of equity.

EXERCISE

The purpose of this exercise is to give you the opportunity to design a small segment of a training course. Your motivation to do so will be increased if you can find someone who needs to acquire knowledge or skill in a specific area. For example, does someone in your family need to learn how to program a VCR? Does a colleague want to learn how to lift heavy objects properly or to use a simple graphics program? Do any of your children or those you are coaching need to learn how to swing a golf club, punt a football, or multiply numbers in their heads? If these real-life situations exist, use them.

Once you have a specific performance goal, use the following steps to design a training program:

1. Determine the person's current knowledge or skill level.
2. Determine if the trainee could perform the task if his or her life depended on it.
3. Does the person have the mental and physical capacity to learn the task?

4. Looking at the person's current level of performance, and the goal, determine the content, the method, and the instructional resources needed. Prepare a session agenda similar to the example presented in this chapter.
5. Build in principles of learning, equity, and transfer of skills.

Discussion Questions

1. Describe the advantages of preparing a detailed lesson plan. Discuss the reasons that many instructors would not want to prepare a plan in such detail.
2. Course developers often face a choice of assigning a content expert to teach a class or of designating a trainer to conduct the session. Under which conditions would you choose the content expert? In which situations would you choose the expert in training?

References

Logan, G.D. 1985. "Skill and Automaticity: Relations, Implications and Future Directions." *Canadian Journal of Psychology* 37, no. 4, 367–386.

Nadler, L. 1990. *Designing Training Programs: The Critical Events Model*. Reading, Mass.: Addison-Wesley Publishing Company.

Nadler, L., and Z. Nadler. 1990. *The Handbook of Human Resource Development*. 2nd ed. New York: John Wiley and Sons.

Pace, R.W., P.C. Smith, and G.E. Mills. 1991. *Human Resource Development: The Field*. Englewood Cliffs, N.J.: Prentice-Hall.

Weiss, H.W. 1990. "Learning Theory in Industrial and Organizational Psychology." In M.D. Dunnette and L.M. Hough, eds., *Handbook of Industrial and Organizational Psychology*, 2nd ed., Vol. 1. Palo Alto, Calif.: Consulting Psychologists Press.

For additional information, consult: Government of Ontario. *The Training Plan*. Toronto: Ministry of Skills Development, 1987.

9

Training
Methods

INTRODUCTION

Training practitioners, teachers, and academics have developed a variety of techniques, ranging from traditional lecture formats to interactive computer-software systems. This chapter highlights the most common of these training systems or techniques. Even though there is now a general trend in training from passive to active learning methods, many of the older techniques continue to be useful. In addition, there is a tendency to mix or combine training methods (e.g., case studies with lecturing) so that trainers need to become skilled in a variety of approaches to learning.

The sections that follow are arranged in rough order, from passive to active, depending upon the amount of trainee input possible or encouraged (see Figure 9.1). No attempt is made to judge or rank these techniques in

FIGURE 9.1 TRAINING METHODS

PASSIVE

Lecturing

Behaviour Modelling

Distance Learning

Technology-based Training
- videoconferencing
- multimedia training

Case Method

Case Incident Concept

Games and Simulations

Role Play

Group Discussion
- trainer-led groups
- peer groups
- technology-aided groups

Action Learning

On-the-job Training

ACTIVE

Apprenticeship

terms of usefulness, as the most appropriate method will depend on the work situation, the nature of the material or skill to be taught, and the characteristics of the trainees.

◆ ◆ ◆

LECTURING

The modern concept of lecturing is rooted in the Middle Ages. Until the late 16th century, books were extremely rare and expensive. Unfortunately, a monk from a medieval monastery would be quite at home in most contemporary lecture theatres as, until recently, comparatively little value was placed on the art of lecturing, especially in higher education. Given that lecturing is the most cost-efficient technique for reaching large numbers of trainees while still preserving some face-to-face contact, however, this archaic method of imparting information is unlikely to disappear. Indeed, there is increasing demand for "good" lecturing in training and education at all levels (Parker, 1993; Gordon, 1988).

THE PRIME PREREQUISITES

Anyone can be taught to master the mechanics of lecturing. To be a great lecturer, however, one has to like people. This inherent attitude is critical to effective information delivery. Most students have been exposed to trainers, teachers, and professors who didn't like them much and who would rather have been somewhere else, e.g., conducting research or on the shop floor. It takes a consummate actor to hide one's inner feelings, especially if lecturing activity is part of a course or other method requiring long-term interaction between teacher and students.

The second prerequisite is that the lecturer must be able to share the students' reality, or put him- or herself into "the students' shoes." For this reason, the best lecturers often are those who share a similar social background or who have had similar academic/work experiences as the trainees or students. Many students have learned to avoid mathematics, for example, often because quantitative disciplines are taught by brilliant individuals who cannot understand why others should have difficulty with their area of specialization.

The concept of understanding and relating to the trainee permeates the entire lecture process. Pace of delivery, type of support material supplied, terminology used, and length of presentation, for example, are all affected by the nature of the audience. As well, the trainees' mindset at any given time of day cannot be ignored. The professor who starts a new topic five minutes before the end of a three-hour night-school class, for example, is not only ineffective as a teacher but causes people to avoid his or her discipline.

No matter how brilliant or competent the lecturer in his or her discipline or trade, then, if the passage of time, student boredom, teacher personality, or the teacher's preoccupation with other matters creates a divide between teacher and student, classroom performance likely will be mediocre. Although the discussion that follows will suggest ways to design an effective lecturing experience, the two prime requisites (liking people and understanding the trainee) remain the cornerstones of classroom teaching.

PREPARING THE LECTURE

"Where do I begin?" is a question asked by most first-time lecturers. The answer is: "First you have to know what you want to do (the objective) and how much information you need to impart." Objective-setting has been covered elsewhere in this text, but on a pragmatic level the lecturer should be able to write a concise statement describing what the trainees will be able to do or accomplish by attending any given lecture.

Although the lecturer is not always the subject-matter expert, usually there is some good reason he or she is called upon to teach. Either through previously gained knowledge or the ability to research, then, the lecturer or teacher will gather and arrange information in a logical manner. Logic could dictate a progression from the general to the specific, or from the specific to the general, depending upon the subject matter.

This information can be transcribed on cards or sheets of paper. An effective technique is to rule off a wide (5–8 cm) margin down the right-hand side of each page. Then detailed information can be placed in the body of the page, while headings are written in the margins.

It takes practice to get the timing of a lecture right. Only through experience can one judge the amount of material needed for any given amount of time.

Renner (1989) has suggested that no more than six major points be illustrated during each half hour of a lecture. In addition, he suggests the lecturer summarize the material at both the beginning and the end, while stopping occasionally to allow students to "catch up" and to write their own summaries. Finally, time should be scheduled for questions and answers.

THE PHYSICAL SETTING

Obviously, each student should be able to see the lecturer. As well, close attention should be paid to heat, light, acoustics, and seating. The optimum seating plan will depend on numbers and space. Again, one must remember the second "prime prerequisite"—"do unto others ..."—the lecturer must put him- or herself in the students' situation. Trainee attention span is often dictated by the physical surroundings; either the lecturer must be sure the setting is appropriate or break the lecture into 10 to 15 minute segments with a short "stretch time" in between.

PRESENT AN APPROPRIATE MIX OF MATERIAL

A lecturer that drones on for an entire hour is rarely effective. Depending upon audience needs, age, and motivation level, the delivery should be punctuated with a variety of supplementary material and/or exercises. Stories, case incidents, graphics, humour, student presentations, videos, and question/answer sessions are but a few of the techniques lecturers use to maintain interest and, perhaps even more important, to instill in the students love or, at the least, respect for the subject matter, trade, or craft. Lecturers not only represent themselves but function as ambassadors for their institution/firm *and* their discipline. A poor lecture, then, not only shows the teacher in a bad light but forms trainee attitudes toward entire sections of curriculum.

◆ ◆ ◆
BEHAVIOUR MODELLING

People learn by observing the behaviour of others. Children watch action figures such as the Teenage Mutant Ninja Turtles and, with no formal training, will leap into "kung fu" positions at the cry of "kowabunga!" Teenagers surreptitiously observe the posturing of the "cool" kids. Administrative trainees watch very carefully how the senior team leader makes a presentation to his or her boss.

The behaviour modelled can be both positive and negative and can range from interviewing skills to hijacking. In 1961, an airplane was hijacked out of Miami, resulting in a wave of copycat terrorist acts. Industry uses behaviour modelling mainly to teach interpersonal skills such as supervision, negotiation, communication, sales, etc.

Models can be anyone—parents, peers, celebrities—although people with authority or charisma are the models most likely to be copied. Sabido in Mexico City ran a popular soap opera showing stars enrolling, studying, and graduating in literacy courses. After watching this popular show, the number of Mexicans enrolled in literacy courses increased from 90 000 to 840 000 in one year (Sabido, 1981).

Behaviour-modelling instruction is founded on four principles of learning: imitation (modelling), behavioural rehearsal (practice), reinforcement (reward), and transfer (Robinson, 1982).

The process is straightforward. A learner observes a model in a particular situation, such as a selection interview or handling a customer with a complaint. This situation can be filmed or conducted live. The model should be someone with whom the learner can identify and should have desirable qualities, such as power or status. Under these conditions, the learner is more likely to want to imitate the model's behaviour.

In addition, the trainees must have sufficient trust in the facilitator to "experiment," i.e., to try new behaviour in front of a group. Sometimes, a traditional and ineffective scenario is enacted to increase motivation to try the new positive model. (John Cleese of Monty Python fame used this technique very effectively in his humorous video series on interviewing.)

The trainee observes the behaviour then attempts to re-enact the scenario. The trainer should have broken down the skills to be learned into a series of critical steps, which can be modelled independently. After viewing the model, the participants practise the behaviour, one step at a time. When one step is mastered and reinforced, the trainer moves to the next critical skill. Specific feedback is given immediately. This step-by-step process results in the solid development of skills and the confidence needed to use them (Georges, 1988).

Transfer of the new skill to the workplace is always the "weak" spot in the training cycle. Old patterns are comfortable and familiar. By "overpractising" or overlearning the skill, however, its use may become automatic. Of course, as was seen in the chapter on transfer, regular reinforcement of newly acquired skills ensures their repetition. When these reinforcers are in place, behaviour-modelling training can have long-lasting and positive outcomes (Buller and McEvoy, 1990).

◆ ◆ ◆
DISTANCE LEARNING

Distance learning and distance education are general terms referring to learning methods in which information is communicated from a central source to individuals or groups at locations separate from the source, usually through the use of technology. The most common methods of distance learning include correspondence courses, which can include audio- and videocassettes, supplemented by workbooks and even supervised off-site exams. Advances in technology have resulted in a variety of methods, such as teleconferencing and computer-managed multimedia packages.

Distance-learning methods are considered valuable for students or employees who live in remote areas; when there is an insufficient number of students enrolled in a course to justify hiring an instructor; for trainees who are less mobile than others because of parenting or work responsibilities; and for trainees who are physically challenged.

In Canada, organizations such as the Open Learning University of British Columbia, Télé-université of Québec, and TV Ontario supply distance education. Many Canadian companies such as the Royal Bank, the Ford Motor Company, and Bell Northern Research use two-way video for communicating and training. In 1990, CIBC announced a new corporate education strategy for 23 000 employees in 73 sites using video-teleconferencing.

Motivation seems to be a big problem in distance learning. Students report feeling isolated and missing the collegial nature of classroom learning (Robinson, 1992). Another problem is the high cost of course development, particularly when advanced technology is used. However, the advantage of nearly universal access overrides concerns about motivation and cost.

◆ ◆ ◆
TECHNOLOGY-BASED TRAINING

Training technology will be broadly defined in this section. Any technology that delivers education or training, or supports the delivery of these subjects, would be included in the definition. The Office of Technology Assessment of the U.S. Congress lists everything from print through to CD-ROM and virtual environments as training technology. However, in corporate life, video tapes are the most frequently used technology in training.

The field of training technology is changing rapidly. This change is sustained by the increase in storage capacity of personal computers, the growth of expert and authoring systems, and the development of "generic" courses. The trend for organizations to "computerize" office procedures facilitates the introduction of computer-based training (CBT). Industries with a high investment in technology infrastructure use CBT more extensively than others (Stahmer, 1991). Combine this technology with the desire of students to control the pace and place of learning and the growth potential of distance learning is obvious. In 1986, 36 000 Canadians were enrolled in home-based study courses (Slade and Sweet, 1989). These numbers represent a huge potential market for training technology.

The following sections examine common technologies in training, beginning with a description of the technology and an assessment of strengths and weaknesses.

VIDEOCONFERENCING

This method consists of linking a subject-matter expert to employees by means of two-way television (video). This allows people at two or more locations to see, hear, and speak with one another. It permits simultaneous meetings in different locations. Videoconferencing is used to bring in an expert from another location, to hold meetings with staff working in various locations, and to communicate corporate information that needs to be rapidly disseminated and accepted.

Unsettled political conditions and incidents like the Gulf War (which made some executives wary of travel terrorism) and decreases in the costs of technology have made videoconferencing more acceptable and affordable. In addition, employees in remote locations and those with limited flexibility, e.g., with child-care arrangements, stand to benefit from this technology, which allows them to be trained at their own workplace.

Companies like Stentor claim that training by live TV reduces travel and labour costs of training by reducing travel time, gets consistent or uniform training quickly to a large number of people, brings the subject-matter expert to all trainers, enhances company revenues by implementing training faster (from 3 months to 2 weeks), and distributes complex information over periods of time.

The disadvantage of this method is that there is less personal attention given to trainees. This problem can be remedied by having a facilitator on-site or by allowing for interactive questioning while training takes place.

MULTIMEDIA (COMPUTER-BASED TRAINING)

"Multimedia" can mean almost anything. "Chalk and talk" are multimedia, so is a slide show with two projectors. A virtual-reality simulator for teaching pilots is also multimedia. However, the term "multimedia" is evolving to mean any instructional delivery system that includes a computer. The Association of Multi-Image International defines multimedia as "presentations of a visual or audio-visual nature that are created using integrated computer technology." This method combines audio, video, computer graphics, and text and is presented via computer disc and associated technologies.

Experts predict that within 10 years, only 5 percent of training will take place in classrooms. They imagine a world in which a wide variety of databases, computer networks, and bulletin boards free individuals to create unique learning packages and experiences, allowing them to solve business problems as they arise (Geber, 1994).

Their vision is being realized. A "smart card" has been developed for distance education in which an employee or student uses the card to register and request learning materials, to link with tutors and other participants, and to study at home (*The Training Technology Monitor*, 1993). Ernst and Young have implemented an interactive multimedia program to train thousands of new accountants each year just in time and at their own pace.

The advantages of multimedia training are significant. Computers can simulate situations where skills, knowledge, or behaviours can be practised and tested. Reports from industrial users of multimedia training suggest that training time is reduced, test scores remain the same, but on-the-job performance is better than that given by conventional training methods (Greengard, 1993).

The main reason that the Hudson's Bay Company uses CBT is that it can standardize training for all its 65 000 employees (Allan, 1993). This method can provide immediate feedback to users. The feedback ranges from a simple prompt indicating that the answer is right or wrong to the execution of another program segment in which trainees are routed through a complex maze of reviews and reinforcements based on their input. Courses can be custom designed for use by pretesting students and, where proficiency is indicated, bypassing some modules.

All the learning senses, not just the eyes, are activated with the use of multimedia. Research has shown that the wider the range of media used, the greater the proportion of students who succeed in learning effectively (Smith, 1986). Mastery of skills is about 25 percent higher using CBT than other methods. Learning time is reduced by 30 to 50 percent (Stahmer, 1991). Trainees can learn at their own pace, with reinforcement and feedback from an endlessly patient tutor. The courseware is available 24 hours a day. This method reduces the need to wait until a group of students is ready to take a course, such as a company orientation program. CBT allows students to track their own progress and test themselves. The technology easily generates tests that can provide legal documentation for proof of competency levels. When an accident or safety incident results in a lawsuit, the employer can prove that the training program was undertaken and that a desired level of competence was reached. These training statistics could reduce corporate liability. As well, the use of computers virtually eliminates cheating. Questions are randomly administered to students with photo identification and secret passwords. After a lapse of time, retesting is done with a different set of questions.

Geographic flexibility is a major advantage to a computer-based technology. Students can learn at their home or workplace. High overhead costs of traditional training (travel, accommodation, training facilities) make technological-based training advantageous to companies with national or international employees. Savings occur at around the 2000-employee level and will reduce costs by 40 percent over other methods (Stahmer, 1991).

Not everything about training technology is positive. Multimedia instructional technology demands more trainee involvement and interaction but, paradoxically, offers less interpersonal contact. Students have learning preferences or styles. If a trainee prefers to be taught by a human, then this technology would disadvantage that employee. However, the technology does reduce some of the weaknesses of human-based training. Students who are too embarrassed to ask a question in class can do so electronically, directly to the instructors, or repeat some basic material without other students knowing. No other student is aware of how slowly one is progressing through the material and how often one is seeking remedial work. Trainers are aware of workers who are reluctant to attend training classes because their limited knowledge of the subject would be exposed. This instructional format reduces these group pressures.

The major disadvantage to the immediate implementation of multi-media training is the cost. Estimates are that it takes 200 to 300 hours of design and development to produce one hour of instruction (Miles and Griffith, 1993). A full-motion colour-and-sound courseware would likely cost $200 000 for 30 hours of instruction. However, for a company training thousands of employees, there are definite cost savings with this method.

◆ ◆ ◆
THE CASE METHOD*

The case method has become one of the most important learning methods of this century, evolving in scope and sophistication since the early 1900s. In 1910, Harvard University began using cases as an additional teaching instrument for business students. Company executives would present actual problems for students to analyze. In 1921, the Harvard Business School published its first book of written cases, outlining a model that has become a preeminent tool for learning worldwide (Schnelle, 1967; Craig, 1987).

The case study differs from teaching theory, allowing students to think for themselves while the teacher functions as a catalyst to learning. Students apply business-management concepts to relevant real-life situations as a case study should "... focus on a contemporary phenomenon within some real-life context" (Yin, 1985, 13). Case studies help develop analytical ability, sharpen problem-solving skills, encourage creativity, and improve the organization of thoughts and ideas (Pearce et al., 1989).

Over 70 percent of business schools use case-simulation methods. Several studies have found that using cases improves communication skills, offers a reward of solving problems, and enables students to better understand management situations (Wright, 1992). In order for the case method to be successful, however, certain requirements must be met. For example, the qualifications of both the students and the teacher (human and social

---

*Although the work has been rewritten extensively, recognition should be given to Daniele Bastarche, who completed the original research for this section while an MBA candidate in the Faculty of Administration at the University of New Brunswick.

factors) affect the ability to analyze cases and to draw conclusions. As well, space and time dimensions are relevant; students need time in order to analyze cases properly. Finally, case studies and discussions work best in an open and informal atmosphere (Craig, 1987).

TYPES OF CASES

Cases may be written in various styles, presenting either single problems or a number of complex interdependent situations. They may be concerned with corporate strategy, organizational change, departmentalization, or any problem relating to a company's financial situation, marketing, human resources, or a combination of these activities. Some case reports describe the organization's difficulties in vague terms, while others may state the major problems explicitly.

In addition to the various styles of writing a case, there are also different methods of presentation. Cases do not always have to be in written form. Sometimes it is more effective to present cases using audiovisual techniques. This approach has advantages for both the students and the teacher in that teachers do not have to do as much research and writing, while students are able to identify better with the characters (Craig, 1987). A second alternative to a written case presentation is the "live" case method. Businesses may contact schools to report certain undesirable symptoms of problems; students then analyze the situation and report back to the company. This approach has been called operational consulting (Schnelle, 1967).

ELEMENTS OF A CASE

Certain requirements should be met when writing a traditional case. The case should be a product of a real business situation. A fictitious case could be regarded with boredom and distrust, as the setting may be unrealistic (Craig, 1987). Ideally, cases should be written by more than one person. Collaboration on the presentation of facts ensures a more realistic situation and helps to reduce biases. Although it is difficult, the case writer must not make assumptions; only facts should be included. "The case writer must report to the best of his/her ability the relevant facts of the situation at the time the decisions needed to be made or the problem existed" (Leenders and Erskine, 1973, 11). The author of a case, then, must relate core issues to the reader, not personal bias.

Case studies often concentrate on the corporate strategy of a company within an industry setting. Businesses do not usually follow predetermined behaviour. "It may well be frustrating when companies do not seem to act like textbook models" (Kenny et al., 1992, 451). The complexity of business situations makes decisions and analysis challenging. In addition, despite their length, most cases do not contain complete information on the organization or all the relevant inputs. This incompleteness is part of the benefit of using the case method, as students must learn to deal with incomplete data (Kenny et al., 1992).

WRITING THE CASE

As a case study is a description of a "typical" management situation, it is often difficult to know what to include and what to omit. Most cases give an overall description of the company and the industry situation. The length of a case report varies. A typical case, however, will be up to 20 typewritten pages. The key issues and the relevant details should be included to give the reader enough information to make a qualified decision. Some case studies disclose what management decisions were made when attempting to solve the organization's problems. Cases vary depending on the intended purpose of the writer and according to the issue being examined.

The objectives of a case are: 1) to introduce realism into the student's learning; 2) to deal with a variety of problems, goals, facts, conditions, and conflicts that often occur in the real world; 3) to teach students how to make decisions—therefore, most cases present situations in which problems are correctable; 4) to teach students to be creative and think independently (Yin, 1985).

WRITING TEACHING NOTES

A teaching note provides communication between the case writer and those who teach the case. In its strictest sense, a teaching note would include information on approaches to teaching a specific case. Some teaching notes, however, are more detailed, containing samples of analyses and computations. In addition, teaching notes may state the objectives of the case and contain additional company information not available to the student (Leenders and Erskine, 1973).

◆ ◆ ◆
THE CASE INCIDENT CONCEPT*

The case-study has become an important method for teaching business, law, psychology, religion, communications, and economics. Much of what has been written, however, concerns the creation of lengthy, detailed, strategically oriented academic material based on concepts undoubtedly made popular by their use at the Harvard Business School.

As most of these cases are excessively long and extremely complex, they have not generally found favour with trainers in business, particularly those training front-line supervisors. There is an offshoot of this technique, however, the Incident Concept, that can be used to great advantage with a wide variety of learners at many levels.

Unlike the typical case study, the case incident—usually no more than one page in length—is designed to illustrate or to probe one specific concept or theory (Wright, 1988). Most management textbooks, for example, include a case incident at the end of each chapter. The case incident, then, has become one of the most accessible ways of injecting an experiential or "real world" component into the traditional classroom/lecture setting.

Case incidents work well in two ways. First, the learners can be divided into groups of between three and seven. One trainee can be assigned the chore of making notes on the discussion, while another can be designated group spokesperson. After the group work has been completed, the instructor can ask each group spokesperson to summarize results. This process can lead easily into a general group discussion.

The second approach is to have the trainees read the case and discuss it as one group. This method is especially useful when an example is needed to illustrate a specific point. The technique here would be to stop the training, ask the trainees to read the incident, and then to lead the full group in a short discussion. As soon as the point has been made, the instructor should continue quickly, so as not to lose the trainees' interest.

Should time be a factor, or if reading skills are poor, the incident can be given out in advance. Advance reading seems to allay the fear of learning by this method, especially when dealing with trainees of varied cultural and social backgrounds.

---

*This section is adapted from P.C. Wright, *The Trainer's Case Compendium*. Bradford: MCB University Press, 1988; and "Simulating Reality: The Case Incident As A Commonly Available Yet Underutilized Resource." *Association of Management Proceedings: Education* 10, no. 1 (1992): 46–50.

Case incidents are useful when one topic or concept needs to be stressed. As they are short, valuable time is not taken up by differences in trainee reading speeds. When larger, more traditional cases are used, advance preparation is necessary as some trainees may become bored, since they will be finished reading before the others. Also, slow readers may become embarrassed. The incident's brevity reduces the differences in reading times so that all trainees can participate without a lot of advance preparation.

The use of incidents leads to improved group discussion and presentation skills; indeed, the team-building aspects of this technique are a valuable precursor to participation in major group projects or longer, more traditional cases, and are a good way of getting shy individuals to speak out; otherwise first exposure to the case-study format can prove frustrating. In addition, sophisticated technology is not required. Incidents are also useful as "changes of pace" if one dominant training technology or method is in use.

The final (and perhaps the most important) advantage of the incident concept is that trainees are able to use their own experiences. If the material is written well, the problem presented in each incident will encourage the application of current knowledge, leading to increased confidence and classroom participation.

There are two main disadvantages to the use of incidents. Some individuals are bothered by the lack of background material. Indeed, at times it is necessary for trainees to make assumptions and instructors may be asked by some groups to "sketch in" the background. Similarly, attempts to use incidents in cross-cultural settings, such as training managers in China, met with mixed results. It is thought that the trainees could not "fill in" the background, since they had limited knowledge of Western society *and* cultural relationships can differ widely across countries.

Incidents have been used successfully in both "high tech" and in more traditional organizations. Supervisors seem to like the "hands on" aspects of solving a specific management problem. Similarly, fourth-year university students have found the incident technique to be a "welcome relief" from the traditional lecture format. Incidents have been found valuable in class sizes of up to 70, although the logistics of handing out paper to a group of that size must be considered. At the more junior college level, while the concept is workable, lack of work/life experiences tends to elicit shallow answers based on speculation and ill-informed opinion.

◆ ◆ ◆
GAMES AND SIMULATIONS

Games and simulations attempt to recreate reality by simplifying situations to a manageable size and structure. These models or active representations of situations are designed to increase trainee motivation, involvement, and, hence, learning. They are also used when training in the real world might involve danger or extreme costs.

There are differences between games and simulations. Games represent reality but tend to be more simplistic, more manual, and less amenable to computer analysis (Clark, 1985). The first management-training game may have been the use of chess to teach military strategy. IBM uses games to teach risk taking (McCallum 1991).

Simulations tend to be operating models of physical or social events, designed to replicate environments. An example of a physical representation used in training is the flight simulator designed to teach pilots to fly. These flight simulators mimic flight exactly but pose no risk to humans or equipment. A social-model simulation example would be the exercise commonly used in business schools. Students are asked to run a company operating in a free-market system and to manipulate factors such as price and production. This simulation is designed to teach students about laws of supply and demand.

Games and simulations incorporate many sound principles of learning: learning from experience, active participation, direct application to real problems, incorporation of knowledge, skills, and values in learning (Saunders, 1988). The risks in the use of games and simulation are the possibility of learning the wrong things; the possibly weak relation to training objectives; the emphasis on "winning" and the resultant overconfidence in one's ability to manipulate the environment (Greenlaw et al., 1962).

◆ ◆ ◆
ROLE PLAY

Role play is a method in which employees are given the opportunity to "try on" or practise new behaviours in a safe situation. The emphasis is on doing and experiencing. This training method is most useful for acquiring skills in human relations or for changing attitudes. By playing the role of another, participants develop empathy for others. For example, a customer-service representative could be given instructions to play the part of a disgruntled client with a major problem. The rep can experience the frustrations of responses like "That's not my department," and "Just fill in that form over there; no, not that one ..."

Role play consists of three phases: development, enactment, and debriefing. A role play must be carefully designed to achieve its objectives. The scenario includes information on the time, place, character relationships, and instructions to the participants. Participants are then assigned roles and given some time to become familiar with the material. The most important stage is the debriefing, which should last two to three times longer than the enactment. In this phase, participants discuss the outcomes, correct learning is reinforced, and connections with previous learning and the real world are made. This is done by establishing the facts (what happened, what was experienced); analyzing the causes and effects of behaviours; and planning for skill or attitude changes.

While playing roles is a natural activity for children ("I'm the dragon, you're the monster"), acting in front of others is openly resisted by most adults. The role of the trainer is crucial. Trust has to be established. Participants should be warmed up by involving them in minor role situations, such as suggesting that a person ask one preset interview question. The trainer can reinforce risk taking and use mistakes as learning opportunities. In fact, trainers could ask people to show all the wrong ways to handle an angry customer. When a critical mistake is made, the trainer can start again or "rewind" the case. In one role play, a police officer was testing ways of talking to a potential suicide victim on a bridge. The officer made the fatal mistake of saying "Go ahead, I dare you," and the role-play partner "jumped." The trainer immediately stated, "Well, that approach didn't work, would you like to try another?" He rewound the case and demonstrated the true value of role playing: the opportunity to practise behaviours in a safe environment (Swink, 1993).

◆ ◆ ◆

GROUP DISCUSSION

Group discussion is one of the primary ways to increase trainee involvement in the learning process. Three techniques will be discussed here—trainer-led groups, peer groups, and technology-aided groups—as each is distinct in organization and requires different facilitation techniques.

TRAINER-LED GROUPS

This type of group discussion is most effective when the leader can convince group members that a collective approach has some advantage over individual approaches to a problem (Gabris, 1989). Thus, the trainer should create a participative culture at the beginning of the learning process. It has been known for some time that group discussion serves at least five purposes:

1. It helps members recognize what they do not know but should know.

2. It is an occasion for members to get answers to questions.

3. It allows members to get advice on matters that are of concern to them.

4. It allows persons to share ideas and derive a common wisdom.

5. It is a way for members to learn about one another as people (Zander, 1982, 31).

The trainer's task, then, is to get the group to "buy into" the process as an activity that is both interesting and useful.

As many training facilities are less than ideal, seating arrangements will vary. Any configuration that puts trainees in close proximity to one another will do, but a circle arrangement with no obvious leader's position or place is probably best. Size of group is important, too; certainly, more than 10 would be hard to handle if everyone is to participate.

The major difficulty with expert-led groups is that comments tend to be addressed to the trainer. When faced with this situation, the best technique is to reflect the questions or comments back to other group members. Not surprisingly, positive reinforcement is critical. Reluctant members are drawn out, while the trainer utilizes the energy of more assertive individuals. When the group strays off topic, the trainer gently refocuses the discussion, supporting the participation while changing the substance (Renner, 1988; Conlin, 1989; Whyte, 1989; Wein, 1990).

PEER GROUPS

As all groups quickly generate a power structure, the key to forming successful peer groups is to ensure that one individual does not dominate the discussion. The trainer does not have to be obvious, e.g., putting all the dominant personalities together; more subtle techniques can be used. For example, group members can be given roles that change with each discussion—scribe, presenter, summarizer, discussion leader. If groups are kept small—four to six seems to work best (Renner, 1989)—then most members have something to do, increasing participation and decreasing chances for some individuals to dominate the process. It is harder to be aggressive when taking notes or trying to summarize the thoughts of others.

This issue is important. As Weisband (1992), suggests, the first person to speak out and to advocate a position might, in many circumstances, influence the entire discussion. In fact, the final outcome can be predicted with some certainty, especially if groups were exposed to preliminary discussions before a group member put forth a first position.

A warning to trainers dealing with groups of mixed educational backgrounds: be aware of reading speed and literacy problems. Often group work requires the participants to read a passage, case incident, or problem. Reluctance or hostility to do so may point to illiteracy. Be gentle, work the informal group process by finding a place in a hallway for someone to quietly read the material, or, if this process is too obvious, summarize the main points before you assign the work. People who don't read well often have excellent memories; with care, they'll get by (Keller and Chuvala, 1992).

Of note, too, is that groups should be assigned a well-defined, easily understood task, one that is "doable" within the allotted time frame. Learning groups should be given every opportunity to "look good" in front of their peers, especially if they have to report back to a class or seminar.

Advanced communication technology is changing the way in which individuals can interact and make group decisions; many social, psychological, and physical barriers are breached. In contrast to face-to-face work, for example, Kiesler and Sproull (1992) suggest that computer-aided group work generates more aggressive and outspoken interaction, more equal participation, and more risk taking and innovation when making decisions. Trainers involved with interactive distance-learning technologies, then, should be prepared to cope with these more assertive behaviours. Also, it has been noted that the process can take longer.

◆ ◆ ◆
ACTION LEARNING

One of the principles enunciated in the chapter on learning was that the most effective way of learning is by doing. This process provides the trainee with opportunities to test theories in the real world. Reginald Revans, the originator of action-learning principles, emphasizes that the learner develops skills through responsible involvement in some real, complex, and stressful problem (Revans, 1982). The action-learning method compels trainees to identify problems; develop possible solutions; test these solutions in a real-world, real-time situation; and evaluate the consequences.

The goals of action learning are to involve and to challenge the student. The cognitive objectives to be achieved are of the highest order: analysis, synthesis. The attitudinal objectives move the trainee from passive observation to identification with the people and the vision of the organization. This method moves students from information receivers to problem-solvers. Action-learning incorporates more of the adult learning principles than any other method of training: motivation, active participation, reinforcement, association, and task significance.

The majority of the time spent in action learning is dedicated to diagnosis of the problems in the field. The problems, and the inherent value systems supporting the problems, are assessed and challenged. This work is always done in groups, and learning by-products include group and interpersonal skills, risk taking, responsibility, and accountability (Revans, 1984). Professions use action learning to train and socialize their students. For example, students in social work are often sent to live and work with coal miners or unwed mothers. These students are encouraged to apply their theoretical knowledge in the field. Industry is using the precepts of action learning when employees take responsibility for quality-improvement projects. Ontario Hydro uses action-learning techniques in strategic planning, quality improvements, and a labour management project. The Faculty of Environment Studies at York University uses it as a change technique (under a different name) to solve problems such as pollution.

◆ ◆ ◆
ON-THE-JOB-TRAINING

The focus in this section is on face-to-face encounters in the workplace that necessitate individualized on-the-job training (OJT). With the introduction of technology and sophisticated job aids, the nature of training has changed drastically, but there are still many situations in which a trainee has to perform a task or series of tasks. OJT, therefore, cannot be ignored, although, again, these activities are only one element in a package incorporating a suitable mix of formal training methods, support systems, and technologies (Marschall, 1990; Sloman, 1989).

WHY WORKPLACE TRAINING?

OJT is important because the responsibility for results lies with the trainer. In academia, if the students don't learn, "it's their fault." The professor rarely is chastised for his or her poor performance. By contrast, in industry the trainer is held personally responsible for results. Trainers, then, are forced to create learning experiences that work.

From an employer's viewpoint, there is ample evidence to indicate that OJT affects both organizational and individual performance. Among factory employees, for example, those who have had OJT and longer experience tend to receive better performance ratings than those without training and with less experience (Nollen and Gaertner, 1991). Younger employees who have experienced some formal OJT appear to be less likely to switch jobs (Lynch, 1991), show improved morale, and are easier to cross-train (Rothwell and Kazanas, 1990).

Employee empowerment is difficult to achieve without OJT. With approximately 30 percent of a new employee's time spent in a learning mode, the human-capital investment during the critical first days at work is substantial (Atkinson, 1991; Herman, 1989; Holtman and Idson, 1991; Barron et al., 1989). Lest the enormous expenditures on workplace training (between $90 and $180 billion yearly in North America) lull one into a sense of security, however, it must be realized that North America is falling behind both Europe and Asia in terms of human-capital investment. As well, much of what we do takes place in large companies; the small-business sector—where most new employment is being created—does a spectacularly poor job of training employees (Bernstein, 1992; Holtman and Idson, 1991; Hanson, 1991; Foegen, 1991; Miller, 1990).

The challenge that lies ahead includes the integration of an increasingly culturally diverse workforce into an increasingly competitive workplace. Managers will need to develop creative approaches to OJT as employees exhibit more language, attitude, and cultural barriers. It is likely, however, that people with the most education *and* access to OJT will be the most successful. Traditional concepts of learning-by-doing are fast gaining respectability (Berry, 1991; Lambrinos, 1991/92; McFee, 1990; Buhler, 1992).

The actual OJT process will not be considered here. Refer to the Appendix for a step-by-step description of this useful technique.

◆ ◆ ◆
APPRENTICESHIP

In Chapter 2, the observation was made that training must "fit" into the work culture or this activity will not be effective, used, or accepted. Consider the following scenario: Newly married Mr. and Mrs. Jones, a middle-class couple, are watching their baby daughter crawl around on the rug. He turns to her (or vice versa) and says: "Isn't she a bright little one, darling? I'll bet she grows up to be a fine journeyman electrician!"

An unlikely statement, indeed, for apprenticeships have never captured the imagination of the Canadian public, politicians, or educators. Except in the construction industry (there are a few other exceptions), apprenticeships have never fit into the Canadian culture. Thus Mr. or Mrs. Jones is much more likely to say: "I'll bet she grows up to be a fine electrical *engineer*," librarian, teacher, or any other occupation traditionally viewed as "acceptable" in middle-class society.

Industry, too, generally has been unwilling to invest in apprenticeships because, in the past, skilled-labour shortages could be made up through immigration. As our standard of living fell relative to other countries throughout the 1980s and 1990s, however, fewer trained individuals migrated to this country. The result is that Canada now faces a critical shortage of skilled labour (Hrynyshyn, 1993). In addition, only 30 percent of our high-school graduates are expected to earn college diplomas or university degrees. In order to remain competitive, politicians and educators must refocus their attention toward the 70 percent who will most likely constitute the much needed pool from which future skilled employees and technicians are drawn (Reynolds, 1993; McKenna, 1993).

To make apprenticeships more acceptable as an alternative to college or university, the prestige of technical studies has to be raised, and hands-on (cooperative) components made more meaningful (Reynolds, 1993). Students and parents must become convinced that the apprentice concept leads to an acceptable living standard and that the training does not lead to dead-end, uninteresting careers (Del Valle, 1993). The oft-touted German example is of particular importance here, as 65 percent of graduating engineers have previous apprenticeship training (Hrynyshyn, 1993).

DEFINING THE CONCEPT[*]

Given the skills shortage crises faced by many industrial sectors, it is likely that increased emphasis will be placed on apprenticeships, as this method is one of the most effective and practical ways of teaching skills occupations.

An apprenticeship can be described as an "integrated" human resource development (HRD) technique that combines on-the-job training with classroom instruction. Training for skills occupations largely involves teaching various skills and the supporting theory (Apprenticeship, 1992). The job-instruction component of apprenticeship training is used to teach the requisite skills of a particular trade or occupation. Classroom instruction, which comprises a relatively minor portion of the program (usually about 10 percent), teaches related theory and design concepts. For example, the 4 1/2-year plumber program includes only three, eight-week in-school sessions. In the classroom, plumber apprentices learn about such things as the physical properties of piping and other plumbing materials, industry codes, safety rules and operating procedures, trade tools and equipment, soldering techniques, and the characteristics of various fittings and piping systems. On the job, the trainees become familiar with relevant codes, regulations, and specifications, and learn to install, service, and test systems and equipment.

In Canada, the present apprenticeship system covers more than 65 regulated occupations in four occupational sectors: construction (e.g., stone mason, electrician, carpenter, plumber); motive power (motor-vehicle mechanic, machinist), industrial (industrial mechanic, millwright); and service (baker, cook, hairstylist). In some of these regulated occupations, apprentices must earn a "Certificate of Qualification" by passing a provincial government examination. Apprentices who pass an interprovincial examination with a minimum grade of 70 percent are awarded a "Red Seal" indicating their qualifications are acceptable across Canada.

---

[*]Although this section has been amended extensively, recognition must be given to Marisa Lauri, who completed the initial basic research while an undergraduate student at Atkinson College, York University.

Apprenticeship training differs from other job-instruction techniques in that it is regulated through a partnership among government, labour, and industry. In Canada, the federal government pays for in-school training and income support; provincial governments administer the programs and pay for classroom facilities and instructors; employers absorb the costs of workplace training; and apprentices initiate the process by finding employers willing to sponsor them.

This partnership can provide an effective and powerful mechanism to match human resources with opportunities in industry, given social and economic constraints. The conflicting goals of each partner, however, can have an impact on the effectiveness of apprenticeship as a training method and a possible solution to shortages of skilled labour. Consensus among the partners and cooperation among program participants are critical elements in the smooth and efficient operation of the system (McKenna, 1993).

Unlike corporate-sponsored training programs that address the specific needs of an organization, apprenticeships are focused on the collective training needs of specific occupations within broad industrial categories (Moskal, 1991). Consequently, the skills learned through apprenticeship training are transferable within an occupation, across a province, and across Canada. For example, in the construction industry, carpenters, electricians, plumbers, and masons are trained to meet standards recognized throughout the trade. This flexibility provides advantages to the worker and the industry when regional fluctuations occur in the supply and demand of skilled labour. The system also is highly dependent on employers, however, for they must accept the responsibility for establishing and maintaining adequate standards of job performance.

In determining acceptable qualifications and performance standards for the future, industry and government must address the special needs of new labour groups like women and minorities, eliminating standards or test criteria that might unjustly limit opportunities. For example, criteria pertaining to physical strength might be relaxed or eliminated by making simple changes in job design. Employers that intend to utilize apprenticeships also will need to become more sensitive to the special needs of working mothers and to the various religious or cultural backgrounds of employees, in that more flexible work schedules may be required to better accommodate those with family or other commitments (Still, 1992).

THE EFFECTIVENESS OF APPRENTICESHIP AS A TRAINING METHOD

The effectiveness of a training intervention can be measured in two ways: its ability to achieve the specified learning objectives, and the contribution of these objectives to an industry's overall goals. If the benefits of apprenticeship training cannot be related to a company's profitability, employers will not be willing to participate. This factor is particularly relevant in apprenticeship schemes that are based on voluntary cooperation among industry, labour, and government. Because industry must take the initiative to make a program work and must also bear most of the cost, employers must be convinced of the cost benefits before a program will be accepted.

The cost-effectiveness of apprenticeship training, however, is difficult to determine with any accuracy. Some early studies indicated that employers are able to recover their investment between the second and third years of an apprentice's term. Obviously, the "break-even" point will vary widely depending on the industry and the depth and quality of training provided. In cases where the expected payback period exceeds the training period, employers may be even more reluctant to invest in a program. In addition, because apprentices' skills are transferable once they are certified, graduates may choose not to continue working with their sponsoring firms. Unfortunately, the high cost of apprenticeship sometimes leads to an exploitation of apprentices by employers who seek to offset their expenses by using them as a source of cheap labour.

THE ROLE OF GOVERNMENT

The role of government is to administer apprenticeship programs and to ensure that the demands and needs of both industry and labour are fairly addressed. Without government intervention and commitment, the system can rapidly deteriorate, providing industry with the opportunity to exploit apprentices. Government also provides funding (provincially) through the various ministries of education or colleges and universities that supply classroom facilities and instructors, and (federally) through the Canada Employment and Immigration Commission, which offers training allowances to apprentices during in-class periods.

Governments also strive to ensure that programs are compatible with general economic and social policies that impact on the business environment and the labour market. For example, adjustments to tax and trade policy, such as the Goods and Services Tax (GST) and the Free Trade Agreement, can cause industry to pursue new business and marketing strategies that can have an effect on economic growth and labour markets. Similarly, changes in immigration policy, human rights legislation, human resource legislation, and subsidization can alter the labour-pool mix and the types of jobs available. Legislation prohibiting discrimination based on sex and other characteristics, for example, has created potential opportunities for women in nontraditional occupations (Brodsky, 1989). Conversely, the redistribution of government funding from public education to public health care creates budget constraints that place a greater economic burden on industry to absorb the costs of training.

A high-priority concern voiced by apprentices is their potential for career advancement. Modifications to the education system could enhance the mobility of apprentices interested in professional careers by eliminating barriers between academic and training programs. Upgrading apprenticeship programs to include general knowledge in language, math, and science, might enable apprentices to apply credits toward higher education or other programs.

THE ROLE OF LABOUR

The interests of labour are represented by Advisory Committees made up of union and selected industry representatives. Some trade unions tend to focus on restricting the numbers of certified tradespeople in order to maintain wage levels and job security for their members. Conversely, a number of unions have established supplementary classroom training programs independent of the formal apprenticeship system in order to train apprentices to meet their own specified criteria. This practice may attest to the perceived ineffectiveness of the present system and its inability to respond quickly enough to changes demanded by industry; however, this activity may also serve as a screening process to restrict the hiring of externally trained workers (who would not meet the criteria) and to help retain members trained in-house.

The cooperation of unions in the system is important, given their power and highly organized structures (Riccucci, 1991). Unions can help ensure that the interests of apprentices are protected in the workplace and that their training meets established standards. Unions can also play a key role in helping to select and train industry trainers to ensure their teaching abilities are as effective as their trade skills.

THE ROLE OF INDUSTRY

The reasons for the traditional lack of interest in apprenticeship programs by industry have focused on cost. Until recently, it was cheaper for companies to hire skilled immigrants from Europe than to train apprentices. Current trends in our labour market, however, are creating new demand. All sectors of Canadian industry will need to focus attention on training skilled workers; apprenticeship training is one of the most viable options. Increasing participation rates might provide the impetus needed to revive and to improve apprenticeship training in Canada.

Industry commitment and initiative are the driving forces behind the success of apprenticeship programs elsewhere because opportunities for trainees must be created, and employers are solely responsible for hiring apprentices and for providing them with adequate training, experience, and wages. Employers can improve the training further by establishing standard qualifications for workplace trainers. While it is important that trainers be highly skilled, it is at least as important that they be competent teachers.

Unfortunately, many managers do not realize the cost benefits of apprenticeship, as it is always difficult to relate training directly to increased productivity and profitability. As a result, some employers have attempted to take advantage of the system by not providing adequate training or resources, preferring instead to keep apprentices in the same jobs long enough to increase their output and contribution to revenues. Employers also have no guarantee that the apprentices they train will remain with them once they have completed their programs. If apprentices choose to leave, their employers will have borne their training costs without receiving the expected benefits.

Industry also responds more rapidly than government to changes in the economy. During past recessionary periods, many employers have quickly reduced their apprenticeship programs to save costs, resulting in an immediate and long-term impact on the labour market (Donnelly, 1994).

Regardless of the support that government agencies and educational institutions may provide, it is still more efficient for businesses to be predominantly responsible for training their own skilled workers. In addition to cost and the many practical considerations (employers already have the tools, equipment, materials, and experts needed for training purposes), industry also is better able to keep pace with changes in technology and product innovation.

THE NEED FOR A NEW MODEL

Despite the recent infusion of government funding, much of Canada's apprenticeship system remains antiquated. Outmoded legislation, outdated curricula, poor pay for teachers, archaic entry and completion regulations, and low-prestige entry modes still combine to discourage many young people from considering careers in the skilled trades (Premiers Council, 1990). If apprenticeship training could be adapted to suit the large number of emerging white-collar and technical occupations (Graham, 1989), the public's image of apprenticeship would be improved and the resulting programs would fit more securely into the Canadian culture. In addition, these programs would be more attractive as vehicles of upward mobility, especially if there were a closer link to the higher education system. Program expansion and enhancement, therefore, would be key elements in creating apprenticeships that meet the needs of current and future industries, while developing attractive and challenging career alternatives for a greater segment of our labour force.

◆ ◆ ◆
METHODS ASSESSMENT

Trainers use a variety of methods in order to achieve the various objectives of the training program. Their preferences may be influenced by developmental costs or difficulties in implementation. Although there is very little information about the relative effectiveness of these methods available, Table 9.1 summarizes the results of one study in which employers were asked to report the use of different instructional methods (Gordon, 1990).

Very few studies have been conducted comparing the relative effectiveness of training methods. Two large surveys of training directors found that they perceived each of nine training techniques to be effective in achieving different types of training goals (Carrol et al., 1972; Newstrom, 1980). For example, the case study was rated as most effective for problem-solving skills, and computer-assisted or programmed instruction best for knowledge retention. Role play was evaluated as the best for changing attitudes and developing interpersonal skills. However, these are only individual perceptions and do not provide information on actual trainee achievements.

TABLE 9.1 USES OF INSTRUCTION METHODS

Method	Percentage Using Method
Video tapes	88.7
Lecture	84.7
One-on-one instruction	72.2
Computer-based	66.0
Slides	55.6
Role plays	54.4
Audio tapes	53.0
Films	47.8
Case studies	46.4
Self-assessment, Self-testing	39.8
Self-study (Noncomputerized)	35.9
Videoconferencing	11.6
Teleconferencing (Audio only)	8.5

The effectiveness of a training method depends entirely upon its efficacy in the achievement of learning objectives.

◆ ◆ ◆

SUMMARY

Obviously, not all existing training methods have been included in this chapter. The major techniques, however, were covered: lecturing, behaviour modelling, distance learning, technology-based learning, multimedia methods, cases and case incidents, games and simulations, role play, group work, action learning, on-the-job training, and apprenticeship. The list is extensive. Each method has its place; the choice varies according to the environment, trainee characteristics, subject matter, budget, past practice (expectations), and trainer skill or preference.

As well, some techniques focus on groups; others are best suited to training individuals. Traditional approaches (e.g., lecturing) have been included along with multimedia and computer-based techniques. The opportunity to mix, adapt, and blend methods should not be ignored. This chapter, then, not only describes most of the workable techniques for passing on knowledge but lays the foundation from which new innovations or adaptations of old ideas might be developed.

E X E R C I S E

Topics: Training, Orientation, On-the-job Training

When TPK, a manufacturer of small appliances—electric kettles, toasters, and irons—automated its warehouse, the warehouse crew was reduced from 14 to 4. Every one of the displaced stockmen was assigned to another department, as TPK had a history of providing stable employment.

Jacob Peters, a stockman with over 15 years of service, was transferred to the toaster assembly line to be retrained as a small-parts assembler. When he arrived to begin his new job, the foreman said, "This may be only temporary, Jacob. I have a full staff right now, so I have nothing for you to do, but come on, I'll find you a locker." As there really was no job for him, Jacob did nothing for the first week except odd jobs such as filling bins. At the beginning of week two, Jacob was informed that a vacancy would be occurring the next day, so he reported for work eager to learn his new job.

The operation was depressingly simple. All Jacob had to do was pick up two pieces of metal, one in each hand, place them into a jig so that they were held together in a cross position, and press a button. The riveting machine then put a rivet through both pieces and an air jet automatically ejected the joined pieces into a bin.

"This job is so simple a monkey could do it," the foreman told Jacob. "Let me show you how it's done," and he quickly demonstrated the three steps involved. "Now you do it," the foreman said. Of course, Jacob did it right the first time. After watching him rivet two or three, the foreman left Jacob to his work.

About three hours later, the riveter started to put the rivets in a little crooked, but Jacob kept on working. Finally, a fellow worker stopped by and said, "You're new here, aren't you?" Jacob nodded. "Listen, I'll give you a word of advice. If the foreman sees you letting the rivets go in crooked like that, he'll give you hell. So hide these in the scrap over there." His new friend then showed Jacob how to adjust his machine.

Jacob's next problem began when the air ejection system started jamming. Four times he managed to clear it, but on the fifth try, he slipped and his elbow hit the rivet button. The machine put a rivet through the fleshy part of the hand, just below the thumb.

It was in the first aid station that the foreman finally had the opportunity to see Jacob once again.

Questions

1. Comment on the strengths and weaknesses of Jacob's orientation and on-the-job training.
2. Outline how the process should have been conducted (you may wish to consult the Appendix).

Appendix to Chapter 9

◆◆◆
THE CRAFT, OR THE ART, OF WORKPLACE TRAINING

Thus far training has been viewed in a relatively abstract way, and we have avoided detailed "how to" prescriptions for getting the job done. Setting the more practical element in an appendix allows for the introduction of step-by-step systems without altering the general flow of the book. The focus here is on face-to-face encounters with trainees, emphasizing on-the-job training (OJT).

◆◆◆
ON-THE-JOB TRAINING

WHAT IS OJT?

Although OJT has been practiced since at least the Middle Ages, the concept was formalized by the U.S. Army during World War II. OJT is the design and application of a series of steps that enable the trainee to perform a job while either working on the job or preparing to work on the job in the immediate future. Thus, for the new employee, OJT is part of the orientation process, while for the experienced person, OJT updates present job behaviour or provides cross-training for flexibility (Koehler, 1992; Tench, 1992).

Sloman (1989) studied three British National Training Award winners that paid particular attention to the OJT delivery. From their programs he developed a set of rules governing "good" on-the-job training:

1. in terms of planning and preparation, OJT should not be managed differently from other types of training;

2. OJT should be integrated with other methods;

3. ownership must be maintained, even when consultants are used;

4. OJT trainers must be chosen with care and trained properly.

WHO TRAINS?

A large percentage of OJT is performed either by experienced employees or by (immediate) supervisors. Regardless of the approach, however, the prime prerequisite is that the trainer like people. Just as Disney Corp. finds it easier to teach friendly people the art of customer service, great training begins with a fundamental attitude of helpfulness and caring. As well, employees or supervisors who are required to train must want to be trainers, be good communicators, and be expert in their skill area. Patience and respect for differences in the ability to learn also are important as the trainer sets the initial mood or climate of the learning experience (Renner, 1989; Tench, 1992). Once suitable individuals are found, they need "training-the-trainer" training and rewards for OJT activities. It is of little use to give training responsibilities to an already busy employee, for example, without restructuring his or her job to include a training element. Nor is increased pay always the most sought after reward (although it doesn't hurt). Recognition, the chance to add variety to the workday, respect from new employees, training certificates, and the prospect of either promotion and/or cross-training all help to make OJT worthwhile for the individual.

HOW TO DO OJT

Given that OJT has been a longstanding weak spot in North American training practice (Stern and Muta, 1990), it is not surprising that little seems to have been written specifically about how to "do" OJT. Even some of the classic examples of training literature have remarkably little to say on the subject (Odiorne, 1970; Nadler, 1982; Laird, 1985).

There are two notable exceptions: Martin Broadwell's fine little book, *The Supervisor And On-The-Job Training*, written in 1969, along with Rothwell and Kazanas's 1990 article, "Planned OJT is Productive OJT." (See the list of references at the end of this chapter.) The latter updates the technique, but Broadwell's work is unique in its emphasis on the trainer and on employee preparation.

Bearing in mind that OJT will be but one element in the training plan, job analysis and determination of objectives will have been completed. As well, the essential psychology about how and why people learn will have been taught as part of a training-the-trainer course (see Chapter 7).

I. THE PREPARATION PHASE

The OJT process consists of a preparation phase and an activity, or doing, phase. As nothing can destroy learning effectiveness faster than an unprepared instructor, Broadwell begins with self-preparation.

Any face-to-face encounter in business needs to be planned, but when training, "prep" becomes especially important. Aside from routine precautions about using the most up-to-date job analysis, manuals, and other information—knowing what you're talking about—the key activity during this preparation phase is to develop a communications strategy that fits the trainee (don't forget to find out what the trainee already knows) or the situation. A lecture, for example, would not be an appropriate method for training groups in the art of lift-truck maintenance. Even when a lecture might be the right approach, support materials like overhead projection and handouts have to be carefully constructed to fit the audience.

As Renner's (1989) *Instructor's Survival Kit* and other publications contain detailed information on this phase, no attempt will be made to reproduce these data here. Instead, an abbreviated "Techniques Chart" is included to illustrate some of the many ways in which OJT can be accomplished:

On-the-spot Lecture:	Gather trainees into groups and tell them how to do the job.
Viewed Performance/ Feedback:	Watch the person at work and give constructive feedback, e.g., the sales manager makes a call with a new salesperson.
Following Nellie:	The supervisor trains a senior employee, who in turn trains new employees (showing the ropes).
Job-aid Approach:	A job aid (step-by-step instructions or video) is followed while the trainer monitors performance.
The Training Step Sequence:	The trainer systematically introduces the task, following a planned sequence.

Each one of these communication techniques requires a different type and level of preparation. The instructor needs to understand the background, capabilities, and attitudes of his or her trainees, as well as the nature of the tasks to be performed, before choosing a technique or combination of techniques.

Note that trial and error has *not* been included here. There are very few circumstances that justify throwing an employee into a new position without proper training. Learning from one's mistakes is not only inefficient, but can be humiliating, dangerous, or lead to poor customer relations.

The second part of the preparation phase concerns the trainee. There are three stages: putting the individual at ease; guaranteeing the learning; building interest/showing personal advantage (Broadwell, 1969).

1. The trainer must remember that the trainee may be apprehensive. Therefore, it is unwise to begin too abruptly. Some small talk may be appropriate to relax the trainee and to set the tone for the training sessions. Most individuals learn more readily when relaxed. A short conversation concerning any matter of interest—the weather, sports, a work-related item—should be effective. Obviously, the topic chosen must be suitable for the situation.

2. When the conversation does turn to the training session, the trainer needs to guarantee to the employee that learning is possible. Again, use a simple statement, "Don't worry about this machine, Sally; in about three hours you'll be operating it almost as well as everyone else. I've trained at least 10 people in this procedure." The trainee now knows that it is possible to learn (i.e., learning will take place) and that the instructor has the ability to teach the process, adding to her confidence.

3. Although the instructor may be interested, the trainee might be apprehensive or may not understand the effect OJT will have on the quality of his or her work life. Developing trainee enthusiasm sometimes is difficult, but pointing out some personal gain helps to create interest. The idea that the training activity will lead to something positive creates the opportunity to design rewards: more self-esteem, easier work, higher-level work, less routine, more control over work, greater opportunity or security. Once the appropriate reward is found (provided it can be obtained), most employees will respond to OJT.

Often, there will be some who resist, however, as training is change and individuals accept change at different rates. This trainee preparation phase will identify those who are not responding. As the trainer is responsible for meeting measurable objectives, it is important to evaluate the likelihood of cooperation among trainees so that individual remedial action can be taken.

One way to defuse resistance is to train employees in order of their perceived enthusiasm. When the resisters see others reaping the rewards of training, they usually agree to be trained, albeit grudgingly. As the instructor does not own the trainees' attitude, only their behaviour, training objectives can be met even though the work situation is not ideal.

II. THE STEPS IN OJT

If the trainee is to perform a task or an operation, he or she should be positioned slightly behind or beside the instructor so that the job is viewed from a realistic angle. The step approach to the OJT process then can be utilized (Rothwell and Kazamas, 1990; Gold, 1981; Broadwell, 1986):

1. Show the trainee how to perform the job.

   ◆ Be sure to break the job into manageable tasks; present only as much as can be absorbed at one time. Remember, too, that individuals learn at different speeds, so some trainees, for example, may be able to learn six or seven sequences at once, while others can absorb only four or five. REPEAT STEP 1 AS NECESSARY; BE PATIENT.

   ◆ Don't forget to tell *why* as well as how.

   ◆ Point out possible difficulties as well as safety procedures.

   ◆ Encourage questions.

2. Repeat and explain key points in more detail.

   ◆ Safety is especially important.

   ◆ Take the time to show how the job fits into any larger systems.

   ◆ Show why the job is important.

   ◆ Show why key points are more important than others.

   ◆ REPEAT STEP 2 AS NECESSARY; BE PATIENT.

   ◆ Encourage questions.

3. Allow the trainee to see the whole job again.

   ◆ Ask questions to determine level of comprehension.

   ◆ REPEAT STEP 3 AS NECESSARY; BE PATIENT.

◆ Encourage questions.

4. Ask the trainee to perform less difficult parts of the job.

   ◆ Try to ensure initial success.

   ◆ Don't tell how. If possible, ask questions, but try to keep trainee's frustration level low.

   ◆ REPEAT STEP 4 AS NECESSARY; BE PATIENT.

5. Allow the trainee to perform the entire job.

   ◆ Gently suggest improvements where necessary, i.e., keep feedback positive.

   ◆ If needed, repeat Step 4 until the trainee feels comfortable.

   ◆ REPEAT STEP 5 AS NECESSARY; BE PATIENT.

6. Leave the trainee to work alone.

   ◆ Tell when and where to find help if necessary; BE PATIENT

   ◆ Supervise closely, then taper off as the employee gains in confidence and skill.

While these steps may seem elaborate, they must be applied with the complexity and possible safety hazards of the job in mind. Very simple tasks may require only one demonstration. As well, employees bring different skills and backgrounds to the workplace. Competent preparation will eliminate overtraining and the resultant boredom and inattention.

CLASSROOM OJT?

This type of training has been discussed in detail in the sections on role play, and behaviour modelling. Although not traditionally part of the OJT process, combinations might occur whereby technology, video, or other methods could be used as part of an OJT process. Training methods, then, should not be viewed in isolation. Training within some work situations may require flexibility and inventiveness.

References

Allan, K. 1993. "Computer Courses Ensure Uniform Training." *Personnel Journal* (June): 65–71.

Apprenticeship. 1992. *Occupational Outlook Quarterly* 35, no. 4, 26–40.

Atkinson, A. 1991. "Training and Control." *CMA Magazine* 65, no. 3, 15.

Barron, J., D. Black, and M. Loewstein. 1989. "Job Matching and On-the-job Training." *Journal of Labor Economics* 7, no. 1, 1–19.

Bell, C. 1992. "The Trainer as Storyteller." *Training and Development* 46, no. 9, 53–56.

Bernstein, A. 1992. "Replenishing Our Human Capital." *Business Week* 386, no. 14, 78–79.

Berry, S.L. 1991. "Apprenticeships: A Medieval Idea Wins a 20th Century Edge." *Management Review* 80, no. 8, 41–44.

Broadwell, M. 1969. *The Supervisor and On-the-Job Training.* Reading, Mass.: Addison-Wesley.

———. 1986. *The Supervisor and On-The-Job Training.* 2nd ed. Reading, Mass.: Addison-Wesley.

Brodsky, M. 1989. "International Developments in Apprenticeship." *Monthly Labour Review* 112, no. 7, 40–41.

Buhler, P.M. 1992. "Managing in the 90s." *Supervision* 53, no. 11, 22–24.

Buller, M., and G. McEvoy. 1990. "Exploring the Long-term Effects of Behaviour Modelling Training." *Journal of Organizational Change Management* 3, no. 1.

Burke, W.W. 1994. *Organization Development.* 2nd ed. Reading, Mass.: Addison-Wesley.

"Business and Workers Must Play by New Economic Rules." *Supervision* 52, no. 11, 9–12.

Carrol, S. J., F. T. Paine, and J. J. Ivancevich. 1972. "The Relative Effectiveness of Training Methods— Expert Opinion and Research." *Personnel Psychology* 25, 495–510.

Clark, B. 1985. *Optimizing Learning: The Integrative Education Model in the Classroom.* New York: New York Press.

Conlin, J. 1989. "Conflict at Meetings: Come Out Fighting." *Successful Meetings* 38, no. 6, 30–36.

Craig, Robert L. 1987. *Training and Development Handbook: A Guide to Human Resource Development.* New York: McGraw-Hill Inc., 414–429.

Del Valle, C. 1993. "From High School to High Skills." *Business Week* 3316 (April 26): 110–12.

Donnelly, E. 1994. "Apprenticeship: A New Dawning?" *Training and Development* 12, no. 13, 18–20.

Farquhar, C.R. 1990–91. "Total Quality Management: A Competitive Imperative for the '90s." *Optimum* 21, no. 4, 30–39.

Foegen, J.H. 1991. "Corporate Education: A New Parochialism." *Business Horizons* 34, no. 5, 55-58.

Frayne, C. 1992. "Improving Employee Performance through Self-Management Training." *Business Quarterly* 54, no. 1, 46–50.

Future of Apprenticeship. 1977. Report of the Symposium, Focus of Apprenticeship, sponsored by the Province of Ontario, Ministry of Colleges and Universities.

Gabris, G. 1989. "Educating Elected Officials in Strategic Goal Setting." *Public Productivity and Management Review* 13, no. 2, 161–175.

Galagan, P. 1993. "Helping Groups Learn." *Training and Development* 47, no. 10, 57–61.

Garavan, T.N., and D. Murphy. 1989. "Indigenous, High Technology

Companies: A Novel Training Intervention." *Journal of European Industrial Training* 13, no. 8, 4–13.

Geber, B. 1994. "The Wonderful World of Cyber Sally." *Training* 31, no. 5, 8.

Georges, J.C. 1988. "Why Soft-Skills Training Doesn't Take." *Training* 25, no. 4, (April): 44–45.

German, C., and C. Heath. 1994. "Career Development 2000." *Training and Development* 12, no. 5, 12–14.

Geroy, G.D., and P.C. Wright. 1994. *Using Skills Needs Assessment in Support of Economic Development Strategies.* Bradford: MCB University Press.

Gold, L. 1981. "Job Instruction: Four Steps to Success." *Training and Development Journal* 35, no. 9, 28–32.

Gordon, J. 1988. "Who Is Being Trained to Do What?" *Training* 25, no. 10, 51–60.

_____. 1990. "Where the Training Goes." *Training.* (October): 51–69.

Graham, G. 1989. "Training The Next Generation." *Computing Canada* 15, no. 15, 29–30.

Greengard, S. 1993. "How Technology Is Advancing." *HR Professional Journal* 72, no. 9 (September): 28–31.

Greenlaw, B., M. Herron, and L. Ramdon. 1962. *Business Simulation in Industrial and University Education.*

Englewood Cliffs, New Jersey: Prentice-Hall.

Haim, A. 1993. "Strategic Planning Unbound." *Journal of Strategic Planning* 14, no. 2, 46–52.

Hanson, H.L. 1991. "Getting Started." *Training and Development* 45, no. 8, 53–56.

Heathman, D., and B. Kleiner. 1991. "Future Directions for Computer-Aided Training." *Industrial and Commercial Training* 23, no. 5, 25–31.

Henry, L. 1989. High-Tech Training for the High-Tech Factory. *Training* 26, no. 4, 26–32.

Herman, S.M. 1989. "Participative Management Is a Double-edged Sword." *Training* 26, no. 1, 52–57.

Holtman, A. G., and T.L. Idson. "Employer Size and On-the-job Training Decision." *Southern Economic Journal* 58, no. 2, 339–55.

Hrynyshyn, T. 1993. "Siemens Chief Critical of Skilled Labour Shortage." *Computing Canada* 19, no. 11, 1.

Huntly, S. 1991. "Management Development—Considerations and Implementation." *Industrial and Commercial Training* 23, no. 2, 20–25.

Isaac, R., A. Cahoon, and W. Zerbe. 1992. "Values in the Corporation—Who Is in Charge?" *International Journal of Value-Based Management* 5, no. 2, 36–45.

Kaupins, G. 1989. "What's So Funny About Training?" *Training and Development Journal* 43, no. 1, 27–30.

Keller, S. and J. Chuvala. 1992. "Training: Tricks of the Trade." *Security Management* 36, no. 7.

Kenny, B., E. Lea, and G. Luffman. 1992. *Cases in Business Policy.* 2nd ed. Oxford: Blackwell Publishers.

Kiesler, S., and L. Sproull. 1992. "Group Decision Making and Communication Technology." *Organizational Behaviour and Human Decision Processes* 52, no. 1, 96–123.

Koehler, K.G. 1992. "Orientation: Key to Employee Performance and Morale." *CMA Magazine* 66, no. 6, 6.

Kuo, C. 1993. "Teaching Lecture Comprehension to Non-Native Science Students." *IEEE Transactions on Profession Communication* 36, no. 2, 70–74.

Laird, D. 1985. *Approaches to Training and Development.* 2nd ed. Reading, Mass.: Addison-Wesley.

Lambrinos, J.J. 1991–92. "Tomorrow's Workforce: Challenge for Today." *Bureaucrat* 20, no. 4, 27–29.

Leenders, Michiel R., and James A. Erskine. 1973. *Case Research: The Case Writing Process.* London: University of Western Ontario Press.

Lookatch, R.P. 1990. "Coaching After the Kickoff." *Bank Marketing* 22, no. 3, 30–32.

Lynch, L.M. 1991. "Mobility of Women Workers." *American Economic Review* 81, no. 2, 151–56.

McCallum, T. 1991. "Scaling the Classroom Wall." *Human Resources Professional* (September).

McFee, T.S. 1990. "Management Climate." *Bureaucrat* 19, no. 1, 3–4.

McKenna, J. 1993. "The Busy Present of Jobs for the Future." *Industry Week* 242, no. 10, 52–56.

Malerba, F. 1992. Learning by Firms and Incremental Change. *Economic Journal* 102, no. 413, 845–59.

Marschall, D. 1990. "Unions and Work-Based Learning: The Rediscovery of Apprenticeship." *ILR Report* 28, no. 1, 7–13.

Memford, A. (1993). "How Managers Can Become Developers." *Personnel Management* 25, no. 6, 42–45.

Miles, K.W. and E.R. Griffith 1993. "Developing an Hour of CBT: The Quick and Dirty Method." *CBT Directions* (April-May): 28–33.

Miller, W.H. 1990. "Human Resources: A Feeble Response." *Industry Week* 239, no. 16, 34.

Moskal, B. 1991. "Apprenticeship: Old Cure for New Labor Shortage?" *Industry Week* 240, no. 9, 30–35.

Nadler, L. 1982. *Designing Training Programs.* Reading, Mass.: Addison-Wesley.

Newstrom, J.W. 1980. "Evaluating the Effectiveness of Training Methods." *Personnel Administrator* 25, no. 1, 55–60.

The New Yorker. 1982. "The Talk of the Town." *The New Yorker* 58, no. 42, 37–53.

Nollen, S.D., and K.N. Gaertner. 1991. "Effects of Skill and Attitudes on Employee Performance and Earnings." *Industrial Relations* 30, no. 3, 435–55.

Odiorne, G.S. 1970. *Training by Objectives.* London: Collier-Macmillan.

Ontario Premiers Council. 1990. "People and skills in the New Global Economy." Report in Brief. Toronto: Queen's Printer.

Parker, J. 1993. "Lecturing and Loving It: Applying the Information-Processing Model." *Clearing House* 67, no. 1, 8–11.

Pearce, John A., Richard B. Robinson, Jr., and A. Zahra Shaker. 1989. *An Industry Approach to Cases in Strategic Management.* Boston: Irwin Publishing.

Phillips, K. 1993. "Self-Development in Organizations: Issues and Actions." *Journal of European Industrial Training* 17, no. 5, 3–5.

Renner, P. 1988. *The Quick Instructional Planner.* Vancouver: Training Associates Ltd.

_____. 1989. *The Instructor's Survival Kit*, 2nd ed. Vancouver: Training Associates Ltd.

Revans, R.W. 1982. *The Origins and Growth of Action Learning.* Gock, Sweden: Bratt-Institute for Neues Lernen.

_____. 1984. "Action Learning: Are We Getting There?" *Management Decision Journal* 22, no. 1, pp. 45–52.

Reynolds, L. 1993. "Apprenticeship Programs Raise Many Questions." *HRD Focus* 70, no. 7, 1.

Riccucci, N. 1991. "Apprenticeship Training in the Public Sector." *Public Personnel Management* 20, no. 2, 181–83.

Robinson, J.C. 1982. *Developing Managers Through Behaviour Modelling.* Austin, Texas.

Rothwell, W.J., and H.C. Kazanas. 1990. "Planned OJT Is Productive OJT." *Training and Development Journal* 44, no. 10, 53–56.

Sabido, M. 1981. *Towards the Social Use of Soap Operas.* Mexico City, Mexico: Institute for Communications Research.

Saunders, D. 1988. *Learning from Experience Through Games and Simulations.* London: SAGSET Publications.

Schmitz, B. 1993. "Virtual Reality: On the Brink of Greatness." *CAE* 12, no. 4, 26–32.

Schnelle, Kenneth. 1967. *Case Analysis and Business Problem Solving.* New York: McGraw Hill.

Slade, R., and R. Sweet. 1989. "Canadian Private Sector Distance Education." In R. Sweet, ed., *Post-Secondary Distance Education in Canada.* Athabasca, Alberta: Athabasca University.

Sloman, M. 1989. "On-the-job-training: A Costly Poor Relation." *Personnel Management* 21, no. 2, 38–42.

Smith, R. 1986. "The Scope and Growth of Distance Education." Regional Seminar on Distance Education. Bangkok: Asian Development Bank.

Stahmer, A. 1991. "Use of Technologies for Training in Canadian Companies." Report 651, *Employment and Immigration.* Ottawa, Canada.

Stern, S., and H. Muta. 1990. "The Japanese Difference." *Training and Development Journal* 44, no. 3, 74–82.

Still, L. 1992. "Breaking the Glass Ceiling: Another Perspective." *Women in Management Review* 7, no. 5, 3–8.

Swink, D. 1993. "Role Play Your Way to Learning." *Training and Development* (May): 91–97.

Taylor, Bernard and Gordon Lippitt. 1983. *Management Development and*

Training Handbook. 2nd ed. London: McGraw-Hill Book Company, 257–266.

Tench, A. 1992. "Following Joe Around: Should This be Our Approach to On-the-job Training?" *Plant Engineering* 46, no. 17, 88–92.

The Training Technology Monitor 1, no. 3 (10 December 1993): 4.

Tucker, R., M. Moravec, and K. Ideus. 1992. "Designing a Dual Career-Track System." *Training and Development* 46, no. 6, 55–58.

Wein, G. 1990. Experts as Trainers." *Training and Development Journal* 44, no. 7, 29–30.

Weisband, S. 1992. "Group Discussion and First Advocacy Effects in Computer-Mediated and Face-to-Face Decision Making Groups." *Organizational Behaviour and Human Decision Processes* 53, no. 3, 352–80.

Whyte, G. 1989. "Group Think Reconsidered." *Academy of Management Review* 14, no. 1, 40–56.

Wright, P. 1988. "The Incident as a Technique for Teaching Undergraduates in Hospitality Management and Food Administration." *Hospitality Education and Research Journal* 12, no. 1, 16–28.

Wright, P. 1992. "The CEO and the Business School: Is There Potential for Increased Cooperation." Presented to the Association of Management in Las Vegas, NV. Published in: *Association of Management Proceedings: Education* 10, no. 1, 41–45.

Wright, P. and R. Dable. 1994. "Humour as a Management Technique: An Introductory Note." *The Specialist (International)* (March): 14–17.

Yin, Robert K. 1985. *Case Study Research: Design and Methods.* Beverly Hills: Sage Publications.

Zander, A. 1982. *Making Groups Effective.* San Francisco: Jossey-Bass Publishers.

10

Equity
in
Training

◆ ◆ ◆

INTRODUCTION

Facilitators of change programs within organizations now face an increasingly diverse workforce. This chapter documents that diversity, identifies access and treatment barriers to the full participation of designated groups, and suggests ways to increase their participation.

Immigration policies and a political strategy that promote a cultural mosaic have resulted in a rapid rise in the percentage of ethnic, cultural, language, and religious minorities in Canada. The ethnic and racial origins of employees in Canada have expanded considerably over the last two decades. The change in the workforce is indeed dramatic. Nearly 25 percent of Ontario's population was born outside of Canada, and visible minorities make up about 16 to 20 percent of Toronto's population (Meade, 1986). Nearly 50 percent of all immigrants to Canada are visible minorities (Meade, 1986). Projections of labour-force participation in Canada to the year 2000 indicate that only 15 percent of new workforce entrants will be white males; the rest will be women and minorities (Jain, 1991). Women will account for 62 percent of this growth (Gemson, 1991).

This diverse labour force reflects the realities of the world, in which Caucasians are a small numerical minority. To illustrate this concept, consider the world as a global village made up of 1000 citizens. The population demographics would be 60 North Americans, 80 South Americans, 564 Asians, 86 Africans, and 210 Europeans. Seven hundred people in this village would not be white. Given that "visible minorities" are in fact the majority, the term will no longer be used in this chapter and will be replaced by "persons of non-European descent."

Learning to understand and connect with a diversity of experiences will enable Canadians to understand the nature of intercountry differences in a global marketplace.

Today, most trainers and educators will have classrooms consisting of students from many nations. In some cases, students will belong to more than one ethnic group. For example, one human resource management (HRM) student was born in China (and identified with the Asians); raised in Jamaica (and spoke with a Jamaican accent); and as a teenager moved to South America, where he learned Spanish and became assimilated in the South American cultural mosaic. Now an adult, he is a highly valued employee in an international marketing department of a Canadian firm. His "differences" are prized by his employer, and illustrate the positive aspects of acknowledging a diverse workforce.

◆ ◆ ◆
ACKNOWLEDGING DIVERSITY

Valuing diversity matters because 85 percent of all workforce entrants by the year 2000 will be other than white males. This labour pool also reflects the customers and clients of organizations.

Many well-meaning trainers claim not to see diversity. Their refrain is "I do not see men or women, blacks or whites. I see students." Being "colour blind" may mean being nondiscriminatory, but it may also mean not taking into account the differences that do exist and not using these differences to enhance learning. For example, women business students, who receive the same education as men business students, rarely study cases in which the CEO is a woman, or in which a key player in a business decision is a competent women. In this case, "equal" ends up perpetuating the inequality that already exists.

Attitudes such as "I see all my trainees the same way," or "I don't see my students as black, white, purple, or green" are not based on reality. Students as well as trainers have social identities that have been formed by their location in gender, race, ethnic, class, and a myriad of other hierarchies (Lee, 1985). These have an effect on the teaching and learning environment.

As experts in behavioural change, most trainers would acknowledge the need to understand the behaviourial expectations of diverse groups. Acknowledging diversity means being aware of the differences in background that students bring to the classroom, understanding that these differences may influence how students learn, and accommodating these learning styles and preferences (Nieto, 1992). These types of accommodations with trainees are part of a trainers' professional repertoire. Trainers already acknowledge and respond to differences among students, based on student levels of experience or learning preferences. Most trainers will realize that some students prefer working in groups, others learn best by films and discussion, others prefer clear learning objectives to be achieved independently, etc. Likewise, affirming diversity means regarding the students as individuals and respecting their differences and preferences. Indeed, the best approach is the individual one, because classifying trainees according to culture or gender in order to make provisions for them would be overgeneralizing and would result in a different kind of stereotyping.

◆ ◆ ◆
THE MEANING OF EQUITY

Equity does not mean that everyone can, say, become the prime minister of Canada. This statement overlooks the fact that some people may not be intelligent or motivated enough to take advantage of available resources or opportunities (education, contacts, etc.) to become prime minister. Equity means that no one should be denied access to resources or opportunities based on irrelevant grounds like race or gender (Wilson, 1991).

Equity does not mean that everyone assimilates into the mainstream culture. Unlike previous generations of immigrants to Canada who "Americanized" their names, perfected their English, and consciously buried symbols of their roots, immigrants today challenge assumptions about assimilation. Officially sanctioned pluralism is encouraged by funding programs and attitudes. The bottom line is that trainees must be given equitable treatment because it is illegal to do otherwise.

◆ ◆ ◆
HUMAN RIGHTS

The Canadian Charter of Rights and Freedoms states that every person is entitled to be treated without discrimination based on certain enumerated grounds: race, colour, religion or creed, sex, marital status, physical handicap, and, within a range, age (18–65). All provinces have enacted similar legislation and some have included other grounds, such as sexual orientation. Large employers are familiar with this legislation, particularly with regard to hiring.

The legislation is not limited to employee selection but also covers selection for training.

ACCESS ISSUES

People in the four designated groups (females, visible minorities—a term still used by governments—aboriginal peoples, and the physically challenged), then, must not only have access to jobs but equitable access to quality training. Discrimination does not end when a person is hired. Access to the supervisor, the orientation program, the coaching and mentoring process, and formal training also must be distributed fairly.

Discrimination in training does exist. According to the Canadian Congress for Learning Opportunities for Women, during 1992–1993 Canadian women received only 34 percent of federal training dollars, even though they make up 44 percent of the labour force and represent more than 60 percent of new entrants in the labour market (Suderman, 1993). The training they do receive is typically for jobs that are low-paying and becoming obsolete.

The most extreme form of access discrimination is withholding training from individuals within certain groups. Women management trainees, for example, may not receive an out-of-city developmental assignment because it is assumed that their husbands would not let them go or that some day they will become pregnant and quit. If fewer target-group members enter and/or successfully complete training (thus triggering an adverse impact), then the training may be viewed as discriminatory under Canadian human rights legislation (Cronshaw, 1991).

This access discrimination may not be conscious at an individual level, but may be systemic. This means that discrimination may not be the result of individual acts of bigotry but may stem from the traditional or historical operating methods of an organization. For example, management training courses may be held only in the evenings or weekends, so the effect is that women, who are the primary care givers in the family, cannot attend without great difficulty or expense.

Less obvious than discrimination in selection for training are the more subtle ways trainees from the designated groups are treated during training.

TREATMENT ISSUES

Employers are not only responsible for ensuring a workplace free of discrimination, but also a workplace free of harassment. Harassment occurs whenever an individual is subjected to mental or physical abuse because the individual is considered different in some way (Jain, 1989). Courts have ruled almost universally that the employer is required to provide a workplace free of harassment as a condition of employment. These rulings mean that the training environment must not be adversely affected by negative comments or actions by managers or instructors.

Treatment of students has been found to differ based on gender and race. Women are expected to be quiet, attentive, and passive, receiving less attention from teachers for either good or bad behaviour. Asian women have reported that faculty expected them to fit the model of the quiet, subservient woman, and so they participated less in class (Jenkins, 1990). Teachers give white students more academically challenging work, as well as more encouragement and praise (Nieto, 1992).

In addition, expectations of performance have a profound effect on student achievement. In a classic study, Rosenthal and Jacobson (1968) gave students a nonverbal intelligence test purported to identify intellectual growth. Their teachers were told that certain students (randomly picked by the researchers) were intellectual bloomers. The subsequent year, these students showed considerable IQ gain and were rated much higher in positive personality traits than other equally intelligent children. The moral is that expectations about abilities to learn have a dramatic effect on learning. Trainers who assume that persons of non-European descent cannot handle quantitative material illustrate this effect in training.

The next section examines some of the dynamics that result in differences in treatment in the training setting.

◆ ◆ ◆

THE ISOLATION OF THE CLASSROOM

From the time of Socrates, the classroom has been idealized as pure: the one place where students and teachers come together in the free pursuit of knowledge (Marcroft, 1990). Learning is condensed to one neutral, autonomous, ahistorical site: the classroom. Separated from outside influences and connected only to each other, students and teachers learn in the isolation of the classroom (Hancock, 1990). Truth is discovered and legitimated as knowledge.

But classrooms are full of students who arrive with connections to the external world, and to the historical world of their own cultures. All cultures are built upon conceptual systems—a pattern of beliefs and values that define how people act, judge, decide, etc. (Mathews, 1973). These systems are transmitted to members of that culture through socialization practices. But these socialization practices, which teach an individual how to behave, also teach members how to learn in particular ways. In other words, different cultures produce different learning styles (Wilson, 1991).

In addition to cultural conditioning, different groups bring their own experiences of school into the training classroom. Typically, women and persons of non-European descent receive less attention from teachers and so learn that the learning process requires them to become passive receivers of knowledge (Wright, 1987). Thus, before the trainer enters the classroom, certain assumptions and beliefs about learning are waiting for him or her.

For example, in general, the non-Western world values group cooperation, group achievement, harmony with nature, the relativity of time, holistic thinking, the pervasive influence of religion, the acceptance of affective (emotional) expression, and the perspectives of other cultures. Students with this orientation do best on verbal tasks and materials that have a human social content, which are perceived as part of a larger picture. Their performance is influenced by the opinions of those in authority (Wright, 1987).

Because Canadian education and training departments are dominated by Caucasians, the dominant educational philosophies are guided by Western world views. These views emphasize individual competition, individual achievement, the mastery and control of nature, adherence to a rigid time schedule, religion distinct from other parts of culture, task orientation with a limit to affective expression, and a feeling of a superior world view (Anderson, 1988). Students who succeed in this environment do best on analytical tasks, learn impersonal material easily, and their performance is not dependent on others' opinions.

Most trainers have been educated and trained in the Western world view. They see themselves as knowing more than the students. Their roles are to fill the students with knowledge and skills. Trainers come into the classroom with one world belief, students with a variety of world perspectives.

Beliefs may underlie specific and probably unconscious acts of discrimination in the training situation.

◆ ◆ ◆

THE NATURE OF DISCRIMINATION IN THE CLASSROOM

Discrimination refers to a belief system and actions, both personal and institutional, directed against individuals or groups based on their gender (sexism); ethnic group (ethnocentrism); social class (classism); age (ageism), etc. (Nieto, 1992). Discrimination always helps somebody and hurts somebody else. Rewards and opportunities are distributed (or withheld) on the basis of whether one belongs to a certain group, regardless of individual merits or weaknesses.

Society, and citizens within that society, classify people according to visible characteristics and then deduce personality and behavioural traits. Stereotypes are the result: "Boys are not as smart as girls; the lower classes need instant gratification; Germans are clean." Note that stereotypes can be both positive and negative (e.g., Asians are perceived to be "good in math, but not good with people"). These stereotypes, when present in the classroom, affect instruction. Stereotypes block learning in organizations (Friedlander, 1983). A learning organization must treasure differences in perception, values, preferences, etc. because these may benefit the organization. For example, the "feminine" values of emotional support and nurturance are valuable for teamwork and mentoring.

The dominant instructional model in North America, the one under which most trainers learned to learn, is the transmission model (Barnes, 1976; Wells, 1982). The task of the trainer in the transmission model is to impart knowledge and skills—which the trainer possesses—to the students, who do not yet have these skills. The trainer controls 1) the content (knowledge), and 2) the pedagogical process. Training from this dominant model often excludes minorities, as illustrated below.

Content. Knowledge and truth, content and subject matter, are perceived to be universal, but in fact, curriculum is ethnocentric (Sarup, 1986). "Adding on" material from different cultures and perspectives by searching for models and practices from other situations is less valuable than infusing and integrating this material into the core curriculum. Trainees appreciate material that appeals to different groups.

Most of the students interviewed in Jenkins's (1990) study participated more when instructors included materials pertinent to their ethnic group. These students were afraid to introduce this kind of material into classroom discussions because they felt that the trainer would not understand the value of these cultural contributions.

However, asking students to speak for their culture is inappropriate. Women and non-Europeans may become very uncomfortable when requested by an instructor to give, for example, the black perspective, or to discuss how a woman manager would have handled a certain situation. The balancing strategy for instructors is to encourage participation by responding positively, allowing time for responses, but avoiding asking individuals of visible groups to act as spokespersons for these groups (Jenkins, 1990). The cognitive development of other students can only benefit from learning about different perspectives (Kitching, 1991).

Pedagogy. Considerable research data suggest that when non-Europeans are in a subordinate group, teaching that takes into account their languages and cultures will significantly increase academic success (Campos and Keating, 1984; Cummins, 1989; Rosier and Holm, 1980). Trainees are more likely to learn with the inclusion of instructional strategies that take into account culturally conditioned learning styles.

Studies of gender and language confirm that men and women speak differently. Men speak more often and for longer periods than women (Phillips et al., 1987). Male parents and teachers interrupt more often, and give more direct commands, than female parents and teachers.

Social class affects style of language more than does gender. Differences in the choice of words, forms of politeness, hesitations, etc. tend to reflect power differences. Less powerful people (regardless of gender) tend to use more "tag" questions ("Do you want to know something interesting? ...Well, ..."). Men, who hold more powerful positions in society, control the content and rhythm of conversations. Those in subordinate positions have to work harder to maintain the conversation by asking more questions, and by supporting and encouraging responses. Thus we have the stereotype that women are good at interpersonal skills such as sympathetic listening, careful questioning, and sustaining flagging conversations (Thorne et al., 1983, Cheshire and Jenkins, 1991).

In the seminar or discussion group, these conversational patterns persist, based on who holds power both within the group and between groups. Thus, men often ignore the comments of previous speakers, make more frequent declarations of fact and opinion than women, and talk more often and at greater length than women. Men use taboo words more often than women (Hall and Sandler, 1982; Smith, 1985), and women interpret this verbal aggression as personal, negative, and disruptive.

As well, a large part of what is communicated is not done so via language but through nonverbal actions. These nonverbal behaviours are culture specific and learned at a very young age. Confusion and misreading of intentions may result from misinterpreting actions that have different meanings for different groups. For example, children in black and other cultures are taught that looking an adult in the eye is a sign of disrespect; North American white children are socialized to believe that looking away from an adult who is talking is a sign of disrespect (Byers and Byers, 1972). The decoding of these communication patterns influences instructor reaction to the student.

Research has shown that other variables in interracial interactions are the amount of distance between the communicators, the amount of eye contact, and tone of voice (Feldman, 1985). These findings are summarized in Table 10.1. All of these studies underline the need for trainers to consider the training environment in terms of the learning styles and communication patterns from the perspective of participants.

Despite the fact that practices and belief systems are deeply ingrained, there are techniques trainers can adopt in order to lessen discriminatory treatment.

◆ ◆ ◆
A MODEL OF MULTIPERSPECTIVE TRAINING

The quality of the interaction between the trainer and the student is the centre of the developmental process. This process can only be enhanced by the elimination of discriminatory behaviour.

Merely presenting trainers with research that documents discrimination and its effects on minority students will not bring about equality. Instead, the reactions of trainers may be defensive. Asking trainers to police their own behaviour (most of which is socialized and unconscious) is difficult. The act

TABLE 10.1 BODY LANGUAGE IN CULTURES WORLDWIDE

Acceptable interpersonal distance in various countries:

0 to 18 inches	Middle Eastern males, Eastern and Southern Mediterraneans, and some Hispanic cultures.
18 inches to 3 feet	Americans and West Europeans.
3 feet or more	Asians (Japanese the farthest) and many African cultures.

It is inappropriate behaviour to touch Asians on the head.

Acceptable length of eye contact in various countries:

0 to 1 second	Native Americans, East Indians, and Asian cultures (least in the Cambodian culture, which believes that direct eye contact is flirtatious).
1 second	Americans (to continue direct eye contact beyond 1 second can be considered threatening, particularly between Anglo- and African-American persons).
1 second or more	Middle Eastern, Hispanic, Southern European, and French cultures generally advocate very direct eye contact.

Variations of handshakes in various countries:

Firm	Americans, Germans
Moderate grasp	Hispanics
Light	French (not offered to superiors).
Soft	British
Gentle	Middle Easterners
Gentle	Asians (for some cultures, though not Koreans, shaking hands is unfamiliar and uncomfortable).
Pointing	Generally poor etiquette in most countries, except in Asian countries where it is considered rude and in poor taste. If pointing is necessary, in Hong Kong you use your middle finger, in Malaysia it is the thumb, and in the rest of Asia it is the entire hand.
Beckoning	The American gesture of using upturned fingers, palm facing the body, is deeply offensive to the Mexicans, Filipinos, and Vietnamese. For example, this gesture in the Philippines is used to beckon prostitutes.
Signs of approval	The use of the "okay" sign, the "thumbs-up" signal, and the "V" for "victory" are among the most offensive to other cultures.
Signaling "no"	This can be confusing. In Mexico and the Middle East, a "no" is indicated by a back-to-forth movement of the index finger.
The left hand	Gesturing or handling something with the left hand among Muslims is considered offensive because they consider this the "toilet" hand.

Crossing legs is in poor taste among most Asians and Middle Easterners. The Russians find it distasteful to place the ankle on the knee.

Adapted with the permission of Lexington Books, an imprint of The Free Press, a Division of Simon & Schuster, from *Bridging Cultural Barriers for Corporate Success: How to Manage the Multicultural Work Force* by Sondra Thiederman, Ph.D. Copyright © 1991 by Sondra Thiederman.

of monitoring behaviour may make the trainer less able to instruct, as energies are poured into how things are being said and done. Also, some "leakage" of this unconscious behaviour may still occur. Notwithstanding these problems, it appears that some conscious control is possible.

- *Use neutral words:* Words that have negative connotations for some groups can be eliminated from the vocabulary, and others can be introduced that are more acceptable. For example, the use of "flight attendant" instead of "stewardess" was an easy transition for most airline personnel and clients.

- *Mirror effective and ineffective behaviours:* Another technique is to mirror trainer behaviour in the classroom. Showing videotapes of individual teaching behaviours will enable educators to become participant observers of their own dynamics.

- *Overcompensate*: Teachers have been able to "overcompensate" for their lack of attention to women in class by deliberately soliciting more contributions from women and reinforcing these comments nonverbally and verbally (Corson, 1992). In this way, women and minorities can be brought in from the margins of the classroom. (More suggestions for increasing the participation of minorities are contained in Figure 10.1. Further suggestions for training in a multicultural environment can be found in Chapter 14, pp. 345–350.)

◆ ◆ ◆
TRAINEES WITH SPECIAL NEEDS

As employers meet targets within an employment-equity program, more and more employees with special needs will be regular participants in the training and development process. Persons with disabilities are described as those with a physical or mental impairment limiting one or more major life activity. The range of disabilities includes sensory impairment (such as vision or hearing loss), motor-skill impairment (such as paralysis or loss of limbs), and learning disabilities (which include difficulties in reading, writing, and using numbers).

Often the "disability" is the principal focus of attention by managers who are not "able" to see abilities. Contrast this attitude with that of McDonalds, which has hired and trained over 10 000 mentally and physi-

FIGURE 10.1 MANAGING PARTICIPATION

The following outlines some practical suggestions to facilitate the equitable treatment of women and minorities in the classroom.

Elicit participation from all

Participating in group discussions is "normal" for Canadians, but for people who have been socialized in Asian cultures, like the Japanese, it is "normal" to listen to the instructor or teacher (Hanamura, 1989). Listening *is* participating; perhaps those who prefer to listen could provide a written summary or reaction at the end of the class.

Hand-raising and turn-taking are culture specific. Some students are more comfortable speaking out in class without waiting for permission. There are ways to manage participation in the classroom through controlling turn-taking and through the design of the seating arrangements. One alternative to the trainer "allowing" students to speak by acknowledging their raised hands is to let the students determine who is next (perhaps by throwing a soft ball to the next speaker). Students will monitor their own and others' participation. Give students strips of coloured paper or beans, each entitling them to one comment or question. Another strategy is to have students answer in groups. Students can discuss answers in small groups before responding to the trainer. Another approach is to have every student write down the answer to the question, and then call on a student to read the written answer.

Responses to comments and questions also determine the level of equitable participation in a training room. Examples of discrimination by response include sounding surprised when a minority student responds well, praising or criticizing men's comments and ignoring women's comments, asking whites analytical questions and asking blacks fact-based questions.

Seventy percent of classroom interaction exists between the teacher and the immediately available students (i.e., those in the front of the room) (Jackson and Lahderne, 1967). This action zone excludes everyone at the rear of the room. The physical seating arrangements in the classroom can affect the behaviour of the students (Hood-Smith and Leffingwell, 1983). Instead of having students in rows facing the trainer, students can be seated in a circle, in tables of four or five, or in two rows along the side walls, each facing the centre, or in herringbone patterns with a wide centre aisle. All these designs increase the level of student comfort, facilitate interaction among all, and allow the trainer to monitor participation. Part of the effectiveness of the learning experience is the ability to interact with the instructor and other students.

Use cross-cultural material

Use source materials that would appeal to the diverse backgrounds of the class. (If you have no time to do this, invite students as a group to contribute their perceptions; build a file). Explain why you are (or are not) using material from a multicultural perspective. Refer to your own experience as one that has shaped your perspective (e.g., "As a woman executive, I..." or "My grandparents, who were...lived at a time when workers did what they were told.")

Use nondiscriminatory language

The use of language that assumes that men are the only actors silences women. Words such as "businessman," "mankind," etc. can be replaced by "executive" or "manager," "humanity," etc. Sexist humour should not be used to lighten up a dull subject. Sexist language, humour, and remarks should be labelled as such if someone is behaving in this way in a class.

Another effective strategy involves teaching people to decode behaviour; in other words, people can be trained to be sensitive to cues and miscues in communication, and more accurately interpret their meaning from the other's perspective (Rosenthal et al., 1979). As illustrated earlier, the recognition that eye contact has different meanings for different racial groups may allow trainers to accommodate variations rather than negatively evaluate them.

Trainers might alter their training methods to adapt to different learning styles. A highly successful premedicine program with a large population of non-Europeans moved from an instructor-focused format of theory first, labs second (with each student competing), to a format of building an environment of family, in which students cooperate. Bonding occurred between students and faculty in a highly supportive atmosphere. Lessons that progressed from practical experiences in the lab to theoretical concepts resulted in greater student retention and learning (Brown, 1986). The teaching model that embraces these concepts has been termed "reciprocal interaction" (Cummins, 1986). The trainer acts not as a transmitter, but as a facilitator. This model works particu-

larly well with adults, who are guided in a collaborative effort to learn meaningful material. Internally motivated students assume greater control over the learning process. This technique empowers the student to continue to learn outside the classroom and back on the job.

The presence of minority staff (trainers) also directly affects the amount and extent of learning among minority students. The minority instructor serves as a role model, as an advocate, ensuring the equitable application of policies and directly influencing the quality of the educational experience (Fraga et al., 1986; Massey et al., 1975; Meier and Nigro, 1976; Salzstein, 1979).

Perhaps because of the dynamics within the traditional classroom, ethnic minorities and women have turned to other centres for learning. There is a rich history of group participation in nonmainstream settings. Organizations such as churches, community centres, women's organizations, and voluntary organizations have provided educational opportunities for centuries. Participation of black Americans in voluntary organizations is higher than any other ethnic group (Florin et al., 1987). The network of farm wives in Québec has provided training for rural women since the 19th century.

These informal settings enhance discussion opportunities for women and minorities. When less formal instructional opportunities exist in a formal teaching setting (such as laboratories or discussion groups), interaction patterns change. There appears to be a more just distribution of interactive opportunities than in the dominant training model.

cally challenged workers in North America, focusing on the abilities of workers and ensuring that they have equal opportunity. Managers undergo sensitivity training to dispel myths about disabilities (McMichael, 1992).

The tools and techniques used to assist special-needs workers to learn vary from the simple and inexpensive to the highly sophisticated. Moving a classroom to the ground floor increases accessibility for everyone, as does providing audio cassettes or lecture notes. Braille printers can produce training manuals. Sound can be amplified within the classroom. Sign-language interpreters can be provided (Reid, 1992). During testing, extra time may be allowed for written tests. Tests may also be given orally, with the answers recorded on tape.

Frequently, funding is available to help employers accommodate those with special needs. For example, the Ontario Ministry of Community and Social Services supports 1500 mentally and physically challenged workers by providing a work-support assistant who coaches the trainee until an acceptable level of proficiency is attained (Goodson, 1991).

Computer manufacturers have created technology designed to serve the trainee with special needs. Adaptive equipment has paralleled the rapid growth of personal computers. Examples of this equipment include software that recognizes speech and eye movements and keyboards with large customized keys for sticks and wands. One researcher estimates that, given the proper equipment, those with special needs can function proficiently in 80 percent of the jobs listed in the *Dictionary of Occupational Titles* (Acosta, 1991).

More information on accommodation strategies and available funds is available from provincial training departments and offices of human rights and employment equity.

◆ ◆ ◆
SUMMARY

Trainers should be aware of practices and policies that systematically discriminate against women and persons of non-European descent. These include factors that reduce access to training and development programs and treatment within these programs. Conscious efforts should be made to include content and methods that elicit participation on an equitable basis.

E X E R C I S E S*

Scenario One

During a human resources training session, one of your participants points out that all the material you have used during the workshop has portrayed situations involving only white male and female employees. A white participant counters this claim by saying that the other person is being oversensitive and goes on to suggest that the problem with minorities is that they want to change Canadian culture, when they should be listening and learning how to get along here.

Questions

1. As a trainer, how do you respond to the claim that your material is biased and does not really portray the diversity of the Canadian workforce?

2. Is the white participant voicing a racist view? How do you respond to the claim?

3. How can you use this situation in a way that will be constructive and educational for all the participants?

Scenario Two

I am a woman who has participated in a series of quality control workshops. I have felt very uncomfortable in these workshops. It's nothing that I can really put my finger on, but I do not seem to participate very much. The trainer is really nice and helpful but does not seem to ask the female participants any questions when a point needs to be illustrated or elaborated on. The other amazing thing is that the trainer seems to always know the names of the men but never refers to the women by name. I always have to remind the trainer what my name is. When we are paired off into groups to work on projects, the men dominate the discussion, either interrupting us or ignoring us. They just don't seem to take our opinions seriously. I end up just sitting there, or taking notes. I do not think this is fair, but I do not know how to get the men to let me participate equally."

Questions

The trainer is most likely unaware that unequal treatment is being given to male and female trainees.

1. Why do you think the trainer is not conscious of this different treatment?

2. How would you respond if this participant came to you with this problem about your session?

3. Why do you think this woman did not speak up during the session about this problem?

---

*These exercises were developed by Dale Hall, Advisor, Sexual Harassment Education and Complaint Centre, and Chet Singh, former advisor, Centre for Race and Ethnic Relations at York University.

References

Acosta, T.M. 1991. "CBT Opening Doors." *CBT Directions* 4, no. 2 (November).

Anderson, J.A. 1988. "Cognitive Styles and Multicultural Populations." *Journal of Teacher Education* 39, no. 2, 2–9.

Barnes, D. 1976. *From Communication to Curriculum*. New York: Penguin.

Brown, M. 1986. "Calculus by the Dozen: A Retention Program for Undergraduate Minority Students in Mathematics Based Majors." Paper presented at the second annual conference of Black Student Retention, Atlanta, Georgia (October).

Byers, P., and H. Byers. 1972. "Nonverbal Communication and the Education of Children." In C.B. Cazden, V.P. John, and D. Hymes, eds., *Functions of Language in the Classroom*. New York: Academic Press, 3–31.

Campos, J., and B. Keating. 1984. *The Carpinteria Preschool Program: Title VII Second Year Evaluation Report*. Washington, D.C.: Department of Education.

Canadian Congress for Learning Opportunities for Women. 1993. Letter to the Editor. *The Globe and Mail* (10 November): A20.

Cheshire, J., and N. Jenkins. 1991. "Gender Differences in the GCSE Oral English Examination. Part II." *Language and Education* 5, 19–40.

Corson, D.J. 1992. "Language, Gender and Education: A Critical Review Linking Social Justice and Power." *Gender and Education* 4, no. 3, 89–101.

Cronshaw, S. 1991. *Industrial Psychology in Canada*. Waterloo, Ont.: Waterloo Academic Press.

Cummins, J. 1986. "Empowering Minority Students: A Framework for Intervention." *Harvard Educational Review* 56, no. 1 (February).

_____. 1989. *Empowering Minority Students*. Sacramento, Calif.: California Association for Bilingual Education, 18–36.

Feldman, R.S. 1985. "Nonverbal Behaviour, Race and the Classroom Teacher." *Theory into Practice* 24, no. 3, 45-49.

Florin, P., E. Jones, and A. Wandersman. 1987. "Black Participation in Voluntary

Associations." *Journal of Voluntary Actions Research* 15, no. 1, 65–68.

Fraga, L., K. Meier, and R. England. 1986. "Hispanic Americans and Educational Policy: Limits to Equal Access." *Journal of Politics* 48, no. 3, 851–76.

Friedlander, F. 1983. "Patterns of Individual and Organizational Learning." In S. Srivasta, *The Executive Mind*. San Francisco: Jossey-Bass.

Gemson, C. 1991. "How to Cultivate Today's Multi-Cultural Workforce." *Employment Relations Today* 26, no. 2 (Summer).

Goodson, L. 1991. "People Who Need People." *Human Resources Professional* 8, no. 3 (March).

Hall, R., and B.M. Sandler. 1982. *The Classroom Climate: A Chilly One for Women?* Washington, D.C.: Project on the Status and Education of Women, Association of American Colleges.

Hanamura, S. 1989. "Working with People Who Are Different." *Training and Development Journal* 44, no. 4 (June): 110–14.

Hancock, L. 1990. "Teacher Comforts." *Village Voice* (July 24): 75.

Harris, L. 1977. "Sex Differences in the Growth and Use of Language." In E. Donelson and J. Fullahorn, eds., *Women: A Psychological Perspective*. New York: Wiley.

Hood-Smith, N., and R.J. Leffingwell. 1983. "The Impact of Physical Space Alteration on Disruptive Classroom Behaviour: A Case Study." *Education* 104, no. 3, 224–230.

Jackson, P.W., and H.M. Lahderne. 1967. "Inequalities of Teacher–Pupil Contacts." *Psychology in the Schools* 3, 204–11.

Jain, H., ed. 1989. "Human Rights: Issues in Employment." In *Human Resources Management in Canada*. Scarborough: Prentice-Hall Canada, Inc.

_____. 1991. *Employment Equity: Issues and Policies*. A study prepared for the Canada Employment and Immigration Advisory Council.

Jenkins, M. 1990. "Teaching the New Majority: Guidelines for Cross-Cultural Communication Between Students and Faculty." *Feminist Teacher* 5, no. 1, 8–14.

Kitching, K.W. 1991. "A Case for a Multicultural Approach to Education." *Education Canada* 27, no. 4, (Spring).

Klann-Delius, G. 1987. "Sex and Language." In U. Ammon, N. Dittmarx, and K. Mattheick, eds., *Sociolinguist*. Berlin: Walter de Gruyter.

Lee, E. 1985. *Letters to Marcia: A Teachers' Guide to Anti-racist Education*. Toronto: Cross Cultural Communication Centre, 8.

McMichael, C. 1992. "Focus on Ability." *Employee Assistance* (July).

Marcroft, M. 1990. "The Politics of the Classroom: Towards an Oppositional Pedagogy." *New Directions for Teaching and Learning* 44 (Winter): 61–71.

Massey, G., M. Scott, and S. Dornbusch, 1975. "Institutional Racism in Urban Schools." *Black Scholar* 7, no. 3, 10–19.

Mathews, B. 1973. "Black Cognitive Process." Unpublished paper. Howard University, School of Social Work, Washington, D.C.

Meade, C.A. 1986. *Employment Equity for Visible Minority Women: A Guide for Employers.* Toronto: Urban Alliance on Race Relations and Ontario Women's Directorate.

Medoff, M.H. 1975. "Discrimination, Blacks and the Apprenticeship Trade Programs." *Negro Educational Review* 26, no. 4, 147–54.

Mier, K.J., and L.G. Nigro. 1976. "Representative Bureaucracy and Policy Preferences." *Public Administration Review* 36, 458–70.

Nieto, S. 1992. *Affirming Diversity—The Sociopolitical Context of Multicultural Education.* New York: Longham Publishing Group.

Phillips, S., S. Steele, and C. Tanz, eds. 1987. *Language, Gender and Sex in Comparative Perspective.* Cambridge: Cambridge University Press.

Reid, R.L. 1992. "On Target: Tools to Train People with Disabilities." *Technical and Skills Training* (July).

Rosenthal, R., and L. Jacobson. 1968. *Pygamalion in the Classroom.* New York: Holt Rhinehart & Winston.

Rosenthal, R., J.A. Hall, D. Archer, M.R. Di Matteo, and P.L. Rogers. 1979. "Measuring Sensitivity to Nonverbal Communications: The PONS Test." In A. Wolfgang, ed., *Nonverbal Behaviour: Applications and Cross Cultural Implications.* New York: Academic Press.

Rosier, P., and Holm, W. 1980. *The Rock Point Experience: A Longitudinal Study of a Navajo School.* Washington, D.C.: Centre for Applied Linguistics.

Saltzstein, G.H. 1979. "Representative Bureaucracy and Bureaucratic Responsibility." *Administration and Society* 10, no. 2, 465–75.

Sarup, Madan. 1986. *The Politics of Multiracial Education.* London: Troutledge & Kegan Paul.

Shade, B.J. 1986. "Cultural Diversity and the School Environment." *Journal of Humanistic Education and Development* 25, 80–87.

Smith, P. 1985. *Languages, the Sexes and Society.* Oxford: Blackwell.

Suderman, B. 1993. "Women Get Short Shrift." *The Globe and Mail* (10 November): A20.

Thorne, B., C. Kramarae, and N. Henley, eds. 1983. *Language, Gender and Society*. Rowley, MA.: Newbury House.

Wells, G. 1982. "Language, Learning and the Curriculum." In W. J. Tikunoff, ed., *Language, Learning and Education*. Bristol: Centre for the Study of Language and Communication, University of Bristol, 205–26.

Wilson, J. 1991. "Education and Equality: Some Conceptual Questions." *Oxford Review of Education* 17, no. 2, 223–30.

Wright, C. 1987. "The Relations Between Teachers and Afro-Caribbean Pupils: Observing Multi-Racial Classrooms." In G. Weiner and M. Arnot, eds., *Gender under Scrutiny*. London: Hutchinson.

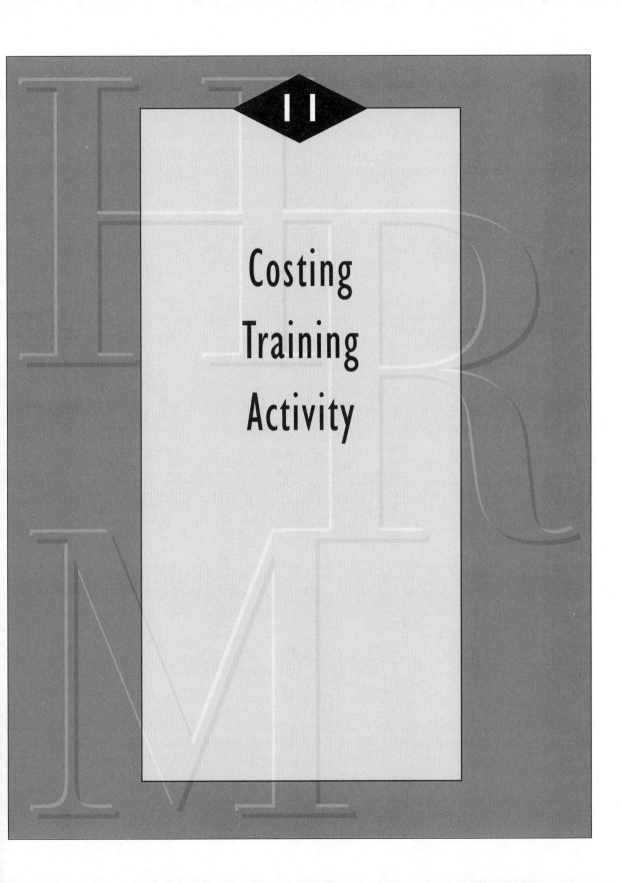

11

Costing
Training
Activity

◆ ◆ ◆
INTRODUCTION

Costing is a complex and time-consuming process that many training specialists traditionally have avoided. The reasons are many; some managers are skeptical about the theoretical underpinnings of costing, while others suggest, rightly, that in business not everything is quantifiable. Indeed, many managers suggest that there are some quality issues—employee motivation, communication techniques, and processes that make people feel good about themselves and the company they work for—that you just cannot put a dollar value on. Still others are afraid that costing (when tied to benefit analysis) might expose some training programs as noncontributors, thus putting their careers at risk (Lombardo, 1989, 63–64; Phillips, 1992).

Trainers who have lost their jobs to budget reductions, or whose departments have been eliminated or drastically reduced, however, tend to be strongly supportive of costing and evaluation, or benefit analysis (Lombardo, 1989). The reasons are obvious; managers "want to hear trainers talking about return, profits and assessment," as too often funding has been wasted on training designs that were too "introspective" and that disregarded the need for more results-oriented development activity (Blanden et al., 1991).

As well, the credibility issue discussed previously must be kept in mind. An educational software-development company on the east coast, for example, was in desperate need of curriculum-development specialists who would work with clients, creating learning packages in a format that could be made into interactive video training modules. Because there were no trained people in the East, this company obtained government assistance, developed a training program, and advertised widely for former teachers and others with appropriate training in psychology and computer expertise. The number of applicants was so large that the screening and interview processes took two months, consuming a considerable amount of valuable management time.

Unfortunately, two weeks before the course was to begin, it was found that "someone" had "forgotten" to add the cost of equipment rental into the budget. Suddenly, the entire project was not financially viable. The course was cancelled.

Consider the embarrassment: the government grant had to be returned; the 15 trainees, some of whom had refused other opportunities, had to be contacted; the company's entire product-development strategy had to be reworked. As the personnel manager said when she sheepishly contacted one of the trainees: "This is one of the worst days in my professional life!" One can imagine, too, that senior management had a few choice words for the person responsible for costing the program.

Costing training activity, then, is important. Professionals who perform this function well turn this traditionally "soft" area of management into something very real. Without costs, benefits can't be measured. Without measurable results or benefits, the entire training function is not credible and is more subject to the "last hired, first fired" syndrome (Lombardo, 1989).

◆ ◆ ◆

A COSTING PHILOSOPHY

Based on the ideas in previous chapters, it should be evident that training activity directed toward measurable objectives must become part of an organization's culture or "way of doing things." To this philosophical stance must be added the determination that training will be considered like any other investment (Bantley, 1991). Training, therefore, becomes an expenditure of capital now, with anticipation that future benefits will occur over and above the initial investment. Training ideas should compete for investment funds with other options, all of which provide some return at some risk. Thus, rate of return on a training proposal is compared with many other possible alternatives.

When decisions about training have to win approval from other managers outside the training function, it is unlikely that arguments about "goodness" or the value of training will prevail (Haislip, 1987); hence the necessity to develop cost (and benefit) calculation techniques that are convincing, thorough, and cost-effective in themselves. The philosophy of exposing training to competitive pressures puts an end to the idea that "training is just something we do." It cancels the fuzzy "how to manage your boss" course and focuses training strategy on the design of competencies and performance-effectiveness criteria (Spencer and Spencer, 1993).

◆◆◆
COMPLEX INTERACTING FORCES

The philosophy and the culture that force training into a category of needs-based investment cannot separate inputs (cost) from outputs (benefits or evaluation). The costs an organization is willing to absorb are directly proportional to the forecasted benefits and the perception of risk, i.e., the perceived probability of actually reaping those forecasted benefits.

Too often, however, the *direct* results of training are impossible to measure, and costing aimed at the wrong level will meet with skepticism. Even if the training initiative passes the budget-review process, many good programs meet all the professional criteria but still have no obvious direct results (Baird and Meshoulam, 1992). For example, how much does supervisory training contribute to profitability? Costing this type of learning activity can be both extremely difficult to figure out and to "sell" to management. There are too many complex variables that might interact to nullify the training. The management style of the supervisor's superior; the physical working conditions; investment in equipment; how the employer introduces change; the state of the organization, e.g., growing, stable, or downsizing—these are but a very few of the variables that affect the ability to manage.

So, under the training-as-investment philosophy, supervisory training is unlikely to be funded. Not so! Kaydos (1991) argues that although an organization's success or failure is derived from many internal or external factors, inevitably these can be reduced to no more than five key performance measures. Further, he suggests that direct costs should not always be the primary focus of management. Affecting both private sector and nonprofit organizations, these performance factors, or measures, might include:

- average order cycle time
- percentage of orders shipped when promised
- time to introduce new products or services
- customer or membership repeat/renewal frequency
- plant office or equipment utilization
- average time to respond to a service order or request for information
- responses to customer audits or questionnaires.

Stressing key performance factors takes the attention away from direct training results (Phillips, 1992), as the trainer is likely to be working as part of a team geared toward improving employee effectiveness, where other nontraining factors are likely to be more important. Many authors insist that training achieves but one small part (usually about 20 percent) of overall effectiveness improvement; the rest is found in changing the environment—support systems, equipment, work methods, and physical conditions (Wright, 1983; Wright and Geroy, 1990; Gordon, 1992).

In this situation, the cost of training tends to be part of a larger budget. The total improvement program is sold to senior management. Training results are hidden and not measured directly; only the key performance factor counts. Simplifying complex situations by using substitute or second-level measures may be a compromise, but the alternative can be what Agresta (1992) calls "paralyzed-in-place," a feeling that the situation is completely intangible (or impossible), therefore no cost data are presented at all.

Once again, one can use the example of supervisory training. Let's suppose that the goal is to reduce the firm's average order-cycle time by some clearly measurable amount. Depending upon the work situation, any number of variables might affect performance. The storage or warehousing system, the telecommunications system, paperwork or order-form flow, job design, the responsibility/authority given to individuals at various levels, production-scheduling techniques, and a host of other factors may need to be studied. To these tangible environmental concerns must be added the manner in which people are managed and supervised.

No matter how sophisticated the systems and the technology, full productivity will not be achieved without attention to human issues and concerns (Perlitz, 1993). For example, supervisory training is often a necessary ingredient in the total productivity- or competitiveness-improvement scenario. But some measurement of productivity is the key performance factor. To attempt a cost/benefit analysis isolating the contribution of training to the whole would be futile. Thus, the cost of training becomes part of an investment that may include changes to many other variables, aimed at improving one or more key performance factors.

Since there may be a temptation in these complex situations to trust technology and to avoid investing in human resources development (HRD), the story of a west coast sawmill and lumber kiln drying operation must be told. In attempting to increase productivity, management invested $5 million in state-of-the-art equipment from Germany. Then they put people accustomed to running chain saws in the bush in charge of the operation, expecting immediate improvements. Predictably, the results were disastrous. The company went bankrupt.

In analyzing the failure, the consultant hired by the firm's creditors contacted the German manufacturer. It appears the training of two or three individuals to the technologist level had been recommended. This process would have involved an orientation at a similar facility in North America and at least two weeks training in the manufacturer's German plant. Then, an experienced engineer would have been sent to the west coast facility to help the newly trained technologists with startup, providing another two weeks of on-the-job training. The manufacturer guaranteed a certain productivity level. Total training cost would have been $50 000, but managers who would finance $5 million in equipment balked at spending an additional one percent on the human resources! The machines were supposed to improve productivity and, indeed, if operated properly would do so. The cost of training could not be *directly* linked to improvements and, therefore, was seen as an expendable frill. Besides, who sends sawmill operators to Europe, a perk normally reserved for managers?

Depending upon the situation, then, costing may be the first step in measuring the direct result of a training program, or this cost can be one variable in a budget designed to enhance a key performance factor. The costing process is similar in both situations, although the task of selling the program to senior management can differ—a topic explored in more detail at the end of this chapter.

◆ ◆ ◆

MEASURING DIRECT INPUTS (COSTS)

The most important issue to remember when costing a training program is not to leave out some item critical to the investment-decision process—like equipment rental for a curriculum-development specialist course. Fortunately, a number of authors have developed checklists to help practitioners prepare cost estimates. Head's (1987) award-winning book consists almost entirely of a wide range of costing sheets, far too detailed to reproduce in this chapter. His costing analysis covers more than 100 pages, including basic cost factors (overhead), data gathering, student, instructor, course development, facility, and maintenance costs. This unabashedly "how to" publication is recommended highly for those wishing to create comprehensive, functional cost worksheets.

A more manageable example has been adapted from Warren (1979), who included a cost worksheet that summarized *direct* costs in sufficient detail for most purposes.

COSTING SHEET

1. **Fixed cost factors**
   i. Overhead—AC/heat/light; space; rental/lease; communications; per input hour   _____
   ii. Supervisory allocation per input hour   _____
   iii. Equipment cost per input hour   _____
   iv. Administrative support cost per input hour   _____
   v. Training unit fringe benefits cost per input hour   _____
   Total fixed costs per input hour   _____

2. **Needs Analysis**
   i. Professional hours ____ @ $____/hour = cost   _____
   ii. Support hours ____ @ $____/hour = cost   _____
   iii. Transportation expenses   _____
   iv. Material   _____
   v. Consulting fees   _____
   vi. Other costs   _____
   Total direct needs-analysis costs   _____

3. **Program Development**
   i. Professional hours ____ @ $____/hour = cost   _____
   ii. Support hours ____ @ $____/hour = cost   _____
   iii. Material   _____
   iv. Consulting fees   _____
   v. Subject-matter expert/management and staff input
   ____ hours @ ____/hour = cost   _____
   vi. Other costs   _____
   Total direct program-development costs   _____

4. Program Delivery
    i.   Administration hours _____
        @ $_____/hour = costs   _____
    ii.   Administrative support hours _____
        @ $_____/hour = costs   _____
    iii. Presentation/delivery hours _____
        @ $_____/hour = cost   _____
    iv.   Technical support hours ____
        @ $_____/hour = cost   _____
    v.   Trainee materials costs   _____
    vi.   Transportation/accommodations/meals
        a. staff   _____
        b. trainees   _____
    vii. Facilities rental   _____
    viii. Equipment   _____
        Total direct program-delivery costs   _____

5. Evaluation/Cost-benefit Analysis
    i.   Professional hours _____
        @ $_____/hour = cost   _____
    ii.   Support hours _____ @ $_____/hour = cost   _____
    iii. Management input hours _____
        @ $_____/hour = cost   _____
    iv.   Trainee input hours _____
        @ $_____/hour = cost   _____
    v.   Transportation costs   _____
    vi.   Material costs   _____
    vii. Consulting Fees   _____
        Total evaluation cost   _____

6. Revision costs
    i.   Professional hours ___ @ $____/hour = cost   _____
    ii.   Support hours ____ @ $____/hour = cost   _____
    iii. Management/staff collaboration hours ____ @
        $____/hour = cost   _____
        Total evaluation cost   _____

7. Total Direct Program Cost
    1 + 2 + 3 + 4 + 5 + 6 = Total Direct Cost   _____

◆ ◆ ◆
INDIRECT COSTS

In many organizations, a measurement of direct costs is acceptable; the indirect costs are absorbed in overall organizational overhead. Any training activity, however, has both opportunity costs (i.e., the trainees could be doing something else) and a measurable labour cost. The *Costing Sheet*, then, might be expanded to include:

i.	total trainee salaries cost	_____
ii.	lost production cost	_____
iii.	replacement cost	_____
iv.	overtime cost	_____
v.	increased supervision cost for iii and iv	_____
vi.	reduced quality cost	_____
vii.	new skills on-the-job training costs	_____
viii.	increased scrap/spoilage costs	_____
ix.	other indirect costs	_____
	Total indirect costs	_____

Obviously, by combining direct and indirect costs, a more complete analysis of the real cost to the organization can be obtained.

What are acceptable cost inputs depends upon the type of training to be conducted and the organization's culture. The trainer will do whatever it takes to create a cost/benefit analysis that can compete for scarce investment funds.

As well, the costing sheet presented here is only one example; it may need to be modified to suit an organization's unique circumstances. One common change would be to recategorize trainee salaries from indirect to direct costs. The idea is not to worry about labels but to design a format that has credibility.

◆ ◆ ◆
MEASURING ALTERNATIVES

Again, depending upon the type of training and the alternative sources available, the person responsible for HRD may need to compare options. One of the foremost North American authorities on costing, Dr. Gary Geroy from the Colorado State University, uses the following simplified comparison worksheet:

Program* _____ **Option name**	**Analyst** _____ 1. _____	**Date** _____ 2. _____
Analysis:		
Needs assessment	_____	_____
Work analysis	_____	_____
Proposal to management	_____	_____
Other _____	_____	_____
Other _____	_____	_____
Design:		
General HRD program design	_____	_____
Specific HRD program design	_____	_____
Other _____	_____	_____
Other _____	_____	_____
Development:		
Draft and prototype	_____	_____
Pilot test and revise	_____	_____
Production and duplication	_____	_____
Other _____	_____	_____
Other _____	_____	_____
Implementation:		
Program management	_____	_____
Program delivery	_____	_____
Participant costs	_____	_____
Other _____	_____	_____
Other _____	_____	_____
Evaluation:		
Program evaluation and report	_____	_____
Performance followup	_____	_____
Other _____	_____	_____
Other _____	_____	_____
Total HRD program costs	$ _____ (Option 1)	$ _____ (Option 2)
Reproduced with the author's permission.		

To complete the analysis, Geroy then combines the cost inputs with an estimate of the value of the HRD program (Performance Value) to the organization to obtain a net benefit—a topic to be discussed later in this chapter.

Program _____	Analyst _____	Date _____
Option	I. _____	2. _____
Performance Value	$ _____	$ _____
Minus Cost		
Net Benefit	$ _____	$ _____

The case study that follows illustrates how this cost-comparison technique works and how different organizations may require cost data at various levels of complexity and detail.

A COST COMPARISON ANALYSIS*

Situation: You are part of an organization that does electronic systems design. It is a "Fortune 500" firm and a leader in its field. A recent reorganization has created a project-management division that places all lead engineers on projects in one group rather than being spread across several operations. The purpose of the reorganization was to allow the engineers to do less "hands-on" technical activity and focus more on theory development, design, and management of others on projects. The management group is now headed up by a manager from your firm with an outstanding record in project management. The group consists of 10 lead engineers. You have been experiencing an alarming rate of turnover in electronic engineers since this group was established. A needs assessment reveals that the engineer types who make up this management group are very unskilled in communicating directions, delegating, and handling people-crisis issues. Data from the exit interviews reveal that inability of project managers to manage crises and the inability to transmit clear guidelines and directions have been the primary frustrations causing individuals to leave. Your needs assessment also confirms that the members of the organization and the management group itself feel that this reorganization was a good decision.

---

*Prepared by Dr. Gary D. Geroy, The Colorado State University at Fort Collins. Reproduced with permission from his client organization.

The crisis in the organization resulting from the high turnover rate is a financial one. It costs the organization approximately $75 000 to find, hire, and relocate an engineer with the appropriate credentials and experience. In the last nine months, your organization has replaced five engineers. At this rate you anticipate you will replace a total of six engineers before the year is complete. You have been asked to recommend a training activity to address the management skills deficiency in this group. The goal is to reduce the turnover rate to two per year.

Your options are to send each project manager in the group to a management development institute which was identified by the president of the corporation, arrange for a vendor-delivered training program in house, or develop a coaching program to help these managers acquire the skills needed. Your director has suggested that the last option might take 9 to 12 months to achieve the desired results. The probabilities are low to none that they will develop the skills needed on their own on the job. Your organization will not consider salaries or other normal employee maintenance costs as training expenses. A budget of $7000 will be provided for materials and $17 000 for consulting fees to support a coaching approach to solving the problem.

The following information is provided to help you make your decision:

Vendor-supplied program:
    15 four-hour sessions delivered on site over a six month period—
    $15 000 per trainee

Management Development Institute:
    80-hour program delivered off site over a two-week period—
    $10 000 per trainee (this includes airfare, lodging, food, and materials)

Materials Budget to Support Coaching Option: $7000

Needs Analysis	10%
Work Analysis	5%
Design	5%
Development	15%
Implementation	50%
Evaluation	15%
	100% allocation

Here is the actual cost-analysis worksheet used by Geroy's client:

COST ANALYSIS WORKSHEET

	M.D. Institute	Outside Vendor	Coaching
Analysis:			
Needs Assessment	$_____	$_____	$ 10,700
Work Analysis	$_____	$_____	$ 4,350
Design:			
Program	$_____	$_____	$ 350
Instructional Aids	$_____	$_____	$ 0
Development:			
Pilot Testing	$_____	$_____	$ 0
Formative Evaluation			
(during the HRD activity)	$_____	$_____	$ 0
Instructional Aids	$_____	$_____	$ 1,050
Implementation:			
Delivery	$ 100,000	$ 150,000	$ 3,500
Management	$_____	$_____	$ 0
Evaluation:			
Summative Evaluation	$_____	$_____	$ 3,000
Training Revision	$_____	$_____	$ 0
Maintenance of Trainee Behaviour	$_____	$_____	$ 1,050
(A) Total	$ 100,000	$ 150,000	$ 24,000
(B) Trainees	10	10	10
Cost Per Trainee (A)/(B) =	$ 10,000	$ 15,000	$ 2,400

This case study is important for four reasons:

1. It shows how the original costing sheet (page 257) can be modified to meet the client's needs. The substitution of a "maintenance of behaviour" category for the nebulous term "Performance follow-up," for example, makes this cost easier to sell. Also, there was no need to make a "proposal to management." The problem was well understood and immediate.

2. Management was not interested in a cost breakdown for either the Institute or the in-house vendor program, hence the single cost entered in the "Delivery" column. In contrast, had this client been a government agency, a detailed breakdown of both bids might have been required.

3. As discussed previously, cost of salaries and benefits, overhead, and cost productivity measures are not included. In this case, the problem had to be solved. Management was not interested in fine-tuning the costs.

4. A nontraining option is being considered. Coaching, an on-the-job learning technique (to be discussed in Chapter 13), is by far the cheapest option. Whether or not coaching is the method finally chosen would require a benefit analysis. The important issue, however, is that traditional training may not be the best investment. All appropriate HRD methods should be considered.

A choice among the three alternatives, then, should not be made without an estimate of the benefits likely to be received under each system.

◆ ◆ ◆
ESTIMATING NET BENEFIT

Estimating net benefits, or return on investment, is one of the most difficult tasks for HRD practitioners (Phillips, 1992; Robinson and Robinson, 1989). How benefits are calculated depends upon the training situation, management needs, and the data available. Because of these difficulties, three examples will be presented here. First, Geroy's case study will be completed. Costs have been calculated suggesting that the coaching option would be the most effective. When the "Net Benefit Value Calculation Worksheet" is completed, however, a different picture emerges.

Using Geroy's benefit estimation method, the Management Development Institute becomes the most attractive option—in quantitative terms. Few managers, however, would make the final decision based on these criteria alone. As previously suggested, there are qualitative concerns that become part of the analysis—reputation of the training institute, past experience, trainee perceptions of the three options, the degree to which the training can be customized, and the time factor—all will be considered before a final decision is made. The key issue is that management has been given a credible tool with which to make a return-on-investment (ROI) decision.

NET BENEFIT VALUE CALCULATION WORKSHEET

	Institute Option 1	Option 2	Coaching Option 3
A. Data Required for Calculations			
(a) What is the desired performance as a result of worker training?	4	4	4
(b) What unit(s) of measure will be used to describe the performance?	reductions per group	reductions per group	reductions per group
(c) What is the dollar value that will be assigned to each unit of measure?	$75,000	$75,000	$75,000
(d) What is the estimated training time to reach the goal?	.04 year	.5 year	1.0 year
(e) What is the current level of worker performance?	0 reduction	0 reduction	0 reduction
(f) How many workers will participate in the training?	10	10	10
B. Calculations to Determine Net Performance Value			
(g) What is the estimated performance level during training? Will trainee produce during training? _____ No = 0 _____ Yes = a + e / 2	0	2	2
(h) What is the length of the period being evaluated (at a minimum this will be the longest "d" of all options under consideration)?	1.0 year	1.0 year	1.0 year
(i) What is the estimate of the total number of units (b) that will be achieved during training? [d × g]	0	1	2
(j) What is the estimate of the total individual performance (or the evaluation period [(h − d) × a] + 1)?	3.84 reduction	3.0 reduction	2.0 reduction
(k) What is the value for the total performance for the evaluation period? [c × j]	$288,000	$225,000	$150,000
(l) What is the net performance value gain? [k + (e × c × h)]	$288,000	$225,000	$150,000
(m) Do you want to calculate the total net performance value of all trainees? _____ Yes = 1 × f __X__ No = Net Performance Value of 1 trainee which is of (1)	$288,000	$225,000	$150,000
Net Benefit	$288,000	$225,000	$150,000
Cost (from Cost-Analysis Worksheet)	$100,000	$150,000	$ 24,000
Final Net Benefit	*$188,000*	*$75,000*	*$126,000*

The second ROI model has been adapted from Gordon (1991, 22–23). It concerns the analysis of a two-week, 12-module learning program for courier van drivers. This example is significant, as there could be no needs analysis—the course had been in place since 1982. If a cost analyst has input into training design, sometimes the objectives chosen for measurement can be written so that benefit calculation is made easier (Long, 1990). Here, the analyst had to work with a mature program using any data he could collect.

Gordon (1991) describes the ROI study, costing about $10 000, carried out by a Memphis-based air freight company, FedEx:

> *The course in question was the company's two-week, 12-module basic training program for new couriers—the people who drive vans (usually) to the front of your office building, take the elevator up to the receptionist's desk or the mail room or wherever, and pick up or deliver your Federal Express packages. The program had been running since the early 1980s.*
>
> *The study tracked three groups of 20 employees each. In the first group were recent graduates of the basic training course—new employees who had completed the course (and been on the job) no more than 90 days before the study began.*
>
> *In the second group were new couriers sent to their job assignments without going through the course. "This meant we were accepting the risk of sending out 20 untrained people," Addicott noted (Addicott was the manager in charge of training). Well, almost untrained. Their managers were told to do no more (and no less) on-the-job training than normal to prepare them for their new jobs. Managers typically ride with new couriers to familiarize them with their routes, teach them how to fill out an airbill, and generally show them the ropes. Also, the "untrained" group received defensive driving and dangerous-goods training, as required by the Department of Transportation. What they didn't get was the two-week course.*

In the third group were veteran couriers who had been with the company for five or more years. FedEx wanted to examine the possible need for recurrency training in matters such as filling out an international waybill and converting pounds to kilos.

Nobody in any group was told about the study. The performance of these 60 people was monitored daily, for 90 days, by their managers. The managers used checklists to track 18 performance indicators, determined by a task force of experts—namely, FedEx managers who oversee couriers. Some of those performance indicators were: accidents, injuries, time-card errors, domestic airbill errors, international air waybill errors, pickup manifest errors, courier-caused wrong-day deliveries, customer complaints, etc.

Ten of those 18 performance indicators were assigned dollar values: cost per error. How did the training department decide that? It didn't. The figures were supplied by the safety department, engineering, finance, and other groups. ("You may find," said Addicott, "that these departments want to get involved with you on something like this. Our finance people actually formed teams to come up with some of these figures.")

In the category of accidents (meaning accidents involving vehicles), for instance, the average cost per incident was $1600, according to the safety department. Given that figure and the data on the checklists turned in by supervisors at the end of the 90-day period, projecting the annual cost of accidents for couriers in each of the three groups becomes a simple exercise in arithmetic: Cost per error X number of errors = total cost of errors. Total cost of errors − number of people in group = total cost per person. Multiply cost per person by four *(because this was a 90-day study) and you have total cost per courier per year.*

For everyone except the five-year veterans, Addicott subtracted 25 percent from that total, reasoning that in the course of a year performance would improve somewhat with experience on the job. In other words, both the trained and untrained couriers would probably get better at avoiding accidents (and at completing waybills and manifests and delivery records) if they simply stayed on the job for a year. The training course should not get undue credit for producing performance differences that are apparent for 90 days but might diminish within six or nine months.

The cost of accidents per employee per year? For a recently trained courier, $399. For an untrained courier, $1920. For a veteran courier, $428.

Using the same formula with all 10 performance indicators that had dollar figures attached, Federal Express determined the annual cost of all errors per courier for each of the three groups. Recently trained: $2492. Untrained: $4833. Veteran: $4064.

What did this tell the company? For one thing, something was very fishy about those veterans. Addicott knew which performance indicators were out of whack (veterans in this study made a lot of domestic airbill errors, for example), but this data alone didn't confirm a need for recurrency training: maybe the problem wasn't that the vets didn't know how to fill out airbills; maybe something else was wrong. When the veterans were debriefed, however, it turned out that there were knowledge problems. For example, some company procedures had changed in the past few years but the veterans' way of doing things hadn't. They were still taking "shortcuts" that used to work under the old airbill system but now created errors. Recurrency training was launched.

The "value" of the two-week course? The difference in errors per year between a trained courier and an untrained one is worth $2341 ($4833 − $2492). The cost of the training program, per courier, is $1890 (including hotel, meals, airfare, mileage allowance, instructor salary, courier salary while training, and "coverage" for the courier while in training— somebody else has to deliver those packages while this person is being trained). Therefore, the ROI for one courier during the first year on the job is $451. In fiscal year 1989, Federal Express sent 1097 new couriers through the training course. Total ROI for the program in 1989: $494 747.

This example shows quite clearly that it is possible to compute ROI, or net benefit, from traditional training activities. The process only works, however, if managers are prepared to accept the inevitable assumptions that have to be made. The FedEx manager (Addicott) subtracted 25 percent of total cost per courier from the cost of employing five-year veterans, "reasoning that in the course of a year, performance would improve *somewhat* with experience on the job." Why a 25-percent reduction—why not 20 percent, or 15 percent, or 2 percent? Obviously in this situation, 25 percent was a believable figure. Perhaps 25 percent made intuitive sense, or perhaps Addicott's reputation is what makes this figure acceptable. The major point here is that benefits estimation is an inexact procedure, another reason why trainers should be concerned about professional credibility.

Credibility, then, is a major issue, perhaps *the* major issue in cost/benefits analysis (Phillips, 1992). The final example illustrates the use of what Phillips (1991) called "soft" data.

A large bank was experiencing an abnormal turnover rate. A training program was designed to counter the turnover problem. The cost of employee turnover needed to be estimated if an ROI was to be calculated. But actual cost calculation was difficult because of the many interacting variables—administrative costs, interviewing, testing, relocation, orientation, increase in supervisory time, initial less-than-optimal performance, on-the-job training—all make up the cost of replacing one person. As the bank did not want to devote the considerable resources necessary to developing a precise calculation, turnover was classified as a "soft" cost and a combination of approaches were used to derive an acceptable figure.

Initially, a literature search was used to determine that another institution in the same industry had calculated a cost of $25 000 per turnover. This figure, derived by an internal-audit unit and verified by a consulting specialist in turnover reduction, was used as a starting point. The application of this statistic to another (even though quite similar) organization was in question, however. HRD staff then met with senior executives:

> to agree on a turnover cost value to use in gauging the success of the program. Management agreed on an estimate that was half the amount from the study, $12 500. This was considered very conservative because other turnover studies typically yield statistics of greater value. Management felt comfortable with the estimate, however, and it was used on the benefits side of program evaluation. Although not precise, this exercise yielded a figure that was never challenged (Phillips, 1991, 337).

The term "never challenged" is significant. Trainers must perform cost/benefit analyses, but they must do so from a position of strength. In this example, senior managers were brought "onside" when they were used as "experts." It mattered little that the turnover cost was set at $12 500, rather than $25 000, as the benefit estimation produced from these data was credible and accepted by those with the power to make investment decisions.

Thus, despite the appearance of quantitative rigour, virtually all but the most simple cost/benefit designs are dependent to a greater or lesser extent on assumptions and expert opinion (Wright, 1990; Geroy and Wright, 1988). As with training, cost/benefit design must fit into the organization's culture (Bushnell, 1990). The arithmetic must be believable so that investors who are accustomed to thinking in terms of present value on future returns and liabilities will see fit to allocate appropriate funding.

◆ ◆ ◆
SUPPORTING THE COSTING FUNCTION

A. COST/BENEFIT TRACKING SYSTEMS

A database that can be used to measure the progress an organization is making toward meeting its objectives is one of the most important facets of a costing system. In particular, historical data can be invaluable when costing new proposals or in negotiating for new funding.

The major weakness in past training design has been the inability to show its contribution to profits. Without a method of collating and reporting successes in financial terms, the HRD professional is reduced to a minor supporting role in the corporate enterprise (Haislip, 1987; Phillips, 1992).

B. COST-REDUCTION SYSTEM

One way to support the HRD function is to constantly reduce training costs and to show that the training system is becoming more effective and efficient (Wright and Kusmanadji, 1993). Although there may be other costs, one checklist, developed by Cawthray (c. 1987), includes a variety of suggestions:

a. Company commitment:
   - press for in-company or on-the-job development leading to reduced reliance upon:
     1. outside consultants,
     2. "prestige" trainers,
     3. off-site training.

b. Instructor costs:
   - use company staff and trainers where possible,
   - use one instructor where one instructor will suffice,
   - reduce preparation costs by using/reusing standard sessions and using course member discussion,
   - reduce travel time off the job,
   - develop in-company skills and training talent,
   - consider technology-based training,
   - keep good records.

c. Material costs:
   - use reusable training materials,
   - let the client/company print the papers, provide the files, etc.,

◆ adapt commercial materials.

d. Course design costs:
   ◆ brief course members before/after courses,
   ◆ assign work before and after courses,
   ◆ reduce "setup" costs by using standard courses and company facilities,
   ◆ evaluate off-the-shelf computer-based training and distance-learning courses.

e. Course direction costs:
   ◆ use company office staff for administrative support,
   ◆ use the lecturer/instructor/trainer as course director,
   ◆ use in-house directors.

f. Course member costs:
   ◆ reduce travel costs and bed and meal costs through in-company short courses,
   ◆ reduce off-the-job costs with short courses,
   ◆ counsel trainees on the need for training—don't send employees to courses automatically or in rotation as "perks."

g. Accommodation costs:
   ◆ reduce "visible" accommodation costs by using client/company teaching and residential accommodation,
   ◆ use shorter courses to reduce overnight accommodation costs,
   ◆ use local community college facilities.

C. ACCOUNTING TREATMENT OF TRAINING COSTS

Once training costs have been identified, they have to be incorporated into the accounting system so that they can be included in the total cost of production or service rendered. There are three ways to administer training accounts:

1. *Allocation of costs.* Costs can be shared with other departments and may, for example, be allocated according to the number employed in a department and its labour turnover or output. The main advantage of this method is its simplicity. Because of that simplicity, it is the most widely used method. However, this method has disadvantages:

◆ it is contrary to the principle that managers should not be held accountable for costs they do not control,

◆ it does not relate to actual use of the training facilities or services,

◆ it gives no incentive to the training unit or professional to reduce costs and to improve efficiency.

2. *Selling the service.* Under this system, the training unit is required to sell its services at competitive rates to the other departments, the aim being to cover the cost of the training department (Phillips, 1992; Long, 1990). The main advantages of this method are:

◆ control over training costs (training costs have to remain reasonable or the training function will price itself out of the reach of consumer departments),

◆ a check on the relevance and efficiency of the training offered (training is carefully evaluated by the departmental managers who are required to pay for it).

The disadvantages arising from a fluctuating demand for training services and the consequent planning difficulties seem to outweigh the advantages of this method.

3. *Policy costs.* Under this system, training costs are regarded as company policy costs and are stated as such in the accounts. They are accumulated and shown as a deduction from the gross profit of the business. This approach is simple but can mean that control over training expenditure is less rigorous than it should be. Use of the method can, however, be justified where training is designed to keep human resources available, irrespective of individual departmental needs, as for example in a company-wide, management-development scheme.

Some form of joint responsibility for, or division of, costs appears to be the best solution. A fixed charge can be made to the departments according to the number of staff undergoing training and the duration and type of training given. This charge should be fixed in advance and be a realistic estimate of the expected cost of training an average employee. The amount is known in advance by the departments utilizing the services. The training department is treated as a profit centre in its own right; it is expected to show a profit on the fixed charges levied. In the company accounts, the training department's profit or loss is credited or debited respectively to the training account in the ledger, to which the total of the charges levied on the departments using the service also is debited. The balance on this training account is then incorporated in the final profit and loss account in the usual way (P & E Consulting, n.d.).

D. RECORD KEEPING

Record keeping is not done for its own sake, but as a communication tool. Evidence needs to be presented that a contribution from training is being made on a day-to-day basis, rather than a once-a-year review before the next year's training plan is written (Brown, 1992). In addition, historical and comparative data can be useful in the identification of opportunities. Even the humble flow chart can be used to advantage, to discourage "duplicate efforts and unnecessarily complicated procedures," and to prevent bottlenecks (Kaydos, 1991, 132, 133).

As Haislip (1987) commented:

> *Remember to record, record, record. The progress reports you submit will keep the pump primed for future interest in new training proposals. They will help keep management's attention on training as a means to greater efficiency in planning, production, sales and service. Eventually, you may even be invited to real, live staff meetings, where your sage advice on all sorts of matters will be highly regarded (66).*

◆ ◆ ◆

REPORTING AND SELLING COST/BENEFIT ANALYSIS

These concepts will be familiar to those who have read Chapters 2 and 3, but they are important enough to be reiterated briefly here. Remember that trainers have clients. In most cases, although these clients are internal members of the same organization, they will react favourably to any business initiative only if it fills a need. As there are often alternative methods of meeting any given need, the training professional must understand how decisions are made within his or her organization and build alliances that can support the view that human resources development (HRD) is a priority investment area.

This widening of the power base is possible only if the trainer can speak the language of business (e.g., quantitatively based decision parameters) and if a broad range of stakeholders at all levels are involved. As in our previously cited example, the senior executives who decided that turnover costs their bank $12 500 per person did not question this figure again; it was theirs, they owned it. The involvement of other interests in the development of cost/benefit analyses will obtain the same results. Note that the original bank's internal-audit function had prepared the $25 000 cost estimate. If this figure had been developed in cooperation with the training function, both groups (owners) would vouch for its validity. The primary strategy for "selling" cost/benefit analyses, then, should be to involve as many potential clients as possible in their preparation.

The reporting function is even more culture sensitive in that how one gets a hearing with the real decision-makers depends on how an organization works. What is certain, however, is the necessity of ensuring that training data and results are integrated into the business reporting system yet are separate enough to give them visibility. An individual or a training unit that is combined or lumped into an overall "Personnel Department" budget is unlikely to have much impact on senior decision-makers. Training or HRD needs to be highlighted. The actual format of this reporting process should vary by organization, according to the manner in which training is handled by the accounting system and according to established feedback mechanisms.

◆ ◆ ◆
SUMMARY

The old adage that trainers are "last hired and first fired" is fast becoming obsolete. The credibility issue, however, has become extremely important. All training activities must be costed as training professionals need to compete for funds. Training is an investment. As resources are always scarce, trainers must convince senior managers that funds spent on training will produce an acceptable return.

This chapter showed how to measure both direct and indirect costs, estimate net benefit and support these activities with cost/benefit tracking systems, cost-reduction systems, and appropriate accounting treatment. As well, the client concept and the necessity to sell the costing system to them was discussed in detail. Finally, the idea that the firm's costing methods must be "owned" by senior management is illustrated by using an example that showed how once a cost (in this case for turnover) was accepted, the figure was never questioned again.

Thus, trainers must be culturally sensitive when selling cost/benefit analyses. There are no set formulae or fool-proof methods of calculating training costs.

E X E R C I S E

Getting the Numbers Right

Herritta Humbolt, Marketing Manager for a large mail-order jewellery firm, looked over the error sheets: 5 percent— not bad when you're 95 percent right! A second look, however, pinpointed the problem. Her shipping department mailed out 20 000 orders every week. Five percent of 20 000 is 1000, that's 1000 unhappy customers every week, 4000 every month, 208 000 every year. Now if everyone told 10 friends about her poor service, 2 080 000 people could be struck off her potential customer list yearly. Obviously she had a big problem, especially since mail-order customers are a special breed. They get hooked on the bargains, each one tending to place at least three orders per year.

Five hundred mistakes every week! What kind of mistakes? A quick analysis showed Herritta that wrong addresses and wrong picks (the wrong jewellery) made up 95 percent of the errors.

Herritta checked the stocking systems and the mailing procedures. Satisfied that nothing much could be done to improve shipping methods—a major systems analysis had been completed last year—she turned her thoughts to training.

A meeting of her three shift supervisors (the experts) set out the following performance criteria:

1. *Keyboarding* (order entry, inventory control) with no more than two errors/day
   - three shifts each with three shippers (266.6 orders/day/person)
   - 4 000 orders/week
   - 800 orders/day; 2 errors = .025 percent error rate

2. *Picking* correct goods to ship
   - 0 percent error rate acceptable

3. Proper order *packing* (no tangles, breakage)

- 0 percent error rate acceptable

4. Proper *shipping* (directly related to keyboarding as address labels were produced automatically from order-entry document)
- 0 percent error rate acceptable

Again, using her panel of "experts," Herritta calculated that each error cost:

- $ 1.00 wasted postage
- $ 1.00 labour wasted shipping original order
- $10.00 labour (management/shippers) to correct original mistake
- $ 4.00 phone/fax charges
- $ 9.50 to send replacement order by courier
- $ 5.00 restocking in inventory
  $30.50

Herritta wanted to add in a large amount for lost goodwill, but the General Manager vetoed the idea, telling her to stick with the hard figures.

Herritta contacted a local consultant who agreed to design a training program. She estimated that 15 hours of specialized keyboard training, followed by 5 hours in-house training in picking/ packing/shipping should be supported by 10 hours of general customer-service training. Her rate would be $160/contact hour for the initial training plus 10 hours @ $100/hour for the evaluation. Additional costs would be $500/day for software rental (15 hours), and $16 per trainee for materials.

Although the training would take place at work on three consecutive weekends, seven computers would have to be rented @ $80/computer/weekend. Wages would have to be added in; average yearly wage was $25 000 + $12 000 in benefits. The shippers were promised time-and-a-half (i.e., 1.5 times their *regular wages*). Salary costs for managers were set arbitrarily at $2000.

Additional costs included: record keeping in the Personnel Unit, invoicing, and extra payroll costs $500 (an estimate); insurance on each of the rented computers @ $12.50/day; lunch for eight, (four lunches) @ $11.50/person; coffee, $25 flat cost (two weekends); overhead (extra heat/lights, etc.), $500 (estimated for the entire course).

Assuming that the objective of no more than two errors per day is reached, calculate the return on investment for this proposed training program.

References

Agresta, R.J. 1992. "Renaissance In Human Resources Development: Can We Afford It?" *The Public Manager: The New Bureaucrat* 21, no. 1, 33–37.

Baird, L., and I. Meshoulam. 1992. "Getting Payoff From Investment In Human Resource Management." *Business Horizons* 35, no. 1, 68–75.

Bentley, T. 1991. *The Business of Training.* London: McGraw-Hill Book Company.

Blanden, M., S. Timewell, S. Laurie, V. Lewis, B. Robins, J. Miller, and L. Simon. "Back To Basics." *Banker* 141, no. 779, 22, 24.

Brown, M. G. 1992. "The Baldrige Criteria—Better, Tougher and Clearer For 1992." *Journal for Quality and Participation* 15, no. 2, 70–75.

Bushnell, D. S. 1990. "Input, Process, Output: A Model for Evaluating Training." *Training and Development Journal* 44, no. 3, 41–43.

Cawthray, B. "Reducing Training Costs." (Outline #174). Chippenham: Marsfield Publishing, 1987.

"Front-end analysis." 1989. *Training* 25, no. 7, 43–45.

Geroy, D. G. and P. C. Wright. 1988. "Evaluation Research: A Pragmatic Program Focused Research Strategy for Decision Makers." *Performance Improvement Quarterly* 1 no. 3, 17–26.

Gordon, J. 1991. "Measuring the 'Goodness' of Training." *Training* 27, no. 8 (August): 19–25.

_____. 1992. "Performance Technology: Blueprint for the Learning Organization?" *Training* 29, no. 5, 24–31.

Haislip, O.L. 1987. "How To Treat Training as an Investment." *Training* 24, no. 2, 63–66.

Head, G.E. 1987. *Training Cost Analysis.* Denver: Marlin Press.

Kaydos, W. 1991. *Measuring, Managing, and Maximizing Performance.* Cambridge, Mass.: Productivity Press.

Lombardo, C.A. 1989. "Do the Benefits of Training Justify the Costs?" *Training and Development Journal* 43, no. 12, 60–64.

Long, R.F. 1990. "Protecting the Investment in People—Making Training Pay." *Journal of European Industrial Training* 14, no. 7, 21–27.

P & E Consulting. A photocopied paper distributed through Marsfield Publishing, England, n.d.

Perlitz, M. 1993. "Why Most Strategies Fail Today: The Need For Strategy Innovations." *European Management Journal* 11, no. 1, 114–21.

Phillips, J. J. 1991. "Measuring the Return on HRD." *Employment Relations Today* (Autumn): 329–42.

_____. 1992. "13 Ways to Show You're Worth It: A Guide to HR Evaluation." *The Human Resources Professional* 4, no. 2, 59–63.

Robinson, D.G., and J. Robinson. 1989. "Training For Impact." *Training* 25, no. 8 (August): 34–42.

Spencer, L.M., and S.M. Spencer. 1993. *Competence at Work.* New York: John Wiley & Sons.

Stewart, J., and B. Hamlin. 1992. "Competence-Based Qualifications." *Journal of European Industrial Training* 16, no. 10, 9–16.

Warren, M.W. 1979. *Training for Results.* Menlo Park, Calif.: Addison-Wesley Publishing Co.

Wright, N. B. 1983. "Seven Assumptions that Block Performance Improvement." *CTM: The Human Element* (October/November): 14–22.

Wright, P.C. 1990. "Validating Hospitality Curricula Within Associated-Sponsored Certification Programs: A Qualitative Methodology and a Case Study." *Hospitality Research Journal* 14, no. 1, 117–32.

Wright, P.C., and D.G. Geroy. 1990. "An Investigation of Qualitative Planning Techniques Acceptable to Owners/Managers of Small Business." *Journal of Small Business and Entrepreneurship* 8, no. 4, 41–50.

Wright, P.C., and K. Kusmanadji. 1993. "The Strategic Application of TQM Principles in Human Resources Management." *Training for Quality* 1, no. 3, 5–14.

12

Evaluation

◆ ◆ ◆

INTRODUCTION

valuation is the link that closes the human resources development (HRD) chain, which began with needs assessment. The processes of needs identification and evaluation share common measurement methods. Needs assessment identifies the problem to be solved; evaluation is the process that determines if the problem has been solved. Stated more broadly, *evaluation* is the procedure that determines the effectiveness of a HRD activity (Pace et al., 1991). This chapter examines the reasons evaluations should be conducted and the reasons they are sometimes not conducted. Four types of evaluations—reaction, learning, behaviour, and results—are described in detail. Methods for assessing the effectiveness of training interventions are presented.

◆ ◆ ◆

RATIONALE FOR EVALUATION

Evaluation of activities is done for many reasons. Often, human resource developers wish to determine the value or effectiveness of a workshop or program in order to assist them in a purchase decision. This form of evaluation, called *summative* evaluation, can be used to assess any aspect of the full program including the instructors, the methods, or the facilities (Smith and Brandeburg, 1991).

More commonly, trainers evaluate programs for *formative* reasons: how can the process and outcomes be improved? A question like this can be answered by assessing participant reactions and changes in outcomes.

In addition to these two reasons, there are several other grounds for assessing the development activity. Managers who make decisions about attendance at programs rely on evaluation information. Trainers can use the objectively measured results of a successful program to increase credibility and funding for other programs. Participants can even benefit from a measurement of learning. As seen in Chapter 5, feedback and reinforcement of learning are powerful tools in motivating the employees to continue using the skills. Evaluation methods that use time-series analysis and control groups help determine whether the training program was responsible for observed changes, or whether other factors caused the change.

In addition, senior executives have a right to expect a cost–benefit analysis of any program, including development programs. The preceding chapter presented a method of conducting a cost–benefit analysis of a change program. This chapter discusses nonfinancial evaluations of HRD activities.

◆ ◆ ◆
BARRIERS TO EVALUATION

Despite these laudable reasons for evaluation, very few HRD programs are subjected to an evaluation. One study reported that the average organization allocates only 4 percent of its development budget to evaluation (Stone and Meltz, 1993). Most of the feedback about a course examines only trainee reactions, not the hard data of impact on organizational outcomes (Dixon, 1990).

Trainers cite many reasons for not conducting evaluations. A study of training professionals revealed that most did not do evaluation because it was too time-consuming or expensive; top management did not care; and the effect of the course was too difficult to isolate among many variables (Grider, 1990).

Some developers fear that the negative results will jeopardize their careers. But results are seldom negative in a simplistic fashion. More often, the program sets into motion diverse situations, where trainees and their managers change many behaviours. Viewing evaluation data in a formative light—designed to improve, not punish developers—mitigates the negative effect.

Trainers have reported that evaluation is the most difficult aspect of their job (Gallagan, 1983). The following sections were written to lessen the perceived difficulty of implementing an evaluation program, but first, a summary of the reasons evaluations are important:

◆ to determine if the program has met the objectives, or solved the problem,

◆ to identify the strengths and weaknesses of a program,

◆ to determine the cost-benefits of the program; related to this, evaluation helps ascertain which change technique is the most cost-effective,

◆ to assist managers in the determination of which employees would most likely benefit from the program,

◆ to reinforce the expected results among the participants,

◆ to use the evaluation data to reinforce the value and credibility of HRD programs.

The evaluation of development programs and activities must be planned at the beginning of the training process. The evaluator should use the data and methods from the needs-assessment procedure and the learning objectives to determine if the desired changes have occurred.

◆ ◆ ◆
TYPES OF EVALUATION

The evaluation of HRD programs usually focuses on the impact of the training activity on the trainee. However, other areas that may be evaluated include the value of the training materials, the effect of the trainer, and the influence of the environment to which the development activity is transferred (Pace et al., 1991).

Training materials are evaluated for their ability to produce the desired outcomes. This process of evaluation starts early in the developmental stage and continues to the transfer-of-skills stage. Trainers are assessed for their knowledge, their ability to communicate this information (presentation skills), and their ability to adapt to learner requirements. However, the principal focus of most evaluation is the impact of training on the trainee.

Kirkpatrick (1983) developed a model of evaluation that researchers and writers still find useful. Kirkpatrick's framework considers the impact of development activity on the trainee in three areas: reaction, knowledge of learning, and skills. His fourth sphere is the impact on the organization (results). To simplify, the four key questions to be answered are:

◆ Reaction—Did they like it?

◆ Learning—Did they learn it?

◆ Behaviour—Did they use it on the job?

◆ Results—Did this change organizational effectiveness?

In a survey of 275 companies in Canada, McIntyre (1994) reported that 75 percent evaluated reaction, 30 percent evaluated learning, 16 percent evaluated behaviour, and only 5 percent examined end results, or the actual return on investment.

The next section examines these four levels of evaluation.

I: REACTION

The measurement of trainee reaction or satisfaction is the most common evaluation method. Estimates of its use by trainers range from 50 to 80 percent (Grider, 1990). This method is used most frequently because it is easy to administer, collect, and analyze the data.

Usually, trainees complete a questionnaire at the end of a program asking them to indicate their satisfaction with the content, the facilities, the trainer, the methods, etc. Critics of this measure of satisfaction call these questionnaires "smile" sheets. They claim that all these forms are measuring is the entertainment value of the trainer or the video. This happiness index, they argue, has little to do with a participant doing a better job after training.

Problems: The problems with self-reporting have been thoroughly discussed in Chapter 4. The self-report form is fraught with problems of reliability and validity. A study by Dixon (1990b) of 1400 trainees concluded that there was no significant relationship between how much participants said they enjoyed the course, how the instructors were rated and how much they felt they learned, and how well they actually did on the performance measure. This is not as surprising as it first appears. Many of us have had the experience of listening to someone tell us how to, for example, change a tire or perform a computer operation, have felt satisfied that we really understood the task, but were then unable to do it.

Also, trainers are rewarded for their personality and energy in the room rather than for the amount learned. Numerous research studies have concluded, with a fair degree of consistency, that four major factors underlie effective instructor behaviour (Cranton, 1989). See Figure 12.1 for a description of these factors.

Another explanation for the lack of correlation between enjoyment and learning is that while having learned something feels good, the process of learning is often arduous. All these reasons make the use of "happiness" sheets suspect. However, management seems to want them; they are

FIGURE 12.1 DIMENSIONS OF EFFECTIVE INSTRUCTION

1. *Presentation skill*—the ability to communicate the content in an interesting, clear, and stimulating manner.
2. *Rapport*—the ability to establish and maintain empathy with, concern for, and interaction with the learner.
3. *Structure*—the tendency to have and follow a clear organization or lesson plan.
4. *Evaluation of learning*—the ability to test in a fair and consistent fashion.

economical and easier than any other form of evaluation, and so they will be used. Their usefulness can be increased by careful design.

Optimizing Reaction Forms: Linking the reaction sheet to the objectives of the programs allows the trainer to measure critical factors, such as the effectiveness of the case method in learning a management skill. An example of a well-designed form is presented in Figure 12.2.

FIGURE 12.2 A REACTION FORM

Course or Session: _____

Instructor: _____

Content:
Please answer the following questions using the scale of:
1. Disagree strongly
2. Agree
3. Agree strongly

_____ The material presented will be useful to me on the job.
_____ The level of information was too advanced for my work.
_____ The level of information presented was too elementary for me.
_____ The information was presented in manageable chunks.
_____ Theories and concepts were linked to work activities.
_____ The course material was up-to-date and reliable.

Instructor:
Please rate the instructor's performance along the following dimensions:
_____ Needs improvement
_____ Just right, or competent, effective
_____ Superior or very effective performance

continued

The instructor:

_____ Described the objectives of the session
_____ Had a plan for the session
_____ Followed the plan
_____ Determined trainees' current knowledge
_____ Explained new terms
_____ Used work and applied examples
_____ Provided opportunities for questions
_____ Was enthusiastic about the topic
_____ Presented material clearly
_____ Effectively summarized the material
_____ Varied the learning activities
_____ Showed a personal interest in class progress
_____ Demonstrated a desire for trainers to learn

Perceived Impact:

_____ I gained significant new knowledge.
_____ I developed skills in the area.
_____ I was given tools for attacking problems.
_____ My on-the-job performance will improve.

Please indicate what you will do differently on the job as a result of this course.

_____

_____

_____

_____

Overall Rating:

Taking into account all aspects of the course, how would you rate it?
_____ Excellent _____ Very Good _____ Good _____ Fair _____ Poor

Would you take another course from this instructor?   _____ Yes _____ No

Would you recommend this course to your colleagues? _____ Yes _____ No

Evaluators should allow lots of time at the end of a program for questionnaire completion so that trainees will respond thoughtfully. Responses should be anonymous. If comparisons of reactions between groups is needed (such as new employees versus skilled employees), a code could be developed. Note too that space should be allowed for more open-ended feedback.

Benefits: Reactions obtained at the completion of a program give the trainers immediate feedback and allow them to make quick adjustments to the next course, but these reaction forms serve many other purposes.

Their most obvious contribution to the HRD function is the positive feedback that can be given to management as a sign that the program is effective (at least in the participants' eyes). Data from many participants balance the effect of the one participant who may complain to top management that he or she thought that the course was useless.

Another benefit of reaction questionnaires is a psychological one. Trainees who have had a chance to comment on the program, make suggestions for improvements, and indicate how much they have learned might be more motivated to transfer that learning to the job than others who leave a program with no input.

To summarize, care in the design of the reaction form will result in useful information for the developers and management. The next factor that can be measured is the amount of learning that has occurred.

II: LEARNING

The measurement of the amount of learning that has resulted from a training program is the second easiest method of evaluation. About 20 percent to 30 percent of trainers use this type of evaluation (Grider, 1990). Learning refers to all those cognitive, attitudinal, and skill components that were thoroughly defined and discussed in the chapter on learning objectives. *The Taxonomy of Learning* is a classification system of objectives that provides useful information on the types of learning that can be measured.

The best way to measure learning is to administer a test at the beginning of the program (pre-test) and then administer the same test at the end of the program. Any gains might be attributed to the course or program. (Improvements on this research design are covered in a later section.) The test can be a paper-and-pencil test of knowledge, such as is found in schools and referred to as quizzes, exams, or tests. These types of tests, familiar to everyone who has attended school, use formats like true–false, multiple-choice, short-answer and essay questions. An array of these options is found in Figure 12.3. The test items listed in Part A of Figure 12.3 are termed objectively scored tests, because there is only once correct answer possible.

FIGURE 12.3 A SAMPLE OF TEST ITEMS

Part A: Objectively Scored Tests

True–False

1. A test is valid if a person receives approximately the same result or score at two different testing times. True .... False ....

Multiple Choice

The affective domain of learning refers to:

1. _____ skills
2. _____ attitudes
3. _____ knowledge
4. _____ all of the above
5. _____ 2 and 3

Matching

For each of the governments listed on the left, select the appropriate responsibility for training and place the letter next to the term:

_____ 1. federal   a. displaced workers

_____ 2. provincial   b. language training

_____ 3. municipal   c. student summer work

Short Answer

Kirkpatrick identified four types of evaluation. These are:

_____

_____

_____

_____

Part B: Subjectively Scored Tests

Essay

Describe how and why the process of needs assessment is a critical step in the measurement of the effectiveness of an HRD intervention.

Oral

The measurement of training has many potential benefits. Identify these benefits. Discuss the reasons why, given these advantages of measurement, most trainers do not evaluate training.

Observation Checklist

The customer service representative:

1. Greeted the customer   _____
2. Smiled   _____
3. Offered to help   _____

continued

Rating Scale

Indicate the degree to which you agree or disagree with the statements below:

Scale: 1. Strongly disagree, 2. Disagree, 3. Agree, 4. Strongly agree

During a selection interview, the interviewer:

1. Used behavioural-based questions   1..............4
2. Looked for contrary evidence   1..............4
3. Used probing questions   1..............4

Diaries, Anecdotal Records, Journals

In your journal, write about your experiences working with someone from a different culture. Record the date, time, and reason for the interaction. Describe how you felt and what you learned.

Part B gives some examples of subjectively scored test items. Test items that are considered subjective are essay questions, oral interviews, journals, and diaries. Here, there might be a few acceptable answers, and markers have some latitude in their interpretation of the "correctness" of the answer.

Tests can also be simulations conducted in realistic situations. For example, a pilot could be tested in a virtual-reality airplane. The skills of a drug counsellor could be tested using actors as "drug addicts." A test could be conducted as a role play (for negotiation skills) or a practice session (for tennis certification). These tests are normally called performance tests.

The development of tests that are standardized, reliable, and valid usually require the services of a psychologist or an educational measurement specialist. Practically speaking, most trainers can do a good enough job by following a few procedures. First, the test items should reflect the learning objectives, which have been specified in measurable terms. (See Chapter 5.) Second, the tests should be given to a pilot group to look for errors, inconsistencies, etc. Third, a group of new employees and a group of very experienced or skilled employees should take the test. The results should demonstrate significant differences between the two groups. Only at this point should trainees be given the test.

Tests are useful for reasons other than evaluating changes in learning. A testing hurdle at the end of a course increases trainee motivation to learn the material (Smith and Merchant, 1990). Trainees at General Dynamics took this hurdle seriously. No employee was allowed access to the Manufacturing Resource Planning software until a competency test was passed (Smith and Merchant, 1990).

The information tests provide to trainers is invaluable. In cases of accidents and litigation, the employer can prove that the employee was trained to the necessary levels. Furthermore, if trainees consistently score low on some aspect, the trainer is alerted to the fact that this component of the course needs to be revised. More information may be required or exercises may have to be added to ensure that learning does occur. At General Dynamics, trainers became extremely motivated because the trainees had to learn and could not be brushed off by hinting that they could "always learn misunderstood material back on the job." It is on the job where the real measurement of the payoff of training begins.

III: BEHAVIOUR

A trainee can enjoy a training course and pass a test and still perform poorly on the job. Organizations that fund training are most interested in seeing that the training is transferred to the job. Behaviour is a conventional term for performance. The evaluation of behaviour is really an evaluation of the application of the learning.

There are several ways to assess if skills learned off the job are transferred to the job. Observers such as subject-matter experts and managers can rate job performance before and after training. An example of such a rating form is shown in Figure 12.4.

Other people who interact with the participant can be asked for their views. Customers can be surveyed by phone or by questionnaire about the effectiveness of the behaviour of the newly trained employee. Video taping on-the-job behaviour is a novel way for subject matter experts to judge performance. Subordinates can be asked in interviews or focus groups to rate a manager's new competence in performance appraisal.

These surveys are usually done some time after the course. There must be time for trainees to become comfortable with newly acquired skills and to be given opportunities to demonstrate them. (The chapter on transfer offers suggestions on methods to increase the likelihood of the newly acquired skills being used on the job.) The time lag for assessment of behaviour ranges from a few weeks to as much as two years, in the case of managerial skills. In these cases, performance-appraisal information should highlight the changes.

FIGURE 12.4   SUPERVISORY RATING FORM

Could you please rate the customer-service representative who reports to you on the following dimensions. Check where you would position the representative's performance on each dimension, indicating your rating before (B) and after (A) the "Quality in Customer Service" course:

The scale to be used in rating performance is as follows:
5—Outstanding
4—Superior
3—Satisfactory
2—Minimum standard
1—Needs substantial improvement

Observation Checklist:

Before   **After**

_____   Greets customers in friendly manner   _____
_____   Serves customers promptly   _____
_____   Uses open-ended questions   _____
_____   Identifies barriers to sales   _____
_____   Other   _____

IV: RESULTS

The most difficult step in evaluating a program is the measurement of its impact on organizational indices. Results in organizational terms refer to quantifiable changes in areas like turnover, productivity, quality, time, profitability, customer complaints, etc. In most instances, the objective is to cost the program and determine the net benefit. The preceding chapter was devoted to procedures for doing this costing analysis.

Sometimes, because of the difficulty of measuring quantifiable results (hard data), evaluators turn to soft data as a substitute. Soft data include measures of work climate, feelings and attitudes, and difficult-to-measure skills like decision-making. The reasoning is that if employees can demonstrate initiative, this will ultimately impact on the organization's bottom line, but it is difficult to assign a dollar value to this, or to prove that changes in attitude do make a difference. However, value can still be determined.

Fitz-Enz (1994) provides a concrete example, using the concept of informed judgment. He asked managers to identify the core competencies of managers. Coaching was one of these. He then asked managers to identify the costs or tangible consequences of poor coaching. Assignments that had to be reworked was one such consequence. The frequency of this happening, the cost associated with the hourly rate of poorly coached employees, etc. were all calculated until managers were able to give a plausible figure to the difference between good and poor coaching. In this way, even soft skills or work processes can be assigned value.

There are several other problems associated with measuring results. Not only does it take more time to collect this data, but the actual effect of the training program on changes is most difficult to assess. In one example, all the senior managers of a firm attended a three-week leadership course. The company had always kept records of productivity, etc. and so could compare operating results before the course and after the course. There were no significant changes in these numbers. The conclusion was that the course was a failure. There are some difficulties with this conclusion, however. At the same time that the managers were being trained, a new competitor with an excellent track record in the United States entered the Canadian market. Customers and market share were being lost. No one will ever be able to determine if more customers would have been lost if managers had not used their new skills in quality management and empowering employees to meet client expectations.

Furthermore, the effects of changing managerial behaviour and organizational culture are not felt for years. During that time, factors such as interest rates and competitor actions may impact operating results.

Tightly controlled experimental designs can solve some of these problems, but they are unlikely to happen in a business environment. The next section discusses ways in which evaluators can appropriate the principles of research and apply them to the real world. This is called action research.

◆ ◆ ◆
ACTION RESEARCH DESIGN

The design of the method to determine if a development activity has "caused" the change in behaviour is important. The design allows managers and developers to state that "Yes, the training program, and not some other factor, resulted in these changes." This section presents an array of designs, from the most commonly used to the best. The differences between these designs can be followed more easily by consulting Table 12.1.

TABLE 12.1 ACTION RESEARCH DESIGN			
DESIGN TYPE	**PRE-TEST**	**PROGRAM**	**POST-TEST**
A. Post Only			
	No	Program	Yes
B. Pre and Post			
	Yes	Program	Yes
C. Post only with Control Group			
Trainees	No	Program	Yes
Control	No	No Program	Yes
D. Pre and Post with Control Group			
Trainees	Yes	Program	Yes
Control	Yes	No Program	Yes
E. Time Series			
Trainees	Yes	Program	Test 1 ⸱ Test 2 ⸱ Test n
F. Time Series with Control Group			
Trainees	Yes	Program	Test 1 ⸱ Test 2 ⸱ Test n
Control	Yes	No Program	Test 1 ⸱ Test 2 ⸱ Test n

Although the evaluation process uses many of the same criteria and methods as research, the focus in evaluation is the effect on the organization (Baird et al., 1983). The focus in pure research, with its controlled conditions in the laboratory, is on the testing of hypotheses.

Design A (in Table 12.1), which consists of assessing trainees only after the program, is the most common form of evaluation in organizations. Unfortunately, it tells us almost nothing about the effectiveness of the course. (Sometimes, knowing how much trainees know after the course is important for certification purposes.) We cannot say that trainees have learned or improved because we do not know what they knew or did before they started training. There is no base line of information. Baseline data is usually collected from the three realms of knowledge or skill, on-the-job performance, and organization results. These correspond to learning, behaviour, and results in Kirkpatrick's model. The establishment of base lines is probably the most important task an evaluator can perform. There has to be a picture, a record of what is happening, before anything changes. This should be as normal a picture as possible—i.e., the records should not be contaminated by strikes or measurements taken around holidays, etc. As is demonstrated in Chapters 4 and 13, sometimes feedback of actual performance results in improved performance. So, if you do no other form of measurement, collect baseline data.

Design B is better, because it does collect this information in some form of pre-test. (The word "test" is used in its broadest form. As noted above, it could be simulations, records, interviews, as well as exams and questionnaires.) By pre-testing participants, information about their knowledge and skills gives us baseline data. A change can be measured. The principal problem with this design is that it cannot be said that training caused the change. For example, at the same time that the sales representatives are taking a sales training course, management may decide to change their compensation package. (Multiple solutions are often implemented when management perceives a performance problem.) However, Design B cannot help the evaluator determine if the training program or the new compensation package changed sales performance.

Design C would provide additional information. Design C uses a control group, which does not participate in the sales training. This control group should be composed of sales representatives who are similar in characteristics, such as experience and education, to those receiving the training. (Candidates selected for future training but not attending the first courses would be ideal.) Both the control group and the trainees (the experimental group) would be measured. If there were differences in performance, it would be tempting to conclude that the sales training was effective. However, unless the two groups were identical on key characteristics, we could also hypothesize that the training group were more motivated to sell (because they wanted the course first). The training may have been irrelevant, except for the possibility that it identified the most eager employees.

Design D could solve this problem. The evaluator would assess all sales representatives before the training program. Then, participants for the first course could be chosen on a random basis. (Those not chosen would be assigned to a later course.) The participants would undergo training. Both the control group and the participants would be tested after training. If the trained group improved on the measures, an organizational analyst could reasonably conclude that the training was effective. In addition, the performance of the two groups could be compared and, in some cases, a dollar value to the improvement could be assigned.

However, because some changes in skills are subject to time lags, as has been shown earlier, the best design would include a series of measures of time. This also silences the criticism that some employees improve simply because of maturation or experience.

Design E portrays a plan in which participants are tested following the course, and perhaps every six months afterward for a period of two years. This helps trainers discern if the training simply boosts skills for a while, and then tapers off.

Design F represents the ultimate in training evaluation. The use of pre-tests and post-tests, using a time series, with both the trainees and a control group, allows evaluators to determine cause and effect. This type of design is rarely implemented. It is simply too expensive and time-consuming for most human resource departments. However, in the long run, developmental programs that are ineffective probably waste more time and money.

◆ ◆ ◆
USING THE RESULTS

The clients of the action-research results include the human resource developers, management who approved and funded the intervention, and potential participants and their managers. Their two questions are: Did it work? and Was it worth it? Trainers may be reluctant to evaluate their efforts objectively; the task is made less difficult by presenting the results in context. Context means that the users of the information must understand the rationale for the evaluation and the limitations of the research design. In addition, users should be given some understanding of the meaning of the information collected.

Raw data is of little use to management, unless they are able to compare them and assign value to them. Comparative information helps determine value. For example, the data that reveal that an instructor is perceived to be competent by 70 percent of the students become more meaningful when other information reveals that other instructors consistently receive a 90-percent competency rating. Also, knowing that a training program resulted in a $50 000 increase in sales only becomes relevant when compared to the costs of other interventions. If, for example, supervisory attention and support for sales representatives result in a net benefit of $10 000, then the effectiveness of a training intervention can be accurately evaluated.

Value also implies significance. In practical terms, is it significant (i.e., does it really make any difference) if health and safety offices scored 72 percent on a safety test, while the control group scored 58 percent? Significance has many meanings. Statisticians use it as a measure meaning that the difference was real and important. (Organizations can use experts or software to tabulate data for significant differences.) This would be the numerical meaning, a first step in determining significance.

A second meaning may be a legislative one. The 20-percent improvement in safety knowledge may be irrelevant if safety officers are required by law to know 100 percent of the course content. But managers may find even 100 percent insignificant if accidents and claims do not decrease as a result of the course. Conversely, some managers want to hear positive comments about the course and weigh these comments as much as changes in job behaviour. The conclusion is not that you can't win; the conclusion is that multiple measures with control groups must be used.

◆ ◆ ◆
PRINCIPLES OF EVALUATION

◆ Evaluation should be planned at the same time that a needs identification is done and an intervention (training course, developmental activity) is designed.

◆ The design should use at least a pre and post measure, with the control group consisting of units or participants scheduled for later interventions.

◆ Multiple measures should be taken. Evaluations should consider measuring not just reactions but learning, behaviour, and results. The measurement of these should look not only at operation figures but should include surveys of observers.

Table 12.2 outlines the levels of evaluation, the data to be collected, and the method of collecting data.

TABLE 12.2 EVALUATION MATRIX		
Level	**Data**	**Method**
Reaction	Opinions	Forms
	Attitudes	Questionnaires
Learning	Knowledge	Objectively Scored Tests (true-false, multiple-choice, short-answer, etc.) Subjectively Scored Tests (essays, papers, interviews)
	Skills	Simulations, role plays,
	Attitudes	Role plays, surveys
Behaviour	Performance	Supervisors, subordinates, customers, etc. complete rating forms or participate in interviews
Results	Hard Data	Records from production, finance, human resources
	Soft Data	Surveys and interviews

◆ ◆ ◆
ISSUES IN EVALUATION

The presentation of the various research designs may have only convinced the readers that training is difficult, costly, and risky. The reaction to these problems is that, in reality, most managers do not conduct evaluations. This short-term cop-out works when profits are high and when the participants are clapping loudly. However, when organizational performance deteriorates and employees become anxious, the training department should have some evaluative data available to prevent the elimination of their function.

The key words in conducting an evaluation in an organization are feasibility and flexibility. Trainers and developers must have some elementary training in the setting of measurable objectives, the measurement of their attainment, and reasonable research designs. With this understanding, trainers should be able to manage a crude evaluation that will answer the critical question: Did the program make a difference?

Coupled with feasible evaluation is the concept of a flexible evaluation. Trainers should look at multiple ways to gather information. Given that there are organizational constraints, trainers should be prepared to be flexible in their approaches. For example, if the company does not want to divide potential trainees into control and trained groups, then the trainer should train in stages. The "control" group simply becomes the next group to be trained (if the program is successful).

Given all these prescriptions for a healthy measurement program, let us use the principles of feasibility and flexibility to design a "model," but practical, program.

A MODEL EVALUATION

The General Hospital is required by provincial law to train all its employees in WHMIS (Workplace Hazards Materials Information Systems). In order to comply with this legislation, and to establish proof that everyone has knowledge of WHMIS (in case of an accident, and subsequent legislation), the General Hospital has devised the following plan for training.

Phase I: Conduct a needs assessment. The General Hospital needs to know not only whether all employees have the required levels of knowledge about hazardous materials, but whether in fact they can apply them on the job. The needs assessment is therefore composed of two parts: a knowledge test and an observation of workplace practices.

The knowledge test consists of 100 items, mainly multiple choice and short answer. An example would be:

> *Carbon monoxide is a*
> 1. *gas*
> 2. *liquid*
> 3. *solid*

The short-answer items asked questions such as "When sulphuric acid is spilled on the skin, what first aid procedures are appropriate?"

Then safety officers were trained to observe safety behaviour of employees on the job, using a standardized checklist.

In these ways, a base line of knowledge and behaviour was established.

Phase II: The training course was conducted (using a combination of presentations, videos, and multimedia interactive computer training).

Phase III: Before leaving the training room, all trainees were required to complete the same knowledge test as previously completed.

A reaction form was designed to measure satisfaction with the content, the instructor, and the learning technologies. Participants were also asked to identify barriers to the implementation of safe practices and to develop, with the help of the instructor, a program to ensure the transfer of the newly acquired skills and knowledge.

Both the knowledge tests and the reaction forms were analyzed to determine the weaknesses and strengths of the program.

Phase IV: One month and then six months after the course, safety officers observed the workplace practices of all employees.

Statistical analysis of the differences before the training course and after the training course established that the course was effective in increasing knowledge about WHMIS and in improving safe workplace behaviour.

Phase V: Records had always been kept on the number of accidents, workers' compensation claims, sick days due to accidents, etc. These were analyzed, comparing the data before the course and after the course. In this way, the trainers were able to show that the WHMIS training course had the following bottom-line impact:

	Before	After
Accidents	1129	351
Sick days	1345	121
Claims	274	107

Students who wish to develop their own model evaluation systems are encouraged to complete the exercises at the end of the chapter.

◆ ◆ ◆
SUMMARY

This chapter examined the reasons why trainers do not conduct four levels of evaluation, and why they should. The evaluation levels of reaction, training, behaviour, and results were described. Problems in each of the measurement steps were identified, and practical solutions proposed.

EXERCISES

1. Since you are reading this text, you are probably part of a course in training and development. Within teams, develop a reaction form that rates the effectiveness of the course, the instructor, the methods, the instructional technology, etc. Design a method to measure the amount of learning that has occurred in one session or module.

2. Return to the exercise described in Chapter 4, "Needs Analysis." Assume that a training intervention occurred and that the reaction to the program has already been assessed. Devise ways of measuring any changes in learning, behaviour, or results. Try to use the same instruments or techniques that established the base line or gap. Design the best or "model" evaluation program will ensure that you can state to management, "These changes are attributable to the training intervention."

References

Baird, L.S., C.E. Schneier, and D. Laird. 1983. *The Training and Development Sourcebook*. Amherst, Mass.: Human Resource Development Press.

Cranton, P. 1989. *Planning Instruction for Adult Learners*. Toronto: Wall & Thomson.

Dixon, N.M. 1990a. *Evaluation: A Tool for Improving HRD Quality*. Belmont, CA: University Associates.

_____. 1990b. "The Relationship Between Trainee Responses on Participant Reaction Forms and Post-test Scores."*Human Resource Development Quarterly* 1, no. 2, 129–37.

Fitz-Enz, J. 1994. "Yes ...You Can Weigh Training's Value." *Training* 31, no. 7 (July): 54–58.

Gallagan, P. 1983. "The Numbers Game: Putting Value on HRD." *Training and Development Journal* 37, no. 8 (August): 48–51.

Grider, D.T. 1990. "Training Evaluation."*Business Magazine* 17, no. 1 (January–March): 20–24.

Kirkpatrick, D.L. 1983. "Four Steps to Measuring Training Effectiveness." *Personnel Administrator* 28, no. 11, (November): 19–25.

McIntyre, D. 1994. *Training and Development 1993: Policies, Practices and Expenditures*. Toronto: The Conference Board of Canada.

Pace, R.W., C.P. Smith, and G.E. Mills 1991. *Human Resource Development: The Field*. Englewood Cliffs, N.J: Prentice-Hall.

Smith, J.E., and S. Merchant. 1990. "Using Competency Exams for Evaluating Training." *Training and Development Journal* 44, no. 8 (August): 65–71.

Smith, M.E., and D.C. Brandenburg. 1991. "Summative Evaluation." *Performance Improvement Quarterly* 4, no. 2, 35–38.

Stone, T., and N. Meltz. 1993. *Human Resource Management in Canada*. 3rd ed. Toronto: Holt, Rinehart & Winston.

13

Management
Development

INTRODUCTION

anagement development is separated from employee training for several reasons: (1) the techniques tend to be different (e.g., coaching, mentoring); (2) in Canada, per-capita training expenditures have tended to be higher for managers than for other employees; (3) management work is less predictable and (directly) measurable than many other jobs; (4) poor managers can have a catastrophic effect on an entire organization's ability to survive. Of all the human resource development (HRD) functions, however, management development is perhaps the most misunderstood and poorly implemented. Yet the single characteristic that distinguishes a successful organization, large or small, from the others is the calibre of the management team (McCallum, 1993).

The problems associated with program design and delivery are many, ranging from the changing nature of management work to organizational politics. In fact, Lees (1992), who regards management development as "the socio-political domain of management," lists 10 reasons why organizations invest in their managers:

1. *Functional—Performance:* the most common superficial rationale, this concept is aimed at improving direct managerial functioning and, by implication, improving corporate performance.

2. *Agriculture:* the desire to "grow" managers.

3. *Functional—Defensive:* the perceived need to acquire a reserve of skills and knowledge for some undefined future.

4. *Socialization:* to develop a common ethos or culture.

5. *Political Reinforcement:* to initiate cultural redesign toward norms as defined by senior management.

6. *Organizational Inheritance:* enhancement of the ability "to climb the corporate ladder."

7. *Environmental Legitimacy:* attempts to gain favour with outside stakeholders by giving out politically correct signals about the environment and other social issues.

8. *Compensation:* management development is used as a form of payment or compensation.

9. *Psychic Defence:* training is seen as a defensive mechanism, protecting the manager from subordinates so they will continue to cooperate.

10. *Ceremonial:* the legitimation and conformation of the social order and/or the progression through the social order.

A management-development program based solely on one or any combination of these concepts will create confusion and in Lees's words "pose massive problems," as the results of investing in management development cannot be evaluated adequately against other more tangible opportunities. Thus, a substantial percentage of the development programs fail to meet either senior management's or the participants' expectations (Whetton and Cameron, 1995).

◆ ◆ ◆
THE STRATEGY FOR MANAGEMENT DEVELOPMENT

Despite, or perhaps because of, the many failures, a new model of management development is emerging. Closely linking the process to strategy formation (Sullivan, 1993), those using the paradigm are adamant that:

> *the only legitimate reason to put in place an executive development program is that it is integral to the business strategy. Any other reason will result, at best, in a series of interesting training programs tangentially related to the business or, at worst, in a variety of expensive activities conveying irrelevant or contradictory messages (McCall, 1992, 25).*

Thus, the focus is not on the individual but toward the cultivation of collective managerial talents, capabilities, and perspectives that will allow the organization as a whole to cope with the future (Vicere and Graham, 1990; Bolt, 1993).

Based on the general concepts outlined in Chapter 2, the practical application of this ideal requires an in-depth understanding of two factors: the characteristics of excellent companies and the nature of managerial work. Without a firm grounding in both these concepts and a commitment to re-engineer current processes, it is unlikely that appropriate strategies will be in place to support effective management development (Vogl, 1993).

As well, it has been stated previously (Chapter 4) that training must fit into the organization's culture, and conscious cultural formation begins with strategy (Geroy and Wright, 1994) in that employees use exhibited corporate values in making career-oriented decisions (Isaac et al., 1994). A major purpose of management development activity, then, is to build commitment to strategic intent (Vicere, 1992), so that strategy-formation activities and management-development processes support one another because both aim to create excellence (Figure 13.1).

FIGURE 13.1   A Model for Management Development

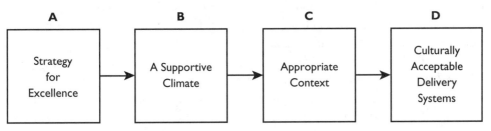

Managers who embark upon an excellence development strategy are therefore more likely to create successful management-development programs, as the behavioural characteristics they wish to instill in employees are known. In these organizations, there is often an intentional effort to expose employees to multiple functions within the enterprise. The success or failure of a management-development program, therefore, seems to be closely tied to the presence of a sustainable business strategy capable of coping with change (Bolt, 1993; Harris, 1993).

Although difficult to achieve, this picture of a strategically driven company is not hard to describe; eight management principles combine to foster the excellence concept:

1. leadership is seen as a "renewable resource" not easily copied or stolen;

2. managers are given autonomy appropriate to their expertise and position;

3. the act, or the art, of management is viewed as a process of interpretation, not as a process of control;

4. involvement, or ownership, is seen as crucial;

5. there is a strong market orientation, which increasingly means a focus on the customer;

6. the absolutes of total quality management (TQM) are accepted and practised;

7. controlled chaos is accepted, fostering innovation and change;

8. integrity or sound business ethics are part of a cultural orientation that leads to respect in the community and enhanced customer relations.*

These eight factors fit into the model as shown in Figure 13.2.

After devising these strategies aimed at creating excellence, management-development structures are put in place to socialize employees into the organization and its culture. The application of these structures—training, job rotation, coaching, etc.—will be discussed in detail later in this chapter, but the key issue here is that they be viewed as symbols of culture in which the rites and rituals of the management role are enacted through design, content, and process (Preston, 1993). Any management-development program, therefore, must be designed with the knowledge that the format will send a message to managers and employees alike. For example, if the programs are used as rewards for those who do not disturb the status quo, all innovation is likely to cease, as managers will find their greatest rewards in the application of established systems and procedures (Stewart and Fondas, 1992).

As suggested previously by Lees (1992), then, the rationale for conducting development activities can be flawed, so that management rites and rituals are self-serving and counterproductive, especially when practised

---

*Holt's 1989 concepts are supported by a variety of sources including: McCall, 1992; McCallum, 1993; Vicere, 1992; Farquhar, 1990–91; Crosby, 1993; Wright and Kusmanadji, 1994.

FIGURE 13.2 The Strategy for Excellence in Management

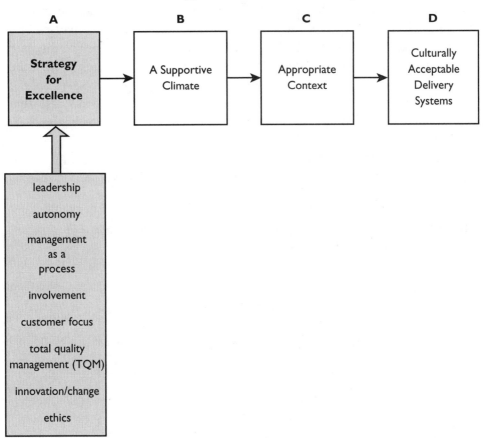

within a poorly functioning or ineffective culture. It is unlikely that truly effective management development can be practised in poorly managed organizations, especially those that are not strategy-driven. Hence, to repeat, of all the HRD functions, management development is perhaps the most misunderstood and poorly implemented.

◆ ◆ ◆

THE CLIMATE FOR MANAGEMENT DEVELOPMENT

The concepts of linking management development to strategy within the context of creating a well-managed company have a practical purpose, for management development will flourish only if the climate or culture is supportive (Figure 13.3). Management development activity must be institutionalized into the cultural fabric of the organization and is a particularly vulnerable activity because programs can be costly and often are directed toward those whose status and salary may make them think they need no more training (Sherwood, 1992). As well, the development of people is rarely given first priority. In fact, it is "difficult to make a good case that development should be a first priority. With no shot at top priority, development must still compete with other compelling issues to make the priority list" (McCall, 1992). The key activities that create an organization's supportive structure fit into that part of the management-development model illustrated in Figure 13.3.

FIGURE 13.3 **Creating a Supportive Climate for Management Development**

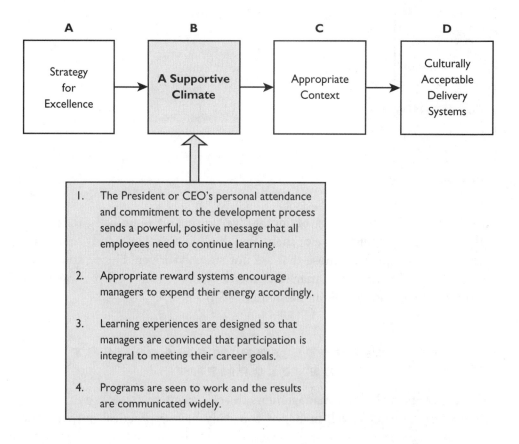

Although nonparticipants should not be completely left out (Harris and Field, 1992), the results of participating should lead to obvious rewards. This approach takes time, as the development program needs to build a track record or history. It must be remembered that it takes 10 to 20 years to develop general managerial talent (Kotter, 1988) and that length of tenure is directly related to high performance. Participation in development activity, therefore, must be given sufficient long-term encouragement so that the program comes to be regarded as an essential part of both executive career plans and the firm's strategic intent (Vicere and Graham, 1990; Slater, 1989).

A common example of failure to institutionalize management development is the use of an overseas assignment. In many organizations, the promise of foreign service is not realized since the managers are forgotten while they are abroad and no suitable position is made available upon their return (Gomez-Mejia and Balkin, 1987). What could be a sought-after opportunity for career enhancement, therefore, can be regarded as a dead end. Senior managers should be aware, then, that every posting, every transfer sends a message to employees. If a technique like job rotation (or any other method) is to be used in a developmental sense, it must be a planned activity that fits into an organization-wide learning-from-experience paradigm (Robinson and Wick, 1992).

◆ ◆ ◆

THE NATURE OF MANAGEMENT WORK

Having described the environment in which management-development programs must operate, attention is now turned to the work managers do, for how we develop managers is closely linked to the importance placed on the various aspects of the manager's role. Stewart's (1984) address to the World Congress on Management Development contained a model of management work that, with some modification, has continued to prove useful in a wide variety of situations. Her concept was based on the analogy that a job is a flexible space surrounded by constraints, enclosing basic, often routine job demands or functions (the core) and an area of choice, or discretion (Figure 13.4).

Jobs are dynamic, so the lines are wavy, representing change. Managers have choices within the job parameter to do or not do some tasks, but no two managers would make identical choices. The choices any individual makes

FIGURE 13.4 The Manager's Job

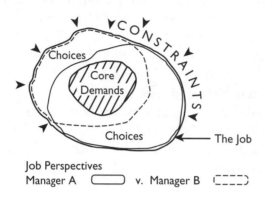

Job Perspectives
Manager A ⬭ v. Manager B ⸤‗‗‗⸥

Source: R. Stewart, *Management Development and Implications for Managerial Choice*, from an address to the World Congress on Management in London, England (June 1984), as reported by Cawthray in Outline 2.14 (c. 1988). Chippenham: Marsfield Publications Ltd.

may emphasize some aspects of the job at the risk of neglecting others, since there are competing demands from:

◆ peers: consulting, planning, etc.;

◆ the boss: accepting responsibility for long-term objectives;

◆ subordinates: coaching, communicating, providing feedback, organizing, etc.;

◆ the system: paperwork, routine obligations;

◆ external forces: accepting/avoiding—innovation, change, fear, insecurity in self, in others;

◆ new technology: re-engineering, change, employee reactions.

At the core of this concept are basic, sometimes routine, job demands or tasks originating from the need to maintain day-to-day activity. Again, these arise from interactions with peers (for assistance or advice), the boss (for effective short-term performance), subordinates (for guidance, training, etc.), the system (conforming with work regulations), external forces (customers, suppliers, the public), and self (meeting personal standards). Depending on the situation, these core activities can be the most visible aspect of the manager's role (Broadwell, 1993).

This whole invariably is surrounded by constraints (Figure 13.4). As might be expected, constraints are factors in the internal and external environments that influence the job holder:

- financial limitations

- company policies

- economic and market conditions

- government legislation

- technological advances/limitations

- demographic considerations

- union activities

- free-trade opportunities and threats.

These largely uncontrollable issues form parameters within which every manager must work. They construct the limitations or emerging opportunities that shape long-term organizational strategy.

It has been predicted that, to survive, most private-sector organizations will need to be re-engineered, in whole or in part, during the next decade, reducing the middle-management workforce by approximately 75 percent. The managerial responsibilities of those who remain will change dramatically, so that two new types of managers—process managers and employee coaches—will emerge. Process managers will oversee a re-engineered process from beginning to end. For example, a process manager might be responsible for managing order fulfilment or product development. Employee coaches will be responsible for supporting and nurturing employees (Hogarty, 1993; Hammer and Champy, 1993).

Even if this drastic scenario is not realized, it is certain that the era of the specialist manager is ending. A new generation of generalists will need to be trained to understand not only finance, accounting, or marketing but economic trends and political issues (Zeidenberg, 1993).

Stewart's (1984) model fits well with the management (core) versus leadership (discretionary) dichotomy. At the core, individuals are taught how to operate within systems that are more or less established. This activity is defined as management. The discretionary portion of the model describes leadership in that a leader takes the organization in directions or into performance parameters never before attempted (Bass, 1985). Obviously there is some overlap, but for our purposes the two functions will be treated separately.

As before, our model takes into account the nature of management work. A management-development program should encompass both core and discretionary elements (Figure 13.5).

FIGURE 13.5 **The Context of a Management Development Program**

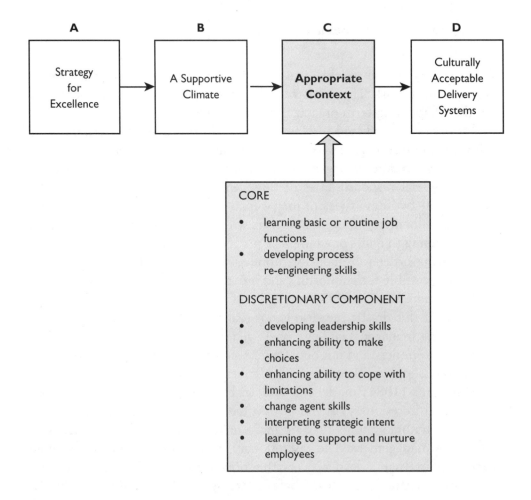

◆ ◆ ◆
THE MANAGEMENT DEVELOPMENT PROCESS

CHOOSING A METHOD FOR MANAGEMENT DEVELOPMENT

As illustrated previously, when developing a method, three major factors must be considered: the firm's long-term strategies as they relate to the development of the work environment or culture, the role of the manager within that culture, and the changing external environment (constraints and opportunities) that inevitably will transform both the organization and the nature of managerial work. The only alternative is to maintain the status quo and continue to offer traditional, course-based, individually oriented learning experiences.

Revolution is underway, however, in the way North American companies use education to improve managerial performance. The shift was caused, in part, by the recent increase in the number of M.B.A.'s, many of whom proved to be poor managers despite their impressive credentials. Senior managers are now looking for programs that give their managers the skills to be effective in the emerging nonhierarchical corporate structure, hence the focus on developing a supportive climate and carefully defining what managers do.

Within this context, Stewart's (1984) analogy has proven useful because two major forces are at work. The first is the need to teach the specific skills required by each level of management (the core); the second is the much broader imperative of cultivating strategic leadership and innovative skills (discretionary activity). In essence, then, effective strategies for individual development are not always the same as effective strategies for organizational development (Pickering and Matson, 1992).

THE CORE: DEVELOPING MANAGERS

Since all management jobs contain routine functions that must be mastered (Figure 13.5), efficient learning processes need to be in place within the organization. The subject matter can range from computer-systems manipulation to more sophisticated concepts like those covered in General Electric's Business Management Course; here, basic concepts such as business strategy, economics, finance, and marketing are taught to potential general managers.

The bulk of the core, however, is usually transmitted through localized in-house training focusing on the specific skills required by each level of management. For example, at the supervisory level the program might cover basic personnel and company procedures, along with interpersonnel problem-solving (Digman, 1986; Noel and Charon, 1992). Here, participants learn the "company way." There is little need for theory-based course work that cannot be applied to day-to-day management. The manager's task is to develop sufficient skill to meet minimum performance levels.

Traditionally, most of the literature and theory concerned with training has focused on the needs and experiences of large-company managers. Yet it is often managers in smaller firms that require the most training. The core skills are most important in this context, as managers in a great many smaller businesses are learning that rejuvenating their organizations hinges on the application of basic principles of good business practice—always with the understanding that there are no panaceas (Steck, 1993). Stewart's (1984) model (Figure 13.4), then, can be adapted to both large and smaller businesses, although the smaller firm may, of necessity, devise a more informal management-development system.

Core skills often are identifiable, tangible competencies. The "how to" of acquiring these basic competencies begins with a well-developed orientation program and continues throughout the manager's career as part of the performance-review process. Although the effectiveness of current appraisal systems has been questioned, one-on-one reviews still play an important role in the mentoring procedure that provides a platform for discussion of achievements (Lester, 1993).

Aside from formal orientation packages, the learning methods employed in the core may vary. In-house courses in larger firms, outside courses, M.B.A. programs, and even board games have been tried (Gunsch, 1993). A key function, however, and one that bridges the core and discretionary concepts, is coaching (see Chapter 6, pp. 119–24). Coaching has two distinct functions:

1. improving performance and skill level,

2. establishing relationships that allow the coach to enhance the trainee's psychological development and ability to accept assignments of ever-increasing complexity and difficulty (Popper and Lipshitz, 1992; Elliott, 1993).

In fact, at senior levels, executive development counselling, or coaching by an outsider, is an alternative with a high success rate because the consultant can assess needs objectively and provide practical developmental support and training techniques (Kessler, 1992). Of course, coaching is ineffective if the organizational culture does not allow the intense person-to-person inter-action necessary to devise individual learning projects that do not threaten the trainee. Hence, the previous emphasis on the type of climate necessary to support development.

When developing basic managerial skills (the core), the key issue is to ensure direct transfer from the "learning venue" to the "work venue." It is unlikely that passive learning will be sufficient. Whatever method is used, participants must engage in activities that require decision-making and actu-ally deal with the consequences of their decisions. If the training does not provide for direct "hands-on" experience (e.g., a coaching assignment), then the time frame between learning and application must be kept to a min-imum (Hoberman and Mailick, 1992).

THE DISCRETIONARY FACTOR: DEVELOPING LEADERS

It has been shown that excellent companies are built primarily on innovation and change. Leadership development, therefore, takes place within the con-text of strategically linked change-management activity (Bramley, 1989). Without an organization-wide commitment to continuous improvement, leadership training is unlikely to flourish—if indeed it exists at all (Colledge and March, 1993).

Within the appropriate setting, however, much can be accomplished. Firms that enhance leadership potential invariably "focus on a broad range of activities (including training), but emphasize on-the-job training as the primary vehicle for development" (McCall, 1992). This learning-from-experience approach is based on action-learning theories suggesting that exposure to rich development opportunities provides the optimum condi-tions for executive development. Learning by doing—through business sim-ulation, wilderness survival trips, interactive team training, even exposure to humanities courses dealing with values central to leadership—is all part of the action design. Job rotation, however, is the main activity that links edu-cation, training, and reforms in the workplace (Raskas and Hambrick, 1992; Rothwell, 1992).

Exposure to many functions within the firm as part of an ongoing career-development program broadens individuals, providing them with multiple perspectives and possibly even multiple areas of expertise. Indeed, the practice of line managers temporarily taking staff jobs has met with some success (Zemke, 1987). A variety of cross-job and project-based experiences can be created, therefore, to create a pool of leadership talent capable of responding to emergencies and rapidly changing business environments, while making the constant incremental changes necessary for corporate survival (McCall, 1992; Miller, 1993).

Of course, some organizations can benefit from job rotation more than others. In highly technical environments, for example, it may be difficult for some employees to be productive in areas for which they are untrained. "The professional rigors of the field [may be] just too great" (Raskas and Hambrick, 1992, 13). Here, short-term assignments and planned observations may prove useful, so that nontechnical managers gain familiarity with technical processes without actually managing the unit or division (Rothwell, 1992).

A practical management-development process, however, revolves around coaching (Yager, 1993). As detailed in Chapter 6, the effective coach works one-on-one with managers at all levels to increase people's ability to lead. Presuming that the organization is committed to excellence, that the climate is conducive to learning, and that the strategic intent of the management-development program is known to both coach and participant, they work together to: (1) identify the changes required in particular areas; (2) provide the perspective necessary to be effective; and (3) develop a plan to try out new behaviours (Cunningham, 1991).

Working from a confidential individual-development needs analysis provides managers with opportunities to learn and to grow through intelligent risk taking and identifies how they should divide their careers between experiences within their own networks (where they might have the most visible impact) and other assignments (that help them rise above their functional experience and training). The nature and the scope of acceptable projects and assignments is unlimited (even including temporary residence at an important customer's work site), but they must be chosen carefully because they should be neither too easy nor too difficult (Elliot, 1993).

Coaching assignments, then, need to be chosen with care and managed carefully, as managers fulfil two distinct roles: superior and mentor or helper.

Job assignments must be challenging and must be chosen with considerable input from the participants. As well, goals should be specific and well understood. Further, participants need to be protected from backlash, especially if they try to change the corporate culture. Criticism should be kept to a minimum, but feedback must be intensive. Finally, more formal program assessment and subsequent refinements should occur at fixed intervals (Harris and Field, 1992; Wexley and Latham, 1991). The key is to create a greater stake in the organization through the expansion of roles, authority, and responsibilities by recognizing that empowering people acts to produce excellence (Gilbert and Whiting, 1993; Smith, 1990).

Two final elements arising from the coaching process are the sometimes elusive assumption that management development is an ongoing process, not a program, and the vital concept of self-development (Smith, 1991). The idea that personal and professional learning is a lifelong activity has permeated our society. Coaching as a developmental method is no exception. Vicere (1992) suggests that leadership enhancement is a cyclical process in which an organization is engaged in "continuous" effort to identify, develop, and integrate a team of strategic leaders. Whittaker (1993) describes coaching as a "continual" transfer of skills, while Yager (1993) and Gaines (1993) also stress the need for "continuous" encouragement. Finally, Wolff (1993) indicates that coaching should become a regular part of a manager's routine. As strategy formation is an ongoing, dynamic phenomenon and as coaching is linked to strategy, similarly, management development must constantly remain flexible and sensitive to both internal and external environmental change.

Just as in sports the coach cannot play the game, in business the coach cannot personally manage every subordinate's career development. Indeed, an increasing number of organizations are creating systems that encourage employees to enhance both skills and leadership capabilities through self-development (Huntley, 1991). As self-development is described fully in Chapter 6, the topic will not be treated in detail here. It should be noted, however, that this model of personal development is not confined to professional life but includes social and recreational achievement. This holistic approach becomes a conscious model for planned achievement (Alder, 1992).

At this point, a final look at our model (Figure 13.6) is appropriate. The methods (delivery systems) we choose must fit into the organization's cul-

FIGURE 13.6 The Delivery of a Management Development Program

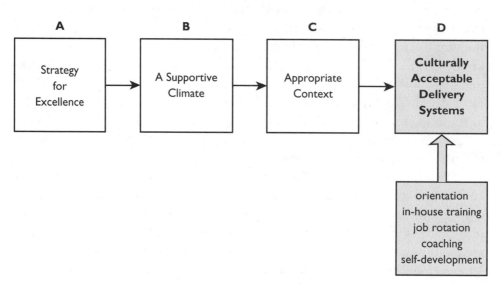

ture and must be able to transfer or develop appropriate skills, knowledge, and attitudes directly related to the core and to the discretionary parts of the manager's job (Figure 13.5). This system is not likely to work well unless the organization's climate is supportive (Figure 13.3), and a supportive climate will not necessarily grow spontaneously. A well-designed strategy for excellence is the best starting point (Figure 13.2). Working backward through the model (Figure 13.1), therefore, illustrates how each function (strategy through delivery) acts as a foundation that supports the next step.

◆ ◆ ◆

THE TRAINER'S ROLE IN MANAGEMENT DEVELOPMENT

Having outlined a two-pronged (skills versus leadership) approach to management development that includes very few traditional, course-based learning experiences, we now examine the role of the trainer. Again, tied to the previous assertion that excellent companies are characterized by their capacity to foster innovation and to manage change, the trainer's emerging role is that of change agent and internal consultant (Christianson, 1989). As early as 1979, Lippitt and Nadler forecast three roles for trainers:

- as learning specialists and instructors;

- as program administrators;

- as contributors to organizational problem-solving.

Their predictions have been accurate, especially the suggestions concerning how trainers might work as internal consultants:

- providing expert advice to management, usually about the appropriateness and value of training options;

- advising management as to what environmental changes are necessary to support and maintain training;

- providing a range, or a continuum, of alternatives;

- taking part in a wide variety of problem-solving processes.

To these roles can be added the need for an increased emphasis on the organizational-development (OD) model (see Chapter 6, pp. 128–130)—1) problem identification; 2) consultation with experts; 3) data gathering and preliminary diagnosis; 4) feedback to stakeholders; 5) joint diagnosis; 6) action; 7) follow-up evaluation and feedback (Svantet et al., 1992)—as OD's focus is shifting increasingly toward measuring productivity, performance, and profit (Van Eynde et. al., 1992). This approach should be designed to mesh with current research in adult development that amalgamates personal and institutional needs into a framework that:

- combines modes of learning into a process of irreversible qualitative change involving planned stages leading toward new personal and professional perspectives;

- develops a global outlook that broadens these life perspectives;

- accounts for organizational environment or culture, stressing that a supportive climate is a critical factor that allows a manager to continue along a developmental path (Morris, 1992).

In specific terms, at the corporate level the trainer focuses on the development of mechanisms that allow for talent to be matched with opportunity—e.g., succession planning, executive review committees, appraisal systems—as well as policies and procedures concerning special assignments, responsibility enhancement, staff assignments, job rotation, and reward systems (McCall, 1992). To this high-level developmental activity is added an individual thrust that includes:

- assessment of leadership potential;

- assessment of strengths and weaknesses;

- assessment of previous experience (McCall, 1992);

- assisting managers to review their jobs and their potential choices;

- discussing (with both superior and subordinate) what learning experiences would help an individual to become more innovative;

- designing career paths;

- advising on an appropriate mix of learning experiences;

- managing the learning process to integrate learning with work;

- creating learning communities and learning groups;

- developing peer learning modules;

- consulting with both superiors and subordinates on the self-directed learning process;

- identifying and cataloguing sources of assistance, both internal and external;

- identifying areas where assistance would be accepted and valued;

- relating learning experiences to individual learning styles and suggesting appropriate changes in direction (Kolb, 1984; Stewart, 1984).

This list must be augmented by carefully targeted training (McCall, 1992) that includes coaching potential coaches, and evaluation.

Evaluation deserves special mention, because few companies bother with it. At the very least, patterns should be noted (both successes and problems) and refinement made in any of the critical variables, e.g., Who was to conduct management development? How? At what point in their careers? Who should coach? "Only if the company has the capacity for systematic reflection and reassessment can ... [management development] programs achieve their full potential ..." (Raskas and Hambrick, 1992, 16).

The challenge for trainers, then, is to respond to changing economic and social climates by creating customized, strategically linked, needs-driven processes designed to meet both individual and organizational goals. They will have to "understand fully the competencies required in the global business environment and the most effective methods for developing these competencies ...," designing learning experiences, both informal and formal, in " ... a more conscious and reflective way." The ideal would be to form a "learning partnership" in which all the stakeholders—top management, managers, professionals, employees, customers, suppliers—share responsibility for designing and implementing the best possible management-development experiences (Mann and Staudenmier, 1991).

◆ ◆ ◆
SUMMARY

Management development is a process stemming from a strategic plan that creates a supportive climate or environment. Only then can appropriate content be designed and delivery systems developed.

The strategic-planning and supportive-climate concepts are more likely to be in place when management attempts to foster the excellence concept by creating an organization in which leadership is regarded as a renewable resource and managers are given autonomy and encouraged to view their craft as a process of interpretation, while fostering innovation and change.

Within this type of environment, trainers can use Stewart's (1984) model of management work to design programs that develop core skills as well as the ability to make decisions within the context of constraints and choices. This discretionary portion of the job presents problems for the trainer, as no two managers will react exactly the same when faced with a complex business situation.

It is logical, therefore, that management development tends to revolve around coaching and self-development. More traditional techniques, like course work, do not have the flexibility to deal with highly individualized work situations.

The trainer's role in this process is to work as an internal consultant, solving both organizational and individual problems through a wide variety of HRD initiatives. Thus, personal and institutional needs are combined into a framework that leads, through planned stages, toward a shared image of excellence.

EXERCISES

Mind Games

"We hire about six new managers a year into this outfit," stormed Mr. Big. "They don't seem to stay very long and they certainly don't show as much dedication to the job as I'd expect in this competitive world! I want you," said Mr. Big, nodding toward the V.P. of Human Resources, "to develop some sort of mind-bending orientation that really puts them through the wringer. When they finish, they'll know they work for a company that means business and expects total dedication!"

"The old man certainly is on the warpath over this one," thought the V.P. "I'd better come up with something good!"

Later that evening, the V.P. began to think about what he should do. Here's his preliminary program:

1. We should pay more attention to our recruiting process, perhaps lengthening it to include two or three interviews and a full battery of tests—we know now what we want (dedication and longevity of tenure), so why not seek out these sorts of people?

2. Let's turn to the military for a model here. We'll break down their personalities and substitute our own. We'll give them lots and lots of routine work to begin with, more than any one person can be expected to handle. They'll have no social life, no outside contacts. To survive they'll have to lean on each other (other newly hired young managers)—that will form a team spirit. They'll all be pushed to the limit of endurance.

3. Then just before they crack (we'll have to be careful here), we'll back off (their egos will be in our hands by then)—they'll be sent off to be trained in one of the firm's branch offices to learn the business from the bottom up. Remember that the recruit has been socialized to think the company way—if we supervise closely, we should be able to solidify our values. As well, we'll ensure that they all start from roughly the same career stage, so they'll begin to think of themselves as the "class" or the "intake" of 199X; that should start them networking.

4. We (this firm) have to become more results-oriented. Any reward our new managers receive should be based on results. This practice should continue throughout their careers.

5. The company should continually reinforce those values that enhance corporate success, e.g., hard work, dedication to the firm, the drive for profit above self-interest. The new recruits must know how they'll be measured, when they'll be measured, and the penalties for poor performance. There can be no surprises.

Everything must be laid out in advance.

6. The good ones will get publicity, both internally and, when we can, in the press. Everybody should be told about successes, so our winners can act as role models for the rest. To be ignored will show our displeasure! In addition, we'll attach these new people to some of our older managers who have made it, as Assistants. Not as Assistant Managers—they might get the idea they're good—but some time as an assistant will cement the behaviour, values, attitudes, and beliefs we want into their psyche. Then they'll be ours in both thought and deed!

"That should please the old man," he thought, "I'll get this typed up in the morning as a 'Draft Proposal'; that way the final report will look like it comes from the old man, not me."

Questions

1. Do you feel that employers have the right to develop career plans like this one? Yes/No. Support your answer.

2. Is it fair to socialize managers to suit the company's purposes. Why/why not? How far should this intense character destruction and buildup (in the firm's image) be allowed to go?

3. Would you be willing to go through the V.P.'s six steps, even if the rewards were substantial? Discuss.

4. Discuss the advantages and the disadvantages of the V.P.'s career-management program.

References

Alder, H. 1992. "A Model for Personnel Success." *Management Decision* 30, no. 3, 23–25.

Bass, B. 1985. *Leadership and Performance Beyond Expectations.* New York: Free Press.

Bolt, J. 1993. "Achieving the CEO's Agenda: Education for Executives." *Management Review* 82, no. 5, 44–48.

Bramley, P. 1989. *Effective Training.* A Monograph in *Journal of European Industrial Training* 13, no. 7.

Broadwell, M. 1993. "How to Train Experienced Supervisors." *Training* 30, no. 5, 61–66.

Brown, J. 1993. "The Management Development Package Deal." *Training* 30, no. 4, 86.

Cadbury, A. 1991. "Ethical Managers Make their Own Rules." In Poff and Walachow, eds. *Business Ethics in Canada.* Scarborough: Prentice-Hall, 72–77.

Cawthray, B. 1987. *Demands, Choices and Constraints.* (Outline 2.18). Marsfield: Marsfield Publications Ltd.

———. c. 1988. *A Strategy for Management Excellence.* (Outline 2.17). Marsfield: Marsfield Publications Ltd.

Christianson, D. 1989. "Responsiveness: Rocketdyne's Winning Edge." *Quality Progress* 22, no. 2, 20–23.

Colledge, M., and M. March. 1993. "Quality Management: Development of a Framework for a Statistical Agency." *Journal of Business & Economic Statistics* 11, no. 2, 157–65.

Crosby. P. 1993. "Quality Leadership." *Executive Excellence* 10, no. 5, 3–4.

Cunningham, S. 1991. "Coaching Today's Executive." *Public Utilities Fortnightly* 128, no. 2, 22–25.

Dennis, A. 1993. "A Way to Build Future Leaders." *Journal of Accounting* 175, no. 5, 70–73.

DeSalvo, G. 1989. "One Training Program—To Go." *Security Management* 33, no. 5, 91–93.

Digman, L. 1986. "How Well-Managed Organizations Develop Their Executives." In Rynes, S. and G. Milkovich. *Current Issues in Human Resources Management.* Plano: Business Publications Inc., 248–57.

Downham, T., J. Noel, and A. Prendergast. 1992. "Executive Development." *Human Resource Management* 31, no. 1, 95–107.

Elkin, G. 1991. "Competency Based HRD." *Training and Development* 9, no. 3, 14–18.

Elliot, K. 1993. "Managerial Competencies." *Training and Development* 11, no. 11, 14–15.

Fairmon, S., and C. Bon. 1993. "Trainee Satisfaction and Training Impact: Issues in Training Evaluation." *Public Productivity and Management Review* 16, no. 3, 299–314.

Farquhar, C. 1990–91. "Total Quality Management: A Competitive Imperative for the '90s." *Optimum* 21, no. 4, 30–39.

Fiebert, G., and J. Tweed. 1989. "Cuts Spawn Internal Consulting." *Computerworld* 23, no. 51, 73.

Gaines, H. 1993. "Ten Ways You Can Help Your Employees Succeed." *Supervising Management* 38, no. 2, 8.

Geroy, G.D. and P.C. Wright. 1994. *Using Skills Needs Assessment in Support of Economic Development Strategies.* Bradford: MCB University Press.

Ghoshal, S. 1992. "A Learning Alliance Between Business Schools." *California Management Review* 35, no. 1, 50–68.

Gilbert, N., and C. Whiting. 1993. "Empowering Professionals." *Management Review* 82, no. 6, 57.

Gomez-Mejia, L., and D. Balkin. 1987. "The Determinants of Managerial Satisfaction with the Expatriation and Repatriation Process." *Journal of Management Development* 6, no. 2, 7–17.

Goodpaster, K. 1989. "Note on the Corporation as a Moral Environment." In Andrews and David, eds. *Ethics in Practice: Managing the Corporation.* Boston: Harvard Business School Press, 89–99.

Gordon, J. 1989. "Tom Peters." *Training* 26, no. 6, 47–56.

Gunsch, D. 1993. "Games Augment Diversity Training." *Personnel Journal* 72, no. 6, 78–83.

Hammer, M., and J. Champy. 1993. *Reengineering the Corporation: A Manifesto for Business Revolution.* New York: Harper Collins.

Harper, M. 1990. "Executive Development and Education: An Evaluation." *Journal of Management Development* 9, no. 4, 7–15.

Harris, S., and H. Field. 1992. "Realizing the 'Potential' of 'High-Potential' Management Development Programmes." *Journal of Management Development* 11, no. 1, 61–70.

Harris, T.G. 1993. "The Post-Capitalist Executive: An Interview With Peter F. Drucker." *Harvard Business Review* 71, no. 3, 114–22.

Hequet, M. 1992. "Executive Education: The Custom Alternative." *Training Magazine* 29, no. 4. April: 38–41.

Hiam, A. 1993. "Strategic Planning Unbound." *Journal of Business Strategy* 14, no. 2, 46–52.

Hoberman, S., and S. Mailick. 1992. *Experiential Management Development: From Learning to Practice*. New York: Quorum Books.

Hogarty, D. 1993. "The Future of Middle Managers." *Management Review* 82, no. 9, 51–53.

Holt, L. 1989. "Project Management Excellence: The Shell Stanney Case." *Construction Management and Economics* 7, no. 3, 217–34.

Huntley, S. 1991: "Management Development Considerations and Implementation." *Industrial and Commercial Training* 23, no. 2, 20–25.

Isaac, R.G., A.R. Cahoon, and W.J. Zenbe. 1994. In H.S. Jain and P.C. Wright, eds., "Values in Corporations— Who Is in Charge?" *Trends and Challenges in Human Resources Management*. Scarborough: Nelson Canada, 251–261.

Jacobs, D. 1989. "Coaching Employees to Perform Better." *Management World* 18, no. 4, 6–9.

Jereski, L. 1990. "The Simmons B-School: Striving to Be The Equalizer." *Business Week* 3160 (May 21): 98, 100.

Jones, J. 1990. *Troubleshooter*. London: BBC Books.

Jubilerer, J. 1991. "Action Learning for Competitive Advantage." *Financier* 15, no. 9, 16–19.

Kessler, B. 1992. "How to Prevent Executive Derailment." *Human Resources Professional* 5, no. 1, 44–7.

Kolb, D. 1984. "From an Address to the World Congress on Management in London, England." (June), as reported by Cawthray, B. c. 1988. *Towards Experiential Learning*. (Outline 2.24). Marsfield: Marsfield Publications, Ltd.

Kotter, J. 1988. *The Leadership Factor*. New York: Free Press.

Lees, S. 1992. "Ten Faces of Management Development." *Management Education and Development* 23, no. 2, 80–105.

Lester, S. 1993. "Appraising the Performance Appraisal." *Training and Development* 11, no. 11, 11–13.

Lippitt, G., and L. Nadler. 1979. "Emerging Roles of the Training Director." *Training and Development Journal* 21, issue 6 (June): 26–30.

McCall, M. 1992. "Executive Development as a Business Strategy." *Journal of Business Strategy* 13, no. 1, 25–31.

McCallum, J. 1993. "The Manager's Job Is Still to Manage." *Business Quarterly* 57, no. 4, 61–67.

McClelland, S., N. Harbaugh, and S. Hammett. 1993. "Improving Individual and Group Effectiveness." *Journal of Management Development* 12, no. 3, 48–58.

Mann, R., and J. Staudenmier. 1991. "Building Transactional Partnerships in Executive Learning through Applied Research." *Training and Development* 45, no. 7, 37–40.

Miller, F. 1993. "Management Development." *Training and Development* 11, no. 8, 16.

Moline, T. 1990. "Upgrading the Consultant." *Journal of Management Consulting* 6, no. 2, 17–22.

Morris, L. 1992. "Research Capsules: A Focus on Development." *Training and Development* 46, no. 11, 25–28.

Morrison, A. 1989. "On-the-Job Training for Managers." *Small Business Reports* 14, no. 7, 62–67.

Mumford, A. 1993. "How Managers Can Become Developers." *Personnel Management* 25, no. 6, 42–45.

Noel, J., and R. Charon. 1992. "G.E. Brings Global Thinking to Light." *Training and Development* 46, no. 7, 28–33.

Parker, B. 1990–91. "The 1990's Challenge." *Management Quarterly* 31, no. 4, 3–7.

Pickering, J., and R. Matson. 1992. "Why Executive Development Programs (Alone) Don't Work." *Training and Development* 46, no. 5, 91–95.

Popper, M., and R. Lipshitz. 1992. "Coaching on Leadership." *Leadership and Organization Development Journal* 13, no. 7, 15–19.

Preston, D. 1993. "Management Development Structures as Symbols of Organizational Culture." *Personnel Review* 22, no. 1, 18–30.

Raelin, J. 1993. "Theory and Practice: Their Roles, Relationship, and Limitations in Advanced Management Education." *Business Horizons* 36, no. 3, 85–89.

Raelin, J., and M. LeBien. 1993. "Learn by Doing." *HR Magazine* 38, no. 2, 61–70.

Raskas, D., and D. Hambrick. 1992. "Multifunctional Managerial Development: A Framework For Evaluating the Options." *Organizational Dynamics* 21, no. 2, 5–17.

Robinson, G., and C. Wick. 1992. "Executive Development that Makes a Business Difference." *Human Resource Planning* 15, no. 1, 63–76.

Rosenberg, A. 1992. "Coaching without Criticizing." *Executive Excellence* 9, no. 8, 14–15.

Rothwell, W. 1992. "Issues and Practices in Management Job Notation Programs as Perceived by HRD Professionals."

Performance Improvement Quarterly 5, no. 1, 49–69.

Sherwood, F. 1992. "Institutionalizing Executive Development and Attendant Problems." *Public Productivity and Management Review* 15, no. 4, 449–61.

Slater, S. 1989. "The Influence of Management Style on Business Unit Performance." *Journal of Management* 15, no. 3, 441–55.

Smith, F. 1990. "Creating an Empowering Environment for all Professionals." *Journal for Quality and Participation* 17, no. 6 (June): 6–10.

Smith, K. 1991. Measuring Your Managers' Skills. *Folio: The Magazine for Magazine Management* 21, no. 9, 106–7.

Steck, R. 1993. "Running Smart." *D & B Reports* 42, no. 1, 40–42.

Stewart, J., and B. Hamlin. 1992. "Competence-Based Qualifications." *Journal of European Industrial Training* 16, no. 10, 9–16.

Stewart, R. 1984. *Management Development and Implications for Managerial Choice.* Excerpt from an address to the World Congress on Management Development in London, England (June), as reported by Cawthray in Outline 2.14 c. 1988, Marsfield: Marsfield Publications Ltd.

Stewart, R., and N. Fondas. 1992. "How Managers Can Think Strategically about Their Jobs." *The Journal of Management Development* 11, no. 7, 10–18.

Sullivan, P. 1993. "Nine Best Practices." *Executive Excellence* 10, no. 3, 3–4.

Svantet, D., M. O'Connell, and T. Baumgardner. 1992. "Applications of Bayesian Methods to OD Evaluation and Decision Making." *Human Relations* 45, no. 6, 621–36.

Van Eynde, D., A. Church, R. Hurley, and W. Burke. 1992. "What OD Practitioners Believe." *Training and Development* 46, no. 4, 41–46.

Vargish, T. 1991. "The Value of Humanities in Executive Development." *Sloan Management Review* 32, no. 3, 83–91.

Vicere, A. 1991. "The Changing Paradigm for Executive Development." *Journal of Management Development* 10, no. 4, 44–47.

Vicere, A. 1992. "The Strategic Leadership Imperative for Executive Development." *Human Resource Planning* 15, no. 1, 15–23.

Vicere, A., and K. Graham. 1990. "Crafting Competitiveness: Toward a New Paradigm for Executive Development." *Human Resource Planning* 13, no. 4, 281–95.

Vogl, A. 1993. "The Age of Re-engineering." *Across the Board* 30, no. 5, 26–33.

Watchorn, W. 1991. "Manufacturing at the Crossroads." *Business Quarterly*, 55, no. 4, 105–10.

Wexley, K., and G. Latham. 1991. *Developing and Training Human Resources in Organizations.* New York: Harper Collins.

Whetten, D.A., and K.S. Cameron. 1995. *Developing Management Skills.* 3rd ed. New York: Harper Collins College Publishers.

Whittaker, B. 1993. "Shaping the Competitive Organization—Managing or Coaching." *CMA Magazine* 67, no. 3, 5.

Wiley, C. 1993. "Training for the '90's: How Leading Companies Focus on Quality Improvement." *Employment Relations Today* 20, no. 1, 79–96.

Wilhelm, W. 1993. "HR Can Make the U.S. a Global Leader." *Personnel Journal* 72, no. 5, 28–29.

Wolff, M. 1993. "Become a Better Coach." *Research-Technology Management* 72, no. 17, 10–11.

Wright, P., and K. Kusmanadji. 1994. "The Strategic Application of T.Q.M. Principles in Human Resources Management." *Training for Quality* 1, no. 3, 5–14.

Yager, E. 1993. "Coaching Models." *Executive Excellence* 10, no. 3, 18.

Zeidenberg, J. 1993. "The Boss Goes Back to School." *Canadian Business* 66, no. 4, 51–53.

Zemke, R. 1987. "Bill Yeomans: Making Training Pay at J.C. Penney." *Training* 24, no. 8, 63–64.

14

Trends

◆ ◆ ◆

INTRODUCTION

Including a chapter about trends is somewhat risky, since the topics must be chosen with great care. No one can forecast accurately what will happen in the future. Many "trends" that are "current" today will be obsolete tomorrow. The task is to separate short-term fancies or fads from the substantive concerns or issues that will have a lasting effect on the discipline, on the way businesses are managed and on society in general.

In terms of human resources development (HRD), we have chosen to include nine topics in this chapter:

- the trainer as consultant;
- the learning organization;
- lifelong learning;
- Total Quality Management (TQM);
- cross-cultural training;
- emerging technology;
- technology management;
- re-engineering; and
- Just-in-time Training (JITT).

Obviously, these are not the only items of concern to HRD professionals. We feel that each of these concepts has an enduring significance, however, that will be reflected in both business and the larger society for some time to come.

◆ ◆ ◆

THE TRAINER AS CONSULTANT

As the pace of change accelerates and competitive forces continue to decrease profit margins, the ritual of setting aside monies for improving productivity through training will begin to be questioned. Although the North American faith in the value of education certainly has "permeated" the corporation (Odiorne, 1987), it is now becoming clearer that between 80 and 90 percent of productivity improvements can be found in the job environment, culture, or process, not in the people who do the work (Wright, 1994a). In essence, then, managers should be concerned with performance, not with performers.

If one accepts the idea (known to organizational development practitioners for many years) that the environment is of paramount importance, allocating funds specifically for training will be viewed with suspicion. Training budgets tend to beget training—and training is aimed at only 20 percent of the performance-improvement possibilities. Similarly, training departments, even if their programs are evaluated on a strict cost/benefit basis, tend to justify their existence through training.

Does this concept mean that training is not a justified business activity? Not at all. What is being suggested is that management should take a much broader approach that focuses on performance improvement, accepting the necessity to train only as part of an overall commitment to improve work performance.

In one large bakery, for example, cakes came down a conveyor on the operator's right; the operator picked up a cake, decorated it, and placed it on another quality-check conveyor to her left. As efficient as that may sound, the left-hand conveyor was too high, so that the cakes tended to be thrown onto the higher finished-goods conveyor as the operator sought to avoid standing up each time. The impact on quality was predictable. Successive attempts by management to train the operators failed, and there was constant friction between Production and Quality Control. In this case, money spent lowering the conveyor would have not only improved quality but created a better work climate as well.

Similarly, a small, very prosperous, family-owned soap manufacturer asked a consultant to design a supervisory training program because work morale was very low. On examining the situation, the consultant found that the firm was hopelessly overstaffed (admittedly a rare occurrence) and that the low morale resulted from boredom. Because management refused to rectify the situation—profits were high and managers felt they were being "kind"—the consultant refused the contract.

There are many similar situations in both the private and the public sectors. Coping with them will require an adaptation of the trainers' role to that of internal consultant, with a mandate and a budget to search out and to improve performance in any way possible. Ideally, an internal consultant would have to prove that his or her services were cost-effective. Funds would tend to be directed, therefore, to areas of greatest potential benefit. If this area happened to be training, training would be conducted. If other activities promised greater returns, monies would be steered away from the training function.

Such a system would have to focus on problems, for to spend money treating symptoms (as many organizations tend to do) would result in sufficient performance improvement to support the consultant's expenses. This trend to organizational problem analysis would greatly improve management's understanding of the overall corporate/organizational culture, enabling sounder decisions to be made in all sectors of the enterprise (Stolovitch and Keeps, 1992). Problems are identified by studying the work environment, by asking the question: "What prevents individuals from doing a good job?" Should this question be asked at all levels in the organization, the answer may indeed be "inadequate training," or it could be "poor ventilation," "poor support systems," or any combination of factors. The key is to discover the real problems and to eliminate them.

In order to make a consultant-based system work, it must become part of the organization's culture. Thus, the system must be introduced with the greatest care. The actual steps involved in altering corporate value systems have been well documented and need not be repeated in detail here (for example, see Neilsen, 1984). Some common pitfalls, however, should be considered. First, it is essential that all levels in the organization be involved in the program. A top-down approach will most certainly encourage failure. Second, the consultant must be trusted by both line managers and staff. A well-known, high-profile individual should be chosen, preferably from inside the company. Third, this individual should report to someone at a very senior level in the organization so as to afford the consultant some protection from organizational politics and to lend prestige to the position (Wright, 1994b).

How can a consulting focus affect the traditional training department? The answer depends on the environment and on the skills of the trainer. If training is found to be a necessary part of improving performance, or if training is obviously necessary to organizational survival, e.g., training temporary sales staff before Christmas, there may be little effect on the training function. If the trainer has sufficient knowledge and prestige to work as a consulting specialist, however, he or she can play a vastly more important role in the organization. Conversely, should training professionals not be able to cope with this broader definition of productivity improvement, they could well find themselves redundant to the organization's needs (Wright and Kusmanadji, 1994).

In essence, the job will evolve toward counselling management in the act of managing change and solving performance problems. It will entail working with line managers at all levels as a facilitator, identifying key individuals (sources of power), and creating links that bring about significant change, leading to measurable productivity/quality improvements (Bennett, 1988). In personnel terms, the task will become one of more effectively integrating the members of the organization in pursuit of the objectives of the organization (Odiorne, 1987). Whether training is involved will be irrelevant.

◆ ◆ ◆
THE LEARNING ORGANIZATION

In his ground-breaking book, *The Fifth Discipline*, Peter Senge (1990) described a learning organization as one

> *where people continually expand their capacity to create the results they truly desire, where new and expansive patterns of thinking are nurtured, where collective aspiration is set free, and where people are continually learning how to learn together (1).*

This definition may seem utopian and esoteric. Indeed, scholars have had some difficulty in crafting an acceptably clear description, and there is much disagreement as to what activities should be included within the paradigm. To clarify the concept, Garvin (1993) offers the following explanation:

> *A learning organization is an organization skilled at creating, acquiring, and transferring knowledge, and at modifying its behavior to reflect new knowledge and insights (78).*

How has this concept developed? As early as 1987, Garavan was concerned with the organization as a learning environment in which individuals could continually interact, make choices, and learn. He regarded such situations, however, as "continued ..., deriving from the organization's necessary reaction to externally imposed pressures" (18). More recent work suggests that the evolution of learning organizations can be best described as a series of waves. First, the main focus of change was on production, or front-line workers. Then (in the second wave) change focused on the management group. These two waves are forecasted to merge gradually into a third, in which learning becomes institutionalized as an all-embracing way of life for both employees and management (Senge, 1992).

The challenge is to implement these high-level precepts—to show how they can be translated into action. In order to apply the concept, therefore, an organization must possess certain characteristics. First, knowledge must be acquired and generated as a variety of learning processes, each of which is linked to a specific source of technological and productive knowledge (Malherba, 1992). As well, learning takes place in a "generative" fashion, emphasizing continuous experimentation and feedback in an ongoing examination of the way the organization defines and solves problems (McGill et al., 1992).

Beginning with an identifiable set of organizational philosophies, attitudes, and approaches, this complex process must be supported by new ways of managing new types of employees (Byrnes and Copacino, 1990). Traditional command-and-control leadership models are seriously deficient (Kiechel, 1990), especially when the need is for employees who think for themselves and identify problems and opportunities, pursuing them through training and involvement (Denton and Wisdom, 1991). A major task of management, then, is to improve the capacity and the willingness of individuals to recognize and to take advantage of large and small learning opportunities (Mumford, 1991), so that as a group, employees continually enhance their capacity to create what they want to create (Galagan, 1991; Senge, 1991).

An organization as an entity, therefore, learns primarily through its employees. Management must make a commitment to acquire knowledge, create mechanisms for renewal, and be open to external influences (Mills and Friesen, 1992). An excellent example of what happens when organizations close themselves off from outside influences occurred during the 1960s and 1970s when the North American car manufacturers, after decades of insular thinking during which few outsiders from other industries were hired into the management ranks, lost substantial market share to more efficient Japanese companies. It has taken more than 10 years for the domestic industry to recover; in the process, thousands of workers have been laid off, plants have closed, and the weakest of the "Big Four" car manufacturers (American Motors) has disappeared.

Managers have little choice, therefore, but to pay close attention to major changes taking place in the environment. But in practical terms, what should managers do? With the realization that any transformation takes time (Garvin, 1993), ideas put forth by Roderick (1993) and Honey (1991) can be modified to help move organizations toward a learning orientation:

♦ Senior management must be persuaded to link learning concepts to corporate philosophies, objectives, and values. Without genuine high-level support, the idea likely will be rejected.

♦ A learning or cultural audit can be used to identify organizational characteristics that inhibit or enhance learning at both individual and group levels. As detailed planning depends upon this high-level analysis, the work of Wright and Geroy (1991) can be used to produce a cultural profile, or an understanding of what is going on within the organization.

♦ A "workshop process" can be used: (1) to help managers (and employees) understand the concept, and (2) to allow full participation in plan formation and implementation. Learning processes must be clarified and adapted for personal use, while simultaneously facilitating self-learning and autonomy in the workplace.

♦ To support learning, a wide range of structures and processes can be created—coaching; networking; mentoring; peer support groups; learning contracts and/or logs; career planning programs—but each, in turn, must be supported by appropriate reward systems and must become part of the performance appraisal or measurement process.

♦ Both employees and managers must be taught how to learn. Learning is a skill that can be analyzed and enhanced by self-completion inventories, practical guides, and special exercises.

◆ New learning skills need to be practised in a team environment, perhaps with the help of temporary tutors, until the whole organization begins to function effectively.

◆ The learning behaviours management wants to encourage must be identified and the "triggers" reinforced. See Table 14.1 for practical examples of this technique.

◆ For each "wanted behaviour," management must look for "reinforcers." As with triggers, reinforcers need to be simple, easy to use, and available or appropriate for immediate application, i.e., used as close to the wanted behaviour as possible, in order to establish an obvious link between behaviour and reinforcer (see Table 14.2).

When the appropriate behaviours become part of the firm's culture, additional behaviour can be added and filtered into the learning system. Similarly, should the process become stale (e.g., some reinforcers cease to be effective), new, fresh reinforcers will need to be generated.

The trigger-behaviour-reinforcer model fosters learning by requiring employees to deal with new knowledge and to consider how this knowledge applies to each individual workplace or station. The result is likely to move learning to a higher level of organizational priority (Garvin, 1993).

As to the training professional, aside from the fundamental task of helping to ensure that learning is part of the conscious day-to-day agenda, what is his or her role within the learning organization? Obviously, the principle function of training is to support the focus and methods that favour widespread, spontaneous learning. This role may require a redefinition of what the training person or unit does, as the type of support needed depends upon the individual's level of responsibility (Kramlinger, 1992).

At the top, for example, the trainer may act as a consultant in the creation of a clan culture—one in which employees perceive that they will be dealt with fairly and listened to seriously. This supportive environment is a prerequisite for learning; all employees with new ideas need to find sponsors who have influence within the corporate power structure (Bahlmann, 1990). The trainer's job at other levels consists of defining and setting up supportive systems and training both employees and managers to use these systems. As suggested earlier, possible examples could be monitoring, coaching, and team building, but self-development and learning to learn are always part of the paradigm.

TABLE 14.1 ENCOURAGING DESIRED BEHAVIOURS

Triggers ('befores')		Desired Behaviours
Invite people to question you. If questions are slow to come, remain silent and just look calmly at people, "willing" them to question you.	→	Asking questions
Seek ideas. Research shows that if you invite ideas, there is an 80 percent probability of an idea being offered.	→	Suggesting ideas
List the alternatives to be explored and say, "Let's go through each of these in turn identifying the pros and cons."	→	Exploring alternatives
Keep asking people, "How could this be done differently/better?"	→	Taking risks/experimenting
Do it yourself by saying, "I'm going to tell you the way I see it and I'd be glad to hear the way you see it."	→	Being open about the way it is
When a mistake has been made, say, "Let's see what we can learn from this" as a lead-in to a nonaccusational exploration of causes and cures.	→	Converting mistakes into learning
Frequently (i.e., at least once a day) say, "Let's ponder how that went. What went well and what could have gone better?"	→	Reflecting and reviewing
Do it yourself. Cut the war stories and anecdotes to a minimum and get into the habit of saying " ... and the lesson I learned was ..." Keep asking other people what lessons they have learned. At the end of a meeting, or other activity, instigate a learning review.	→	Talking and learning
Ask, "What are you going to do about it?" and "What additional learning opportunities would you like and what are you going to do to get them?"	→	Taking responsibility for one's own learning and development
Do it yourself. Say, "I can see how I could have done that better." "I have made a mistake and this is what I learned from it."	→	Admitting inadequacies and mistakes

Source: P. Honey, "The Learning Organization Simplified." *Training and Development* 9, no. 7 (1991): 30–33. Reprinted with the author's permission.

TABLE 14.2   REINFORCING DESIRED BEHAVIOURS

Desired Behaviours		Reinforcers ("afters")
Asking questions	→	Provide full answers. If you don't know the answer say, "That's an interesting question. I haven't got an answer now. I will find out and let you know by (a specific time not too far into the future)."
Suggesting ideas	→	Bend over backwards to support and build on ideas from other people. If that isn't possible, give full explanations about why and why not, and solicit some more ideas.
Exploring alternatives	→	Say, "Thanks. That has been an interesting process. I don't think I would have arrived at the same conclusion if we hadn't examined all the pros and cons."
Taking risks/experimenting	→	Say, "Well done giving that a try." If it led to an improvement, add, "If you hadn't had the courage to try that we would never have discovered (whatever)." If it didn't work out, add, "It's only by experimenting that we can find out what works and what doesn't. What are you going to try next?"
Being open about the way it is	→	Say, "I'm delighted you've been so honest/candid." When you have heard bad news, limit yourself to asking questions and resist the temptation to become defensive or to "shoot the messenger!"
Converting mistakes into learning	→	Comment on how analyzing the mistakes has led to valuable lessons learned and summarize the lessons and what you are going to do about them.
Reflecting and reviewing	→	Congratulate people on time well spent. Say, "For me, this has been another illustration of the worth of pausing to review together. Quality reviews lead to quality conclusions."
Talking about learning	→	Make a note of what people said they had learned and find an early opportunity to refer to it. "I've been thinking about what you said and ... " "Have you thought anymore about ... ?"
Taking responsibility for one's own learning and development	→	Show enormous interest in what they have done/are proposing to do. Put it in your diary as a "bring up" note. Ask what, if anything, they would like you to do to help.
Admitting inadequacies and mistakes	→	Say, "Let's talk about how to improve on that in future." Avoid all recriminations. This is the "reward" for openly admitting an inadequacy/mistake. Only punish mistakes that were concealed and mistakes that reoccur because the agreed improvement plan has not been carried out.

Source: P. Honey, "The Learning Organization Simplified." *Training and Development* 9, no. 7 (1991): 30–33. Reprinted with the author's permission.

◆ ◆ ◆
LIFELONG LEARNING

Both self-development and learning to learn can be subsumed into the general concept of lifelong learning, a major thrust in adult-education practice and philosophy for more than two decades. The need for continuous upgrading is made even more necessary by employment systems that focus on empowerment, in which employees join management in planning, implementing, and monitoring quality programs. Here, learning flows up as well as down in an organization and work methods are constantly changing (Kramlinger, 1992; Rubinstein, 1993).

It is widely agreed that lifelong learning is a basic ingredient to an organization's becoming competitive within the global economy. Authors have repeatedly listed the concept among the behaviours necessary for coping with rapid changes in technology, information systems, and society (for example, see: Sullivan, 1993; Purcell, 1992; Cutler, 1992/93; Matthews, 1991; Gordon, 1989).

As well, the application of a lifelong learning philosophy appears to have tangible results, although the corporate will to adopt such a program probably means that other progressive management practices are in place, so it is impossible to determine direct causal relationships. However, since 1987, when the "learning for life" program was begun at Honeywell, productivity has increased by 40 percent, work-in-progress inventory has decreased by 60 percent, order to customer delivery times and scrap/re-work rates have been reduced by 50 percent. In addition, Motorola Inc., Borg-Warner, and Corning, all exemplary companies, have designed lifelong learning into their fundamental corporate practices (Nopper, 1993; Naisbitt and Aburdene, 1991; Goodnight, 1989).

As usual, the how, or the methodology, used to implement these schemes varies considerably. Honeywell, for example, includes a 16-hour "skills for success" program that enables employees to refresh their study habits. Classes are offered on site during the late afternoon. The practice at Motorola includes a major retraining focus every 7 to 10 years, while Borg-Warner has developed a continuing education/lifelong learning centre, utilizing the resources of nearby universities.

Regardless of the method, it is certain that widespread employee involvement in program design helps create a supportive learning environment. The trainer's role is to work with line personnel and employee advisory committees, making training more efficient by conducting it as close to the workplace as possible, thus saving the nearly two-thirds of training budget spent on travel and lodging (Cohen, 1991; Gordon, 1989).

This approach will free monies for direct uses like the development of special support programs to help employees create lifelong learning habits and attitudes. In addition, as initial training is likely to become a tool for identifying employees' relative strengths and weaknesses for remediation, in-depth training and/or retraining may not occur until after an employee has been on the job for some time, but may reoccur several times during a career. The trainer's role, therefore, may become increasingly significant over time (Cohen, 1991), as HRD professionals involve themselves with functions viewed as essential to organizational survival.

◆ ◆ ◆
TOTAL QUALITY MANAGEMENT*

The term "Total Quality Management" (TQM) is currently in vogue. Although the name may change from time to time, it is felt that a focus on quality will continue to persist as one of the major functions critical to organizational survival. While it is important to outline the role of training in this area, the TQM approach should be viewed as one of a series of ever-changing initiatives. Future modifications to quality-improvement practices may make the term obsolete.

TQM places HRD in a pivotal position, as the process often requires significant changes in the way people work. TQM literature, however, typically contains only superficial information about new approaches to HRD. Fortunately, some HRD professionals have had to become involved in TQM, attempting to provide guidance on how to transform traditional practices into TQM-oriented HRD (e.g., Rossett and Krumdieck, 1992; Cocheu, 1989).

As TQM requires the involvement of all stakeholders in an organization, the concept moves far beyond former piecemeal approaches to quality improvement, which often were limited to other inspection and/or quality-

---

*This material has been modified from: P. Wright and K. Kusmanadji. The strategic Application of TQM Principles in Human Resources Management" *Training for Quality*, no. 3 (1993): 5–14. This material is reproduced here with the permission of MCB University Press.

control methods carried out by a specialized department. Although this search for quality is not a new concept, TQM can require major organizational changes (Armitage, 1992; Fine and Bridge, 1987).

Employees, then, need to be empowered by driving decision-making power down to those who can do the most for quality improvement. Thus, TQM requires that employees at lower levels share managerial responsibility, again moving away from conventional command-and-control procedures to a more participative style of management.

As far as the HRD function is concerned, these issues inevitably require "major changes in the way the HR functions are run and in the type of systems they create and operate" (Bowen and Lawler, 1992). TQM-driven programs need organization-wide support and each function needs to be quality-oriented. Therefore, the training unit should be required, first, to apply quality principles to its own activities (Hendricks and Triplett, 1989; Rossett and Krumdieck, 1992).

As well, most TQM advocates emphasize the importance of training and development (e.g., Oakland, 1989; Schonberger, 1992; Tenner and DeToro, 1992). It has been argued that without proper employee training, the act of empowerment in TQM is meaningless (Gandz, 1990). Training and development are primary methods of reinforcing employee commitment to the consistent delivery of high-quality products and services. Accordingly, leading TQM companies invest heavily in training and development at all levels. In the absence of proper training, many TQM systems that are excellent at identifying and quantifying the cost of performance problems are ultimately unsuccessful, because there is no way of changing the behaviours that caused deficiencies in the first place (Kiess-Moser, 1990; Regalbuto, 1992).

Another important area of interest to HRD specialists—career development—traditionally has followed a linear path. An employee is moved up through a single function in a hierarchical structure. In a TQM environment, however, this practice is no longer appropriate.

With empowerment, employees' roles change as they assume more responsibility. In addition, they are required to work in unit or cross-functional teams. Consequently, career paths and job ladders tend to become diversified as cross-functional careers become possible (Gandz, 1990). Through the use of project teams and direct involvement with various internal clients, HRD professionals can both set an example of interdisciplinary cooperation and gain increased influence throughout an organization, especially when mentoring and other strategically driven career-planning processes are put in place.

The critical role of HRD in implementing TQM is also apparent from the pervasive nature of HRD, as training affects the entire organization. More importantly, HRD systems and practices continually impact on employees at all levels. Since employee participation and related issues are critical to TQM, strong, positive support from the HRD function is indispensable.

◆ ◆ ◆
CROSS-CULTURAL TRAINING*

The presentation of training for those about to work in other cultures is fraught with difficulties, because business practice is culture-specific. Westerners have played a dominant role in the development and dissemination of much of current management theory—theory that has been practised as part of the Western work experience. If the transfer of Western business activities to other cultures is to succeed, careful preparation is needed. Part of the preparatory activity is the development of briefing opportunities that will begin in the process of orienting the trainer to the target or host culture.

Even though many multinational companies have initiated some form of intercultural preparation for people who are sent overseas, they seem to be only in the initial stages of developing cross-cultural training for the broader spectrum of employees. Human resource management (HRM) specialists presently are facing the task of adapting all HRM functions, e.g., recruiting, compensation, and training (Derderian, 1993).

The international business arena requires individuals who can perform effectively in more than one culture. Intercultural training helps these employees withstand the culture shock of working abroad and improves job performance. The most effective, least costly cross-cultural activity is targeted toward the individual and the specific job. In most cases, skills need to be developed in understanding differences in communication patterns and management styles, since these attributes are unlikely to be acquired at school, during normal social interaction, or at work (Odenwald, 1993).

---

*Although updated and adapted extensively, the major outline for this section stems from P. Wright, G.D. Geroy, and S.M. Dingle. "Briefing the Management Trainer: The First Step In A Successful Cross-cultural Experience." *Training and Management Development Methods*, vol. 2, no. 1 (1988): 2.23–2.32. All material reproduced with permission from MCB University Press.

The cost of failure is high, in that each year in North America $2 to $2.5 billion is wasted when overseas postings fail. Multinational firms, therefore, are spending more on cross-cultural training. Furthermore, as the trend toward globalization gathers momentum, training professionals are becoming more involved in transborder operations (Lissy, 1993). These individuals must prepare themselves for this expanding role.

Despite increasing awareness of the importance of cross-cultural training, however, only a minority of firms (30 to 45 percent) provide this training for potential expatriates (Dunbar and Katcher, 1990), or their families—a major contributing factor in expatriate assignment failure (McEmery and DesHarnais, 1990). The training professional or manager, then, must be prepared to promote and/or to conduct cross-cultural preparation activities. Hence, this section focuses on preparing or training the trainer to begin the process of cross-cultural training within an organization.

In presenting this material, it must be understood and accepted that culture is not on the periphery but is central to international business permeating every aspect of the organization (Guptara et al., 1990; Li, 1992). The training professional who is to be part of a global or intercultural initiative may need to actively participate in, manage, or preside over projects that take place in various parts of the world. No one can be an expert in all cultures, but in order to design (or have someone else design) a cross-cultural training program, certain preparations must be made, otherwise the trainer will have no way to determine if his or her firm's program is adequate.

Although this preparatory phase may take a number of forms (e.g., using purchased material from a cross-cultural training firm), we have chosen to present a prototype of a self-prepared briefing document. The advantage of this approach is its low cost and the necessity that trainers prepare their own material. The disadvantage is that considerable time must be set aside for research.

The underlying suppositions behind the preparation of a self-briefing document are that Western management theories have arisen from a specific set of philosophical precepts. For example, Western practitioners expect individuals to be motivated through methods that stress individual needs and expectations. In addition, North Americans and Europeans tend to harbour a pragmatic outlook to both work and life, while believing in the value of technology, change, and the myth that, with hard work, anything is possible. These and other perspectives on life may not be translated easily from one culture to another. Indeed, conscious or unconscious ethnocentrism, the belief that one's native lifestyle is the "best" or the most appropriate for everyone, can result in value judgments that cause misperceptions about other cultures. With proper preparation, however, trainers can be made ready for the shock that invariably comes when they are thrust into a cross-cultural encounter. The well-researched briefing document represents an initial, but integral part of this preparation process. The model presented in Figure 14.1 conceptualizes this procedure. It can be used as a checklist to guide the preparation of oneself or others.

FIGURE 14.1 Self-briefing Model

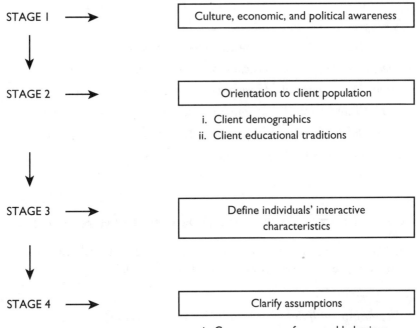

STAGE 1 ⟶ | Culture, economic, and political awareness |

STAGE 2 ⟶ | Orientation to client population |

    i. Client demographics
   ii. Client educational traditions

STAGE 3 ⟶ | Define individuals' interactive characteristics |

STAGE 4 ⟶ | Clarify assumptions |

    i. Consequences of assumed behaviour
   ii. Connections between norms, roles, and behaviour

CULTURAL, ECONOMIC, AND POLITICAL AWARENESS PROFILE

An overview should comprise the first portion of any briefing material. The trainer who is preparing others can use this technique to arouse interest. This concept is useful for preparing to enter into any host culture. For example:

There is widespread agreement in the XYZ country, both offi-cially and among individuals, that modernization is extremely important. The "central thrust" has been toward an economy characterized by considerable reliance on market forces. Despite these intentions, modernization has to proceed within the context of economic fragmentation, as China's provinces tend to be economically separated because of poor transporta-tion and as inefficient, small factories are allowed to survive under the protection of internal trade barriers and regional monopolies.

At the personal level, it must be remembered that the XYZ people, like most others, have been shaped by their cul-ture. The political structure and social processes very much affect what people are expected to do and what they are willing to do. The essence of life revolves around the development of correct interpersonal relationships. In business, this is shown by the formation of an extensive network of friends and con-tacts that exists for long-term mutual benefit.

ORIENTATION TO CLIENT POPULATION

I. Demographics. At this point, the prospective cross-cultural trainer should study his or her host country work group. For example:

The group with which we will be working consists of 116 trainees, of whom 5 are women. The average age is 39, but ages range from 22 to 51 years. As to work experience, the amount varies greatly—from 1 to 33 years. Thirty-nine per-cent (n = 45) either list their professional title as "engineer," or have graduated from an engineering college, institute, or university.

2. *Educational Traditions.* As knowledge of employees' educational background may be critical to the success of some projects, the following type of information might be included:

> *All the trainees have progressed through the traditional XYZ education system—a system that stresses conformity, lectures, learning by rote, and memorization, although they are not as passive as folklore suggests. In general, the trainees' mathematical ability is likely to far exceed Western norms. The major skill deficiency, from the Western manager's viewpoint, is lack of reading comprehension and writing ability in English.*

DEFINING INDIVIDUAL INTERACTIVE CHARACTERISTICS

Here, the trainer begins to learn some of the target culture's specific characteristics:

> *Early, ground-breaking research by Triandis (1983), produced a list of factors that should be taken into account when designing cross-cultural training interventions. His hypothesis was that we are programmed by our culture and that to prepare properly for intercultural interaction, it is necessary that certain specified subject areas be understood:*
>
> 1. *There will be a wide range of acceptable and unacceptable behaviours or norms for different kinds of social situations.*
> 2. *Role structures, including role perceptions, can differ among cultures.*
> 3. *Subtle behaviours can express general intentions and attitudes.*
> 4. *Individuals within the host cultures may have self-concepts that are quite different from the Western norm.*

5. *Certain kinds of behaviours will be acceptable or rejected in the host culture.*

CLARIFYING ASSUMPTIONS

The Western-born trainer is likely to be a product of a business culture that stresses individualism and motivation through individualistic rewards. If this, sometimes unconscious, bias is translated into management styles, management/employee interactions may become strained. In general, it must be remembered that most host cultures not only want to import technology but desire to control and use the technology. Thus, the recipients of Western investment may have their own agendas.

USING THE BRIEFING DOCUMENT

Armed with sufficient background knowledge to interact intelligently with experts and/or those native to the host culture, the trainer now can design or manage the design of a cross-cultural preparation program from a position of strength. As the typical intercultural training program lasts only three days, it is important to design a customized program, staffed with facilitators who have had direct (hands-on) international experience in the area of future operation.

The self-briefing document, although it can be used as background reading for training sessions, provides the trainer with a base from which to investigate systematically which approach will best suit the organization. As cross-cultural training is likely to increase in importance, the self-briefing procedure provides a practical guide, or contingency framework, for determining the method and the vigour of intercultural preparation most effective in various circumstances.

◆ ◆ ◆
EMERGING TECHNOLOGY

As with other sections in this chapter, it is difficult to foresee precisely where technology is headed. One obvious common thread in almost all technological training applications, however, is the computer. It is likely that computer-based and computer-aided HRD will become more sophisticated with time, although simplicity of use will continue to be important. For example, while presentation may be as basic as displaying printed material or diagrams on screen to be read or viewed by the trainee, the trend seems to be toward providing feedback in the form of questions. More advanced systems can include pre-tests, information provided as required, review questions, and other feedback mechanisms. When appropriate skill requirements are met, the system can provide a test or evaluation exercise. Computer-enhanced training systems are expected to remain popular as organizations are facing rapid change (with the resultant need for increased training) in an era of reduced profitability (Heathman and Kleiner, 1991).

As telecommunications are developed into operational information highways, Henry (1989) has suggested that technically advanced learning systems will be transferred from training centres into individual employee cubicles and offices. This view is supported by Geroy (1994), in that he sees the advent of user-based information networks and enquiry-controlled bulletin boards that allow access to both general and specific learning material. These advances will likely herald a new explosion in self-learning (for example, see Garavan and Murphy, 1989), although much still needs to be done in creating user interfaces and effective indexing systems (Emrich, 1990).

Perhaps the most exciting of all the emerging technologies is virtual reality. Trainers have not yet gained widespread experience with this technique, since appropriate software is not readily available. It is likely that sophisticated virtual-reality products will soon become commercially available (Schmitz, 1993). As many HRD professionals feel that simulation is a powerful training technique (Fritz, 1991), it is likely too that virtual environments will become more commonplace in the future.

◆ ◆ ◆

THE TRAINER AS TECHNOLOGY MANAGER

Within all organizations, there will be forces that urge the adoption of new technology and those that regard inevitable change from a negative viewpoint. As well, technical competence and the ability to use and to accept technology vary with both the individual and the organization's subculture. It would be rare, for example, for a trainer in a business setting to lecture

◆

almost exclusively. Similarly, sophisticated technology-based learning methods are used only rarely in university classrooms.

As many companies have not included technology acquisition in their strategic plan, the trainer acquires yet another role, that of determining which of the new technologies should be considered seriously and which are fads (Coffman, 1987). The decision to commit an organization to the whole-sale adoption of one technology or another, then, must be taken with great care, for there are costs and other practical factors to consider.

For example, one large corporation had a division responsible for main-taining gas furnaces. In order to keep repair technicians current with the latest technical changes and safety procedures, it was decided to invest thou-sands in audio-activated slide projectors. A self-taught upgrading program was developed, in which each technician would receive a tray of slides and an audio tape each month.

The tapes were professionally moderated by a local radio announcer from scripts prepared by technical specialists. The program was well received and the results, in terms of behavioural changes (i.e., furnaces were repaired more expertly), were beyond expectation.

While this initiative was being prepared, however, corporate headquar-ters was ordering video cameras, VCRs, and screens for all corporate-level presentations. In addition, there was serious thought being given to linking each regional office by some sort of closed-circuit TV. Even though the training program was a success, several senior managers questioned the wisdom of adopting a technology that was out of step with corporate strategy and seen by the uninitiated as obsolete. The training director coun-tered that videos were too costly to prepare (although he didn't have exact cost estimates) and that flexibility was required; a few slides could be changed and a tape patched when minor adjustments were needed. At cor-porate headquarters, there was some discussion about forcing the training people into line, but after some grumbling, the issue died.

A tempest in a teapot? Probably, although a training director does not need to alienate senior managers. He should have taken the initiative, attempting to forge a corporate technology strategy by beginning the process from the bottom up. Then, not only would he have covered his division in political terms, but as one knowledgeable in technology management (at least the communications side), he would be seen as a valuable internal con-sultant—one with whom senior managers could consult in the future.

Given that many of the current generation of managers know little about technology, Shostack (1989) has devised a six-step process that (with some adaptation), trainers can apply:

1) Behave as if one has no knowledge at all; ask "why?" shamelessly.

2) Leave decisions about actual hardware (brands, etc.) to the experts; the type of "box" means little.

3) Be suspicious of the most advanced hardware. Don't let a manufacturer experiment in your company.

4) Assume that communication between people and technology doesn't work; make the vendor provide proof that a nontechnical person can accept.

5) Live by the rule that all budgets must be doubled and all installation times tripled.

6) If the project runs late, do not add more people; plan the implementation in detail before installation starts.

In summary, the future is likely to see advances in the management of technology and in the technology of management. Successful trainers will learn how to use technology, taking a leadership role that will influence the degree and the direction of technological change, by using technology to add value to processes and product in the drive to create sustainable competitive advantage.

◆ ◆ ◆

THE TRAINER AS PERFORMANCE ENGINEER

Directly related to the consulting concept, performance, or human competence engineering, takes the paradigm one step further—into the realm of re-engineering. This process is so drastic, proponents predict that organizations of the future will have little resemblance to what we know today.

For more than 200 years, companies have been built according to classic economic theory that industrial work should be subdivided into very basic tasks. Now that we are entering the postindustrial business age, many companies will be built, or redesigned, according to the theory that tasks should be redefined into coherent business processes—the end-to-end activities that create value for customers. The technique used to accomplish this process is known as business re-engineering: the radical redesign of business processes to achieve dramatic improvements in performance. This procedure is thought to be the basis for the next major revolution in business, much as Adam Smith's specialization of labour was in the last. Even the most successful contemporary organizations must adopt and apply the principles of business re-engineering or they will be overshadowed by the successes of the companies that do (Hammer and Champy, 1993).

Business re-engineering means starting over from the beginning, forgetting how work was done in the past, while deciding how work can best be done now. Job titles, organizational departments, divisions, etc., do not matter. Business re-engineering is associated with characteristics such as individualism, self-reliance, the willingness to accept risk, and a propensity for change—characteristics that traditionally have been associated with great business innovators. In some ways, re-engineering is about making large organizations as responsive as small ones. Often the attributes businesses need to be successful are those they lose as they become large organizations. The key is to remain, or to become, a large-scale organization, remaining flexible, responsive, and dynamic while maintaining low overhead (Randall, 1993).

Because re-engineering significantly changes the way work is performed, the process has a "ripple effect" on every aspect of the organization. Business re-engineering changes people's jobs, the kind of people working at these jobs, how people are measured and compensated, how people are regarded by one another, and their values and attitudes. Re-engineering focuses on teams rather than on end tasks, compensating workers for their contribution to business performance rather than on their position in a hierarchy (Vogl, 1993).

Many misconceptions surround re-engineering. Often these are associated with the perceived necessity for complete organizational restructuring, upgrading of technology, the necessity to develop TQM systems, etc. For example, there is a perception that for a company to re-engineer, every function in every department must change simultaneously. This concept is false, impractical, and very disruptive. Often companies re-engineer two or three processes at a time so that only the areas being re-engineered are in chaos. Other work units remain stable until it is their turn to be re-engineered. Only companies in severe trouble should attempt to re-engineer everything at once.

Another misconception is that re-engineering means building new computer systems. Although re-engineering is facilitated by technology and re-engineered processes often require new computer systems, the idea of rethinking a process comes before technology is taken into consideration. In successful re-engineering projects, the technology is considered an enabler rather than a solution and the information-systems staff plays the role of catalyst.

Although TQM has some characteristics of re-engineering, e.g., an emphasis on customers and business processes, the two concepts are very different. TQM stresses the improvement of a process or procedure, while re-engineering focuses on the identification of that which has become inefficient and advocates starting over.

Finally, some managers feel that re-engineering changes organizations in "normal" proportions and, therefore, can be managed by "normal" management styles. This notion is false. Re-engineering attempts cannot succeed without the intense focus they demand and without the management tools and techniques required for change (Vogl, 1993).

Indeed, successful re-engineering requires the acknowledgment that work based on fragmentation and specialization cannot respond to a dynamic business world (Byrne, 1993). Re-engineering experts suggest that managers have no time to waste on isolated, incremental improvements that may or may not solve business problems. These methods fail because they try to fix problems that are associated with old management theories that no longer work in today's business environment. Instead, companies must start over and reorganize work based on the demands of today's markets and the power of today's technologies (Hammer and Champy, 1993). Although re-engineering can be a long and difficult process, it often results in dramatic improvements in how the organization responds to customer needs and expectations (Janson, 1992/93).

Many people, however, view re-engineering as a magical solution rather than as an opportunity to tackle fundamental issues. While the end results of re-engineering are alluring, the process can collapse without sound plans (Krpan, 1993). For example, some companies merely tinker with well-entrenched business processes. Others try to drive radical process change from the bottom up and get stymied by functional managers defending traditional interests. For some, re-engineering is just one of many change programs on the corporate agenda. Managers of re-engineering need to meticulously plan organizational change in order to succeed (Stanton et al., 1993).

As we are in the middle of a technological revolution, employees often lack the skills employers require. Thus, employee resistance to technological change is common when companies are involved in re-engineering projects. Resistance can come from employees content with the traditional way, from middle managers threatened by job loss, or from a company president who fears he or she might not be able to guide the organization through the re-engineering process (LaPlante, 1993).

Of course, the training professional must be aware of skill deficiencies and be able to devise remedies, but other analytical skills and knowledge will be mandatory. Aside from the ability to manage change, knowledge about key business processes, job structures, management systems, and corporate values will be needed to eliminate unnecessary tasks, steps, and departments by giving employees the tools and expertise to perform multiple tasks (Stanton et al., 1993).

Trainers will need to review the processes to be re-engineered and identify the people who will be affected, while helping to form change-management support teams to aid technical specialists directly involved in re-engineering business processes. These teams will identify the groups affected by re-engineering, construct detailed charts of key stakeholders in each group, decide what type of change these stakeholders will have to make, and help these people understand and accept the change (Stanton et al., 1993).

To make meaningful contributions toward this goal, training professionals must position themselves in one of three key roles: leader, process owner, or re-engineering team member. The leader's role requires someone who has enough authority over the stakeholders to ensure that re-engineering can happen. A re-engineering leader might be a general manager of a division, because the process might address concerns that fall outside the company, affecting the customer, and inside the company, affecting business processes. Only a senior training manager or director is likely to be involved at this level.

Similarly, the process owner, responsible for re-engineering a specific process, assembles a re-engineering team, obtains the resources the team requires, deals with bureaucratic problems, and works to gain the cooperation of other managers (Hammer and Champy, 1993). Depending upon the industry and the product, a senior trainer might be involved here. It is as part of the re-engineering team, however, that trainers should never fail to be included, for this team performs the actual re-engineering work. Not only do training professionals have needs-analysis and research skills that are vital to team success, but to remain aloof from the re-engineering process is to be marginalized within the new organizational power structure.

Finally, as stated previously, it is expected that re-engineering will reduce the middle-management workforce by 75 percent. The managerial responsibilities of those who remain will change dramatically, so that two types of managers will emerge: process managers and employee coaches. Process managers will oversee a re-engineered process from beginning to end. Employee coaches will be responsible for supporting and nurturing employees. Because re-engineering demonstrates that managing is not that important, the concept is very difficult for middle managers to accept (Hogarty, 1993; Hammer and Champy, 1993). Thus, trainers will be needed to redefine the management-development process so that both the core and the flexible portions of the managers' job reflect the new order.

◆ ◆ ◆ ◆
JUST-IN-TIME TRAINING

A concept that might be viewed with skepticism by many training managers, just-in-time training (JITT), would allow access to training materials on an immediate, as-needed basis. Gerber (1994), for example, sketches the scenario of a manager, who having been criticized by her boss, seeks immediate help by accessing the training unit's databases and by:

1. picking modules from a multimedia course in sexual harassment for review at home;

2. printing out two articles on the same topic for reading on the train trip home;

3. checking the list of colleagues who have the expertise that she needs, so she can contact them personally later;

4. calling up a refresher course in decision-making the company way;

5. broadcasting a call for help on an internal electronic bulletin board, the responses to be checked later on e-mail.

All the while, database use was being monitored by the training unit to see what could be learned in terms of future training needs, programs, and other services.

This type of JITT is unavailable to most managers. Indeed, some of the "services" outlined in the example might not be thought of today as "training" at all. To be successful in the future, then, trainers will have to define their roles much more broadly, casting aside stereotypes that limit what a trainer or training department is prepared to do.

◆ ◆ ◆
SUMMARY

The risky business of deciding what is a trend and what is a fad has produced nine descriptions of what we feel are the most likely techniques that trainers will continue to develop and use over the long term. To repeat, these nine topics include:

1. the trainer as consultant;

2. the learning organization;

3. lifelong learning;

4. Total Quality Management (TQM);

5. cross-cultural training;

6. emerging technology;

7. technology management;

8. re-engineering;

9. Just-in-time Training (JITT).

Each of these methods will affect training and the trainer. For example, the trainer as consultant and re-engineering will change the trainer's job substantially. In fact, the term "trainer" may disappear, as these professionals move from developing people to enhancing performance in the broadest possible sense, i.e., changing how entire organizations operate.

Other trends affect the training function more directly. Cross-cultural training, emerging technology, and JITT, for example, will not only change what we do but how we do it.

The obvious question concerns whether we have chosen the techniques correctly. To illustrate: as this book was being written, interest in TQM seemed to be waning. Will TQM stand the test of time, or will it virtually disappear like transactional analysis and many other fads of the past? Despite the risk of being wrong, however, we have tried to present a cross-section of the major trends that should be studied if one is to become a proficient manager of human performance.

E X E R C I S E

The Future of Training

Rhona Pringle came down the stairs from the kitchen, opened the airlock, and let herself in. She pressed her hand to an identification window. The scanner read her palm print, identified it, and opened the inner door. They were all there, as usual, old friends waiting patiently to help her in her work: a computer console that could be connected by satellite transmission to anywhere in the world; a cordless video telephone with a large screen that would follow her as she walked around the room; data banks that provided instant-display capability; her own photocopy machine capable of copying directly from the computer screen, from her data banks, or from a large television screen where hundreds of channels could be tuned in. And don't forget George! George was her pet robot. He could make coffee, vacuum the floors, change computer paper, and do all manner of fetch-and-carry jobs.

"Morning, George," said Rhona, as she entered.

"Mornnninggg ... RRhonna," answered George, as he recognized her voice.

"Coffee, please," instructed Rhona.

"Yeess ... RRhonna," and the machine turned to do her bidding.

While Rhona had been sleeping, her e-mail had been receiving messages from the other side of the world. She scanned these briefly, sorted them into priority order, and put an automatic dialing card into the phone. The screen lit up and she could see her co-worker, seated at his own console some 400 kilimetres away.

"Morning, Paul."

"Good morning, Rhona. I see that we have a problem in Nigeria with the ... " (the next few minutes were spent deep in highly technical conversation).

"Okay," agreed Rhona, "that's the course of action we'll take—(noticing a flashing light)—I have a conference call coming in, Paul. See you later."

Rhona's automatic camera focused on her. The large television screen divided itself into four equal squares, three containing the images of colleagues. The fourth was her boss. "How's the weather in Canada, Rhona?" "Cold!" was the reply. "You remember Bob from Argentina? And I think you've met Hee Lee from Singapore. This is our new operative in England, Jeff Forbes." The five-way conversation went on for some 20 minutes, decisions were made, deals struck, and personal friendships formed.

After the conference call, Rhona checked her bank balance and called up the latest satellite weather information on the ski resort where she had reservations for the weekend. She then placed her week's shopping order and reserved an appointment at the hairdresser—all through her computer terminal. Chores out of the way, Rhona settled down to work once more.

The phone beeped. "Listen, Rhona (it was the boss again), you know that new virtual-reality package you developed to help our client sell his high-tech tennis racquets? It's been accepted for use by the Executive Committee."

"Wonderful news! I worked on that for months!"

"Congratulations, buddy, I knew you could do it." The boss' smile lit up the screen. "But now we have to develop some sort of training for his sales reps; they have to be brought up to speed on your system. As you know, they're scattered throughout the world; each one works out of the home. I don't need the details now, but I need the concept. How are we going to train these characters? Let me have some ideas by this afternoon, will you? I have a meeting with the client tomorrow morning."

"Okay, boss, leave it with me. I'll see what I can do and get back to you. Bye."

"Bye." The face faded from the phone screen.

Question

1. All the technology mentioned in this case (with the possible exception of George) is available now. Use your imagination—put yourself in Rhona's place and develop some training alternatives to help the client's far-flying sales reps learn how to operate Rhona's new software package.

References

Armitage, H.M. 1992. "Quality Pays." *CGA Magazine* 96, no. 1, (January): 30–37.

Bahlmann, T. 1990. "The Learning Organization in a Turbulent Environment." *Human Systems Management* 9, no. 4, 249–56.

Bennett, R. (1988). "The Right Role." In R. Bennett (ed.), *Improving Trainer Effectiveness.* Aldershot: Gower, 45–69.

Bowen, D.E., and E.E. Lawle. 1992. "Total Quality-Oriented Human Resources Management. " *Organizational Dynamics* 20, no. 4, 29–41.

Bowen, D.E. and L.E Greiner. 1986. "Moving From Production to Service in Human Resources Management, " *Organizational Dynamics* 14, no. 12 (Summer): 34–45.

Byrne, J.A. 1993. "Re-engineering: Beyond the Buzzword." *Business Week* (24 May): 12–14.

Byrnes, J., and W. Copacino. 1990. "Develop a Powerful Learning Organization." *Transportation and Distribution* 31, no. 11, 22–25.

Cantwell, R. 1984. "Coping in a Multicultural Environment." *Conferences Proceedings: Global Strategies for Human Resource Development.* Alexandria, VA: American Society for Training and Development.

Carr, C. 1987. "Injecting Quality into Personnel Management." *Personnel Journal* 66, no. 9, 45–51.

Caudron, S. 1991. "Training Ensures Success Overseas." *Personnel Journal* 70, no. 12, 27–30.

Cocheu, T. 1989. "Training for Quality Improvement." *Training and Development Journal* 41, no. 1 (January): 56–62.

Coffman, L. 1987. "How to Keep Good Programs Alive." *Training* 24, no. 10, 77–80.

Cohen, S. 1991. "The Challenge of Training in the Nineties." *Training and Development* 45, no. 7.

Cutler, L. 1992/93. "Diversity: Key Element in New Administration." *Public Manager* 21, no. 4, 31–33.

Denton, K., and B. Wisdom. 1991. "The Learning Organization Involves the Entire Workforce." *Quality Progress* 24, no. 12, 69–72.

Derderian, S. 1993. "International Success Lies in Cross-Cultural Training." *HR Focus* 70, no. 4, 9.

Dunbar, E., and A. Katcher. 1990. "Preparing Managers for Foreign Assignments." *Training and Development Journal* 44, no. 9, 45–47.

Emrich, M. 1990. "Future Training with a Pair of Practical Visionaries." *Manufacturing Systems* 8, no. 1, 30–35.

Fine, C.H., and D.H. Bridge. 1987. "Managing Quality Improvement." In M. Sepehri (ed.), *Quest for Quality: Managing the Total System* Norcross, Georgia: The Institute of Industrial Engineers, 66–74.

Fritz, M. 1991. "The World of Virtual Reality." *Training* 28, no. 2, 45–50.

Galagan, P. 1991. "The Learning Organization Made Plain. " *Training and Development* 45, no. 10, 37–44.

Gandz, J. 1990. "The Employee Empowerment Era." *Business Quarterly* 55, no. 2, 74–79.

Garavan, T.N. 1987. "Promoting Natural Learning Activities Within the Organization. " *Journal of European Industrial Training*, 11, no. 7, 18–22.

Garvin, D. 1993. "Building a Learning Organization." *Harvard Business Review* 71, no. 4, 78–91.

Gerber, B. 1994. The wonderful world of Cyber Sally. *Training* 31, no. 5, 8.

Geroy, G.D. 1994. "Personnel Communication." Dr. Geroy is Professor in Charge, Human Resource Development, The Colorado State University of Fort Collins.

Goodnight, R. 1989. "Continuing Education, Lifelong Learning at Borg-Warner." *Training and Development Journal* 43, no. 10, 74–76.

Gordon, J. 1989. "In Search of Lifelong Learning." *Training* 26, no. 9, 25–34.

Gravan, T.N., and O. Murphy. 1989. "Indigenous High Technology Companies: A Novel Training Intervention." *Journal of European Industrial Training* 13, no. 8, 4–13.

Green, C. 1992. "Canada: Stand and Deliver." *Business Quarterly* 57, no. 1, 94–98.

Guptara, P., K. Murray, B. Razak, T. Scheehan. 1990. "The Art of Training Abroad." *Training and Development Journal* 44, no. 11, 13–18.

Hammer, M., and J. Champy. 1993. *Re-engineering the Corporation: A Manifesto for Business Revolution.* New York: Harper Collins Inc.

Heathman, D.J., and B.H. Keiner. 1991. "Future Directions for Computer-Aided Training." *Industrial and Commercial Training* 23, no. 5, 25–31.

Hendricks, C.F., and A. Triplett. 1989. "TQM: Strategy for '90s Management."

Personnel Administrator 34, no. 12, 42–48.

Henry, L. 1989. "High-tech Training for the High-tech Factory." *Training* 26, no. 8, 41–43.

Hogarty, D.B. 1993. "The Future of Middle Managers." *Management Review* 82, no. 9, 51–53.

Honey, P. 1991. "The Learning Organization Simplified." *Training and Development* 9, no. 7, 30–33.

Janson, R. 1992/93. "How Re-engineering Transforms Organizations to Satisfy Customers." *National Productivity Review* 12, no. 1, 45–53.

Johnston, C.G., and M.J. Daniel. 1991. *Customer Satisfaction Through Quality— An International Perspective.* Ottawa, Ont.: The Conference Board of Canada, Report 74–91–E.

Kiechel, W. 1990. "The Organization that Learns." *Fortune* 121, no. 6, 133–36.

Kiess-Moser, E. 1990. "International Perspectives on Quality." *Canadian Business Review* 17, no. 3, 31–33.

Kramlinger, J. 1992. "Trainer's Role in a Learning Organization." *Training* 29, no. 7, 46–51.

Krpan, J. 1993. "Re-engineering the Right Way: Ten Tips." *CMA Magazine* 67, no. 5, 14–15.

LaPlante, A. 1993. "Rightsizing Angst." *Forbes* (7 June): 94–104.

Lawrence, H. 1989. "High-tech Training for the High-tech Factory." *Training* 26, no. 8, 41–43.

Li, L. 1992. "The Strategic Design of Cross-cultural Training Programs." *Journal of Management Development* 11, no. 7, 22–29.

Lissy, W. 1993. "International Issues." *Compensation and Benefits Review* 25, no. 1, 17.

Lobel, S. 1990. "Global Leadership Competencies: Managing to a Different Drumbeat." *Human Resource Management* 29, no. 1, 39–47.

Malherba, F. 1992. "Learning by Firms and Incremental Change." *Economic Journal* 102, no. 413, 845–59.

McEmery, J., and G. DesHarnais 1990. "Culture Shock." *Training and Development Journal* 44, no. 4, 43–47.

McGill, M., J. Slocum, and D. Lei. 1992. "Management Practices in Learning Organizations." *Organizational Dynamics* 21, no. 1, 5–17.

McMillan, C.J. 1992. "Quality Management: Lessons from Japan." *Business Quarterly* 57, no. 1, 111–14.

Matthews, I. 1991. "Facing the Educational Challenges." *Canadian Banker* 98, no. 3, 48–54.

Mills, P., and B. Friesen. 1992. "The Learning Organization." *European Management Journal* 10, no. 2, 146–56.

Mumford, A. 1991. "Individual and Organizational Learning." *Industrial and Commercial Training* 23, no. 6, 24–31.

Naisbitt, J., and P. Aburdene. 1991. "New Leadership." *Executive Excellence* 8, no. 3, 10–12.

Neilsen, E. 1984. *Becoming an OD Practitioner*. Englewood Cliffs: Prentice-Hall Inc.

Nopper, N. 1993. "Reinventing the Factory with Lifelong Learning." *Training* 30, no. 5, 55–58.

Oakland, J.S. 1989. *Total Quality Management*. Oxford: Butterworth-Heinemann Ltd.

Odenwald, S. 1993. "A Guide for Global Training." *Training and Development* 47, no. 7, 22–31.

Odiorne, G. 1987. *The Human Side of Management*. Lexington: Lexington Books.

Purcell, L. 1992. "Lifelong Learning: Training Takes a Step Ahead." *Insurance and Technology* 17, no. 11, 36–40.

Randall, R.M. 1993. "The Re-engineer." *Planning Review* 21, no. 3, 8–21.

Raynor, M.E. 1992. "Quality as a Strategic Weapon." *Journal of Business Strategy* 13, no. 5, 3–9.

Redding, S.G. 1980. "Cognition as an Aspect of Culture and its Relation to Management Processes—An Exploratory View of the Chinese Case." *Journal of Management Studies*.

Regalbuto, G.A. 1992. "Targeting the Bottom Line." *Training and Development* 46, no. 4, 29–38.

Roderick, C. 1993. "Becoming a Learning Organization." *Training and Development* 11, no. 3, 13–14.

Rossett, A. and K. Krumdieck, 1992. "How Trainers Score on Quality." *Training and Development* 46, no. 1, 11–16.

Rubinstein, S. 1993. "Democracy and Quality as an Integrated System." *Quality Progress* 26, no. 9, 51–55.

Schonberger, R.J. 1992. "Total Quality Management Cuts a Broad Swath—Through Manufacturing and Beyond." *Organizational Dynamics* 20, no. 4, 16–28.

Senge, P. 1990. *The Fifth Discipline*. New York: Doubleday.

———. 1991. "Learning Organizations." *Executive Excellence* 8, no. 9, 7–8.

———. 1992. "Building Learning Organizations." *Journal for Quality and Participation* 15, no. 2, 30–38.

Shostack, G.L. 1989. "Six Lessons for Managing Technology." *Journal of Business Strategy* 10, no. 4, 52–55.

Smith, A. 1991. "Not Such Splendid Isolation." *Industrial Society* (March): 9–12.

Stanton, S., M. Hammer, and B. Power. 1993. "Re-engineering: Getting Everyone on Board. *IT Magazine* 25, no. 4, 22–27.

Stolovitch, H. and E. Keeps, eds. 1992. *Handbook of Human Performance Technology: A Comprehensive Guide for Analyzing and Solving Performance Problems in Organizations.* New York: National Society for Performance and Instruction.

Sullivan, P. 1993. "Nine Best Practices." *Executive Excellence* 10, no. 3, 3–4.

Sumsky, N. 1992. "Justifying the Intercultural Training Investment." *Journal of European Business* 4, no. 1, 38–43.

Tenner, A.R., and I.J. DeToro. 1992. *Total Quality Management, Three Steps to Continuous Improvement.* Reading, Mass.: Addison-Wesley Publishing Company, Inc.

Thornburg, L. 1992. "Pay for Performance: What You Should Know." *HRM Magazine* 37, no. 6, 58–61.

Triandis, H.C. 1983. "Essentials of Studying Cultures." In D. Landis, and R. Brisbin, eds, *Handbook of Intercultural Training.* New York: Pergamon Press.

Vogl, A.J. 1993. "The Age of Re-engineering."*Across the Board* 30, no. 5, 26–33.

Warrington, M.B., and J.B. McCall. 1983. "Negotiating a Foot into the Chinese Door." *Management Decision* 21, 46–82.

Wigglesworth, D. 1988. "The Indonesian Pilot Project." In P.C. Wright, ed. *Training for Success,* a special edition of *The Journal of European Industrial Training* 12, no. 6 (June): 27–32.

Wills, G. 1991. "Venn and the Art of Lifelong Management Development." *European Journal of Marketing* 25, no. 4, 65–85.

Wright, P. 1994a. "A Policy Alternative to Externally-sponsored Management Development and Skills Training Programs Devised at Small Business." *Journal of Small Business and Entrepreneurship* 11, no. 3, 49–59.

Wright, P. 1994b. "The Cultural Mosaic." In J.K. Prior, ed.*The Gower Handbook of Training and Development.* 2nd ed. Aldershot: Gower, 113–30.

Wright, P. 1985. "Andragogy and Vocational Education in China." *Canadian Vocational Journal* 21, no. 2, 32–39.

Wright, P., and G.D. Geroy. 1991. "Experience, Judgement and Intuition: Qualitative Data-gathering Methods as Aids to Strategic Planning " (a monograph). Bradford: MCB University Press.

Wright, P., and K. Kusmanadji. 1994. "The Strategic Application of TQM Principles to Human Resources Management." *Training for Quality* 1, no. 3, 5–14.

Index

Dictionary of Occupational Titles, 240
Direct-inputs, 253
Disabilities,
    myths about, 240
    range of, 237
Discrimination, 230
    defined, 233
    unconscious, 233
Disney Corporation, 213
Distance learning,
    methods, 188
    motivation, 188
Diversity,
    acknowledging, 228ff.
    racial and cultural, 227
Dixon, N.M., 282
Documentation, general methods, 80ff.
Dofasco, 4, 49
Downsizing, 49, 251
Dreher, G., 123

Economic measures, 75
Education,
    continuing, 53
    cooperative, 5
    vocational, 23
Educational traditions, 349
Effective instruction,
    dimensions of, 283
Effective performance, 75
    obstacles to, 78
    rewards for, 78
Effectiveness,
    improvement, 252
    key measures of, 65
    of training, 139
Electronic Performance-Support System (EPSS), 127ff.
    goals of, 127
Employee coaches, 311
Employees,
    entry-level skills, 147
    perceptions of, 68
    postcourse behaviour, 156

training avoidance, 52
Employers,
    legal responsibility of, 62
    mission of, 129
    moral obligation of, 63
Employment and Immigration Canada, 46
Employment equity, contracts, 46
Empowerment, 67, 202, 344
Entry-level jobs,
    skills, 147
    training for, 42
Environment,
    business, 67
    global, 51
    multicultural, 237
Environmental analysis, 10
Environmental variables, 12
Equity,
    defined, 229
    principles of, 14
    in training, 225ff.
Ernst and Young, 190
Estimating net benefit, difficulties of, 261
Ethics, business, 306
Ethnocentrism, 233
Evaluation, 100ff., 277ff.
    barriers to, 280
    behaviour, 288
    coaching, 120
    defined, 279
    difficulty of, 280, 281
    feasibility and flexibility, 296
    formative, 279
    four levels of, 282
    issues in, 295
    learning, 285
    matrix, 295
    a model of, 296, 297
    negative results of, 280
    principles of, 294
    process of, 281, 291
    rationale for, 279

reaction to, 282
    results of, 289
    types of, 281
Excellence concept, eight principles of, 306
Excellence development,
    counselling, 315
    strategy, 305
Executive review committees, 319
Expatriates, 346
Expectancy, individual, 143
Expectancy theory, 14
Expenditures training, 9, 21, 202
Experience, 316

Failure analysis, 253
Federal government, responsibilities, 46ff.
Feedback, 72, 84, 143, 151, 152, 174, 214, 337
Feminine values, 233
Finning Ltd., 160
Firestone, 51
Firing, 79
Fitz-Enz, J., 289
Focus-group, 83
Following Nellie, 214
Follow-up assignment, 158
Follow-up report, 158
Ford Motor Company, 188
Formal interview, 83
Frayne, C., 118
Free Trade Agreement, 207
Full-service training organization, 23
Functional analysis, 68, 69
Funded clients, 44

Gaines, H., 317
Games and simulations, 197ff.
    definition of, 197
    risks of, 197
Gap analysis, 118
    identification, 73
Gender, studies of, 234

To the owner of this book

We hope that you have enjoyed *Managing Performance Through Training & Development,* and we would like to know as much about your experiences with this text as you would care to offer. Only through your comments and those of others can we learn how to make this a better text for future readers.

School _____ Your instructor's name _____

Course _____ Was the text required? _____ Recommended? _____

1. What did you like the most about *Managing Performance Through Training & Development?*

   _____
   _____
   _____

2. How useful was this text for your course?

   _____
   _____
   _____

3. Do you have any recommendations for ways to improve the next edition of this text?

   _____
   _____
   _____

4. In the space below or in a separate letter, please write any other comments you have about the book. (For example, please feel free to comment on reading level, writing style, terminology, design features, and learning aids.)

   _____
   _____
   _____

Optional

Your name _____ Date _____

May Nelson Canada quote you, either in promotion for *Managing Performance Through Training & Development* or in future publishing ventures?

Yes _____ No _____

Thanks!

- - - - - - - - - - - - - - - - FOLD HERE - - - - - - - - - - - -

MAIL ⇒ POSTE

Canada Post Corporation / Société canadienne des postes

Postage paid
if mailed in Canada

Port payé
si posté au Canada

**Business
Reply**

**Réponse
d'affaires**

0107077099   01

Nelson

TAPE SHUT

0107077099-M1K5G4-BR01

TAPE SHUT

Nelson Canada
College Editorial Department
1120 Birchmount Rd.
Scarborough, ON M1K 9Z9

PLEASE TAPE SHUT. DO NOT STAPLE.